INTRODUCING
NLP

Like the creative composer, some people are more gifted at living than others. They do have an effect on those around them, but the process stops there because there is no way of describing in technical terms just what it is they do, most of which is out of awareness. Some time in the future, a long, long time from now when culture is more completely explored, there will be an equivalent of musical scores that can be learned, each for a different type of man or woman in different types of jobs or relationships, for time, space, work, and play. We see people who are successful and happy today, who have jobs which are rewarding and productive. What are the sets, isolates, and patterns that differentiate their lives from those of the less fortunate? We need to have a means for making life a little less haphazard and more enjoyable.

Edward T. Hall
The Silent Language

NEURO-LINGUISTIC PROGRAMMING

INTRODUCING
NLP

*Psychological Skills for Understanding
and Influencing People*

JOSEPH O'CONNOR & JOHN SEYMOUR

Foreword by Robert Dilts and Preface by John Grinder

To all pragmatic idealists and the spirit of curiosity

HarperElement
An Imprint of HarperCollins*Publishers*
77–85 Fulham Palace Road
Hammersmith, London W6 8JB

The website address is: www.thorsonselement.com

and *HarperElement* are trademarks of
HarperCollins*Publishers* Limited

Published by Mandala 1990
Revised edition by The Aquarian Press 1993
This edition published by Element 2002

36

A catalogue record for this book is
available from the British Library

ISBN-13   978-1-85538-344-9
ISBN-10   1-85538-344-6

Printed in Great Britain by
Clays Ltd, St Ives plc

CONTENTS

CHAPTER I

Sets a context and maps out the main ideas of NLP: how we get from
our present reality to where we want to go, outcomes, communication,
how to gain rapport, and how we build our unique ways of
understanding the world.

CHAPTER 2

Deals with how we use our senses internally to think, how language
relates to thought, and how you can tell the way in which other
people are thinking.

CHAPTER 3

Deals with our states of mind, how they are evoked, and how we can use these stimuli or anchors to gain access to our resourceful states of mind at will.

CHAPTER 4

This is about thinking in terms of systems rather than simple cause and effect. It contains some of Robert Dilts' recent work, how environment, behaviour, capability, beliefs and identity fit together.

CHAPTER 5

Describes how language sets limits on our experience and how we can go beyond those limits. The Meta Model patterns are a way of asking key questions to clarify what people say.

CHAPTER 6

How to use language in artfully vague ways that accord with other people's experience and allows them access to their unconscious resources – called the Milton Model after the world famous hypnotherapist, Milton Erickson. There is a section on metaphor, another on changing the meaning of experience, and a third on how we perceive time subjectively.

CHAPTER 7

Explores more NLP patterns, including conflict, alignment, values
and flexibility in the context of business. How to make meetings run
more effectively and how to reach agreement in difficult situations.

CHAPTER 8

Focuses on NLP in therapy and personal change, and describes three
classic NLP techniques: the swish, the phobia cure, and internal
conflict resolution.

CHAPTER 9

This chapter is about our thinking strategies. There are some practical examples, including the famous NLP spelling strategy. There is a strategy for musical memory, and a creative strategy modelled on Walt Disney.

EPILOGUE

This is a brief, speculative exploration of how NLP reflects change in our culture; how the process of change in the internal world of our thoughts reflects the increasing rate of change in the external world.

REFERENCE SECTION

A source of practical information and advice on choosing NLP books and courses.

FOREWORD

It is always a pleasure to see dedicated and serious students of NLP put their talents to work. In this case, Joseph O'Connor and John Seymour have done an exquisite job in presenting fundamental NLP principles and tools in an easily accessible form. The book is written in an enjoyable conversational manner yet manages to preserve the richness and sophistication of the material it is portraying – thus satisfying Albert Einstein's famous dictum, 'Everything should be made as simple as possible, but not any simpler.'

More importantly, this book provides an *up-to-date* introduction and overview of NLP, incorporating the latest developments in the field as well as reviewing the most important NLP basics. Congratulations to two people who are helping to lay the groundwork for NLP in the next decade!

Robert B. Dilts
Santa Cruz, California
December 1989

PREFACE

Reasonable men adapt themselves to the world.
Unreasonable men adapt the world to themselves.
That's why all progress depends on unreasonable men
George Bernard Shaw

History, when recorded, has much in common with the song of the purveyor of the latest miracle cure, the diplomat and the apologist. How could it be otherwise?

The oral traditions of people in intact cultures before orthographies are introduced are both a comfort and a challenge to them: a comfort in their orderliness and the imperative flow of events; a challenge to the singers who bear witness to the chaos that ultimately must fit the meter and length of their chanted chronicle. No doubt, after a time, blessed amnesia steals upon them and they sing with utter conviction.

Gregory Bateson warns us of the lethal triangle of technology, the propensity of our species to replace natural living physical context (the forests of the Amazon Basin) with artificial context (the streets of New York), and conscious planning without the balance of unconscious process. Tom Malloy (in his brilliant novel *The Curtain of Dawn*) corrects the speech impediment of Charles Darwin who said 'survival of the fittest' where he would have spoken less falsely to have said 'survival of the fitters'.

These two men, O'Connor and Seymour, have set out to make a coherent story out of an outrageous adventure. The jungles through which Richard Bandler and I wandered in our explorations are bizarre and wondrous. These fine and well-intentioned men will show you glimpses of an English rose garden, trimmed and proper. Both the jungle and the rose garden carry their own special attractions.

What you are about to read never happened, but it seems reasonable, even to me.

John Grinder
December 1989

INTRODUCTION

This book is an introduction and guide to the field known as Neuro-Linguistic Programming, or NLP. NLP is the art and science of excellence, derived from studying how top people in different fields obtain their outstanding results. These communication skills can be learned by anyone to improve their effectiveness both personally and professionally.

This book describes many of the models of excellence that NLP has built in the fields of communication, business, education and therapy. The approach is practical, it gets results, and it is increasingly influential in many disciplines all over the world.

NLP continues to grow and generate new ideas. We, the writers, are aware that in contrast, books are fixed and static. Every book is a statement relative to the time it was written. It is a snapshot of the subject. However, just because a person will be different tomorrow is no reason not to take a photograph today.

Think of this book as being rather like a stepping stone, allowing you to explore new territory and continue an exciting lifetime journey. It represents the authors' personal understanding of NLP and is not a definitive or official version. Such a version will never exist, by the very nature of NLP. This is an introduction and we have made many choices about what to include and what to leave out. The result is one of many possible ways to organize the material.

NLP is a model of how individuals structure their unique experiences of life. It is only one way to think about and organize the fantastic and beautiful complexity of human thought and communication. We hope that with two of us writing, this description of NLP will have a dimension of depth, which would not be the case if there was only one author. Depth is perceived by focusing both eyes on an object. The world is flat when viewed through one eye alone.

NLP represents an attitude of mind and a way of being in the world that cannot adequately be passed on in a book, although some sense of it will come from reading between the lines. The enjoyment of a wonderful piece of music comes from listening to it, not from looking at the score.

NLP is practical. It is a set of models, skills and techniques for thinking and acting effectively in the world. The purpose of NLP is to be useful, to increase choice and to enhance the quality of life. The most important questions to ask about what you find in this book are, 'Is it useful? Does it work?' Find out what is useful and what works by trying it out. More important, find out where it does *not* work and then change it until it does. That is the spirit of NLP.

Our aim in writing this book is to satisfy a need that we perceived in talking to the growing number of people who are becoming interested in NLP. We set out to write a book that would provide an overview of the field. It would share our excitement at the insights into how people think and the changes that are possible. It would cover many of the most useful skills, patterns and techniques in a way that makes them readily available for use as tools for change in a changing world. After a first reading, it would continue to be useful as a reference book. It would give practical guidance in buying other NLP books to follow up particular interests and applications. And it would offer guidance in choosing NLP training courses.

This aim was so daunting, given the 'elusive obviousness' of NLP, that neither of us was prepared to tackle it on our own. Combining our resources gave us the courage. How far we have succeeded depends on how useful you find this book.

We particularly want to encourage you to explore further in the field of NLP, and to use these powerful ideas with integrity and respect for yourself and others, to create more choice and happiness in your personal and professional life, and in the lives of others.

We originally planned a chapter of stories about how people discovered NLP and their experiences using it. We soon decided that this would not work, second hand experience has entertainment value, but little direct impact. Instead, in the spirit of NLP, we urge you to create your own chapter of interesting experiences using NLP.

NLP is best experienced live. Read the menu, and if you like what you read, enjoy the meal.

A photograph never was the person.
A stepping stone is not the journey.
A musical score is not the sound.
There is no magic, only magicians and people's perceptions.

THANKS AND ACKNOWLEDGEMENTS

We would like to thank many people for inspiration and help with this book.

First, we want to give credit and recognition to the originators of NLP, Richard Bandler and John Grinder.

We would also like to thank John Grinder for reading the manuscript, giving very useful feedback which we have incorporated, and for writing the preface.

We also want to give credit and recognition to the many other people who extended the ideas, especially Robert Dilts, who has been influential in developing NLP in many directions over the past decade. Our thanks and appreciation to Robert for permission to use his material on strategies and the Unified Field. He has been particularly helpful, given freely of his ideas and has inspired us greatly.

David Gaster has also given us a great deal of help and encouragement with this book. Thank you David, may your flights always bring you joy.

We would also like to thank Sue Quilliam and Ian Grove-Stevenson, for setting us on the right track at the beginning.

Our thanks to Norah McCullagh for much typing, to Francis Vine for research, to Michael Breen for his help in compiling the information on NLP books, and to Carole Marie and Ruth Trevenna for suggestions and encouragement at difficult times.

Many thanks to Eileen Campbell and Elizabeth Hutchins at Thorsons, for their support and concern.

Our acknowledgements to John Fowles and Anthony Sheil Associates Ltd for permission to quote 'The Prince and the Magician' from *The Magus* by John Fowles, published by Jonathan Cape and Sons.

And lastly we owe a debt of gratitude to the inventors of that wonderful machine, the Macintosh computer, for making the actual writing of this book so much easier.

Joseph O'Connor
John Seymour
August 1989

INTRODUCTION TO THE
SECOND EDITION

Right from the beginning, it was our intention systematically to update this book. We want to keep it aligned with NLP, which is spreading and shifting its boundaries. By its very nature it will never stay static. So it is with great pleasure that we have worked on this new edition. The original edition realized a dream we had, and the feedback has indicated that we largely met our outcome: the book is now established as a useful introduction and overview of the field. This new edition continues that dream.

We have made a large number of small changes and a small number of large ones. The first we hope will make a overall difference and add to the quality. The large changes are the addition of new material and an updated resources section. There is a section now on metaprograms. These patterns are coming more to the fore, especially in a business context, so the book needs to reflect this. We have expanded the beliefs chapter, and the modelling section of the last chapter, and would like especially to thank Michael Neill for his contribution to these last two.

The NLP Organizations Worldwide section has been an obvious candidate for updating. It has been revised and expanded to bring in the many new NLP Institutes that have grown up all over the world in the last two years. Our listing is as comprehensive and accurate as we can make it at this time. NLP has grown so rapidly in Germany that a whole book has been published that is devoted to listing German NLP Institutes and trainers. Rather than duplicate this work, we have referred to this book in the listing.

NLP books continue to be published at a rapid rate, so this may be the last edition in which we will have space to make a list with brief comments as a guide.

Changing the main text of the book has been more difficult than we imagined. NLP is like a hologram. Every part connects to every other part. It is a systemic model. To the extent that this book mirrors the systemic nature, changing one part has meant others need to be changed too in sympathy as the reverberations echo down the pages and unwind the skein (to mix a metaphor).

However NLP spreads, there are two ideas that stay constant. NLP embodies the attitude of fascination with people. How do they do what they do? Secondly, the modelling skills: looking constantly for excellence in the world so you can model it and use it. Excellence is all around, sometimes so obvious that we miss it. NLP is about always increasing the choices you have, and we understand by acting and experimenting, not by thinking about it.

We would like also to thank Jay Erdmann and Michael Neill for their help. Also Michael Phillips of *Anchor Point Magazine* for his help in compiling the NLP organization listing for America. Also Liz Puttick, our editor at Thorsons. And finally all the many friends who gave us feedback and suggestions for this revised edition. Please write to us with your thoughts if you are so moved. Our address is at the end of the book.

Joseph O'Connor
John Seymour

London, January 1993

I

WHAT IS NEURO-LINGUISTIC PROGRAMMING?

As I sat wondering how to begin this book, I remembered meeting a friend a few days before. We had not seen each other for some time, and after the usual greetings, he asked me what I was doing. I said I was writing a book.

'Great!' he said. 'What is it about?'

Without thinking, I replied, 'Neuro-Linguistic Programming.'

There was a short but meaningful silence. 'Same to you,' he said. "How's the family?'

In a sense my answer was both right and wrong. If I had wanted a conversation stopper, it worked perfectly. This book does deal with a way of thinking about ideas and people that goes by the label of Neuro-Linguistic Programming. However, my friend wanted to know what I was doing in a way he could understand and share with me. And he could not relate my reply to anything he knew about. I knew what I meant, but I did not put it in a way he could understand. My reply did not answer his real question.

What then is NLP? What are the ideas behind the label? The next time someone asked me what the book was about, I said it was about a way of studying how people excel in any field and teaching these patterns to others.

NLP is the art and science of personal excellence. Art because everyone brings their unique personality and style to what they do, and this can never be captured in words or techniques. Science because there is a method and process for discovering the patterns used by outstanding individuals in any field to achieve outstanding results. This process is called modelling, and the patterns, skills and techniques so discovered are being used increasingly in counselling, education and business for more effective communication, personal development and accelerated learning.

Have you ever done something so elegantly and effectively that it took your breath away? Have you had times when you were really delighted at what you did and wondered how you did it? NLP shows you how to understand and model your own successes, so that you can have many more of those moments. It is a way of discovering and unfolding your personal genius, a way of bringing out the best in yourself and others.

NLP is a practical skill that creates the results we truly want in the world while creating value for others in the process. It is the study of what makes the difference between the excellent and the average. It also leaves behind a trail of extremely effective techniques for education, counselling, business and therapy.

SANTA CRUZ, CALIFORNIA 1972

NLP started in the early seventies from the collaboration of John Grinder, who was then an Assistant Professor of linguistics at the University of California, Santa Cruz, and Richard Bandler, who was a student of psychology at the university. Richard Bandler was also very interested in psychotherapy. Together they studied three top therapists: Fritz Perls, the innovative psychotherapist and originator of the school of therapy known as Gestalt, Virginia Satir, the extraordinary family therapist, who consistently was able to resolve difficult family relationships that many other therapists found intractable, and Milton Erickson, the world-famous hypnotherapist.

Bandler and Grinder did not intend to start a new school of therapy, but to identify patterns used by outstanding therapists, and pass them on to others. They did not concern themselves with theories; they produced models of successful therapy that worked in practice and could be taught. The three therapists they modelled were very different personalities, yet they used surprisingly similar underlying patterns. Bandler and Grinder took these patterns, refined them and built an elegant model which can be used for effective communication, personal change, accelerated learning, and, of course, greater enjoyment of life. They set down their initial discoveries in four books, published between 1975 and 1977: *The Structure of Magic 1 and 2* and *Patterns 1 and 2*, two books on Erickson's hypnotherapy work. NLP literature has been growing at an increasing rate ever since.

At that time John and Richard were living very close to Gregory Bateson, the British anthropologist and writer on communication and systems theory. Bateson himself had written on many different topics – biology, cybernetics, anthropology and psychotherapy. He is best known for developing the double bind theory of schizophrenia. His contribution to NLP was profound. Perhaps only now is it becoming clear exactly how influential he was.

From these initial models, NLP developed in two complementary directions. Firstly, as a process to discover the patterns of excellence in any field. Secondly, as the effective ways of thinking and communicating used by outstanding people. These patterns and skills can be used in their own right, and also feed back into the modelling process to make it even more powerful. In 1977 John and Richard were giving very successful public seminars all over America. NLP grew quickly; in America to date, more than 100,000 people have done some form of NLP training.

SANTA CRUZ, 1976

In the spring of 1976 John and Richard were in a log cabin, high in the hills above Santa Cruz, pulling together the insights and discoveries that they had made. Towards the end of a marathon 36 hour session, they sat down with a bottle of Californian red wine, and asked themselves, 'What on earth shall we call this?'

The result was Neuro-Linguistic Programming, a cumbersome phrase that covers three simple ideas. The 'Neuro' part of NLP acknowledges the fundamental idea that all behaviour stems from our neurological processes of sight, hearing, smell, taste, touch and feeling. We experience the world through our five senses; we make 'sense' of the information and then act on it. Our neurology covers not only our invisible thought processes, but also our visible physiological reactions to ideas and events. One simply reflects the other at the physical level. Body and mind form an inseparable unity, a human being.

The 'Linguistic' part of the title indicates that we use language to order our thoughts and behaviour and to communicate with others. The 'Programming' refers to ways we can choose to organize our ideas and actions to produce results.

NLP deals with the structure of human subjective experience; how we organize what we see hear and feel, and how we edit and filter the outside world through our senses. It also explores how we describe it in language and how we act, both intentionally and unintentionally, to produce results.

MAPS AND FILTERS

Whatever the outside world is really like, we use our senses to explore and map it. The world is an infinity of possible sense impressions and we are able to perceive only a very small part of it. That part we can perceive is further filtered by our unique experiences, culture, language, beliefs, values, interests and assumptions. Everyone lives in their unique reality built from their sense impressions and individual experiences of life, and we act on the basis of what we perceive our model of the world.

The world is so vast and rich that we have to simplify to give it meaning. Map making is a good analogy for what we do; it is how we make meaning of the world. Maps are selective, they leave out as well as give information, and they are invaluable for exploring the territory. The sort of map you make depends on what you notice, and where you want to go.

The map is not the territory it describes. We attend to those aspects of the world that interest us and ignore others. The world is always richer than the ideas we have about it. The filters we put on our perceptions determine what sort of world we live in. There is a story of Picasso being accosted by a stranger who asked him why he did not paint things as they really are.

Picasso looked puzzled. 'I do not really understand what you mean,' he replied.

The man produced a photograph of his wife. 'Look,' he said, 'like that. That's what my wife really looks like.'

Picasso looked doubtful. 'She is very small, is she not? And a little bit flat?'

An artist, a lumberjack and a botanist taking a stroll through a wood will have very different experiences and notice very different things. If you go through the world looking for excellence, you will find excellence. If you go through the world looking for problems you will find problems. Or as the Arabic saying puts it, 'What a piece of bread looks like depends on whether you are hungry or not.'

Very narrow beliefs, interests and perceptions will make the world impoverished, predictable and dull. The very same world can be rich and exciting. The difference lies not in the world, but in the filters through which we perceive it.

We have many natural, useful and necessary filters. Language is a filter. It is a map of our thoughts and experiences, removed a further level from the real world. Think for a moment what the word 'beauty' means to you. No doubt you have memories and experiences, internal pictures, sounds and feelings that let you make sense of that word. Equally, someone else will have different memories and experiences and will think about that word in a different way. Who is right? Both of you, each within your own reality. The word is not the experience it describes, yet people will fight and sometimes even die believing the map is the territory.

Our beliefs also act as filters, causing us to act in certain ways and to notice some things at the expense of others. NLP offers one way of thinking about ourselves and the world; it is itself a filter. To use NLP you do not have to change any of your beliefs or values, but simply be curious and prepared to experiment. All generalizations about people are lies to somebody, because everyone is unique. So NLP does not claim to be objectively true. It is a model, and models are meant to be useful. There are some basic ideas in NLP that are very useful. We invite you to behave as if they are true and notice the difference that makes. By changing your filters, you can change your world.

Some of the NLP basic filters are often referred to as *Behavioural Frames*. These are ways of thinking about how you act. The first is an orientation towards *outcomes* rather than *problems*. This means finding out what you and others want, finding what resources you have, and using these resources to move towards your goal. The problem orientation is often referred to as the 'Blame Frame'. This means analysing what is wrong in great detail. It means asking questions like: 'Why do I have this problem? How does it limit me? Whose fault is it?' These sorts of questions do not usually lead anywhere useful. Asking them will leave you feeling worse than when you started, and does nothing towards solving the problem.

The second frame is to ask *How* rather than *Why* questions. How questions will get you an understanding of the structure of a problem. Why questions are likely to get you justifications and reasons without changing anything.

The third frame is *Feedback* versus *Failure*. There is no such thing as failure, only results. These can be used as feedback, helpful corrections, a splendid opportunity to learn something you had not noticed. Failure is just a way of describing a result you did not want. You can use the results you get to redirect your efforts. Feedback keeps the goal in view. Failure is a dead end. Two very similar words, yet they represent two totally different ways of thinking.

The fourth frame is to consider *Possibilities* rather than *Necessities*. Again this is a shift in focus. Look at what you can do, what choices are available, rather than the constraints of a situation. Often the barriers are less formidable than they appear.

Finally, NLP adopts an attitude of *Curiosity* and *Fascination* rather than making *Assumptions*. This is a very simple idea and has profound consequences. Young children learn tremendously quickly, and they do it by being curious about everything. They do not know and they know they do not know, so they are not worried about looking stupid if they ask. After all, once upon a time, everybody 'knew' the earth went round the sun, that something heavier than air could not fly, and of course to run a mile in less than four minutes was physiologically impossible. Change is the only constant.

Another useful idea is that we all have, or can create, the inner resources we need to achieve our goals. You are more likely to succeed if you act as if this were true than if you act the opposite.

LEARNING, UNLEARNING AND RELEARNING

Although we can consciously take in only a very small amount of the information the world offers us, we notice and respond to much more without being aware. Our conscious mind is very limited and seems able to keep track of a maximum of seven variables or pieces of information at one time.

This idea was outlined in 1956 by the American psychologist George Miller in a classic paper called *The Magic Number Seven, Plus or Minus Two*. These pieces of information do not have a fixed size, they can be anything from driving a car to looking in the rear-view mirror. One way we learn is by consciously mastering small pieces of behaviour, and combining them into larger and larger chunks, so they become habitual and unconscious. We form habits so we are free to notice other things.

So our consciousness is limited to seven plus or minus two pieces of information, either from the internal world of our thoughts, or from the external world. Our unconscious, by contrast, is all the life-giving processes of our body, all that we have learned, our past experiences, and all that we might notice, but do not, in the present moment. The unconscious is much wiser than the conscious mind. The idea of being able to understand an infinitely complex world with a conscious mind that can only hold about seven pieces of information at once, is obviously ludicrous.

The notion of conscious and unconscious is central to this model of how we learn. In NLP, something is conscious when it is in present moment awareness, as this sentence is right now. Something is unconscious when it is not in present moment awareness. The background noises that you can hear were probably unconscious until you read this sentence. The memory of your first sight of snow is almost certainly out of conscious awareness. If you have ever helped a young child learn to ride a bicycle, you will be aware of just how unconscious that skill has become in yourself. And the process of turning your last meal into hair and toenails is likely to remain forever unconscious. We live in a culture which believes that we do most of what we do consciously. Yet most of what we do, and what we do best, we do unconsciously.

The traditional view is that learning a skill divides into four stages. First there is unconscious incompetence. Not only do you not know how to do something, but you don't know you don't know. Never having driven a car for example, you have no idea what it is like.

So you start to learn. You very soon discover your limitations. You have some lessons and consciously attend to all the instruments, steer, co-ordinate the clutch, and watch the road. It demands all your attention, you are not yet competent, and you keep to the back streets. This is the stage of conscious incompetence when you grind the gears, oversteer and give cyclists heart attacks. Although this stage is uncomfortable (especially for cyclists), it is the stage when you learn the most.

This leads you to the stage of conscious competence. You can drive the car, but it takes all your concentration. You have learned the skill, but have not yet mastered it.

Lastly, and the goal of the endeavour, is unconscious competence. All those little patterns that you learned so painstakingly blend together into one smooth unit of behaviour. Then you can listen to the radio, enjoy the scenery and hold a conversation at the same time as driving. Your conscious mind sets the outcome and leaves it to your unconscious mind to carry it out, freeing your attention for other things.

If you practise something for long enough you will reach this fourth stage and form habits. At this point the skill has become unconscious. However, the habits may not be the most effective ones for the task. Our filters may have caused us to miss some important information en route to unconscious competence.

Suppose you play a passable game of tennis, and wish to improve. The coach would probably watch you play, then start changing such things as your footwork, how you hold the racquet, and the way you bring the racquet through the air. In other words he would take what was for you one piece of behaviour – hitting a forehand drive – break it down into some of its component parts, and then rebuild it so you hit a better forehand drive. You would go backwards through the learning stages to conscious incompetence and you would be unlearning before relearning. The only reason to do this is to build in new choices, more efficient patterns.

The same happens in learning NLP. We already have communication and learning skills. NLP offers to refine your skills and give you more choices and more flexibility about using them.

The Four Stages of Learning

1. Unconscious Incompetence
2. Conscious Incompetence
3. Conscious Competence
4. Unconscious Competence

Unlearning is 4 to 2
Relearning is 2 back to 4 with more choices

We shall be exploring different models of learning later in the book.

THE THREE MINUTE SEMINAR

If NLP were ever to be presented in a three minute seminar, it would go something like this. The presenter would walk on and say, 'Ladies and gentlemen, to be successful in life you need only remember three things.

'Firstly, know what you want; have a clear idea of your outcome in any situation.

'Secondly, be alert and keep your senses open so that you notice what you are getting.

'Thirdly, have the flexibility to keep changing what you do until you get what you want.'

He would then write on the board:

Outcome

Acuity

Flexibility

and leave.

End of seminar.

First is the skill of knowing your outcome. If you do not know where you are going, it makes it hard to get there.

An important part of NLP is training in sensory acuity: where to place your attention and how to change and enlarge your filters so that you notice things that you had not noticed previously. It is present moment sensory awareness. When communicating with others, this means noticing the small but crucial signals that let you know how they are responding. When thinking, that is, communicating with yourself, it means heightened awareness of your internal images, sounds and feelings.

You need the acuity or sensitivity to notice if what you are doing is getting you what you want. If what you are doing is not working, do something else, anything else. You need to hear, see and feel what is happening and have a choice of responses.

NLP aims to give people more choice about what they do. Having only one way of doing things is no choice at all. Sometimes it will work and sometimes it won't, so there will always be situations you cannot cope with. Two choices will put you in a dilemma. Having a choice means being able to use a minimum of three approaches. In any interaction, the person who has the most choices of what to do, the greatest flexibility of behaviour, will be in control of the situation.

If you always do what you've always done, you'll always get what you've always got. If what you are doing is not working, do something else.

The more choices, the more chance of success.

The way these skills work together is rather like what happens when you hire a rowing boat to explore a stretch of water. You decide where you want to go: your initial outcome. You start rowing and notice your direction: sensory acuity. You compare this with where you want to go and if you are off course, you change direction. You repeat this cycle until you reach your destination.

Then you set your next destination. You can change your outcome at any point in the cycle, enjoy the journey and learn something on the way. The course is likely to be a zig-zag. Very rarely is there an absolutely clear, straight path to where you want to go.

OUTCOMES

'Would you tell me, please, which way I ought to go from here?'
'That depends a good deal on where you want to get to,' said the cat.
'I don't much care where . . .' said Alice.
'Then it doesn't matter which way you go,' said the cat.

Alice in Wonderland, Lewis Carroll

Let us begin at the beginning with outcomes or goals. The more precisely and positively you can define what you want, and the more you program your brain to seek out and notice possibilities, the more likely you are to get what you want. Opportunities exist when they are recognized as opportunities.

To live the life you want, you need to know what you want. Being effective in the world means producing the results you choose. The first step is to choose. If you do not, there are plenty of people willing to choose for you.

How do you know what you want? You make it up. There are some rules for doing this, so that you have the best chance of success. In NLP language, you choose a well-formed outcome. That is, an outcome that is well-formed in terms of the following criteria.

First, it must be stated in the positive. It is easier to move towards what you want than away from what you do not want. However, you cannot move towards something if you do not know what it is.

As an example, think for a moment of a kangaroo.

Are you thinking of a kangaroo?

Good.

Now stop thinking of a kangaroo while you finish reading this page. Do not let the idea of a kangaroo come into your mind for the next minute or so. Are you not thinking of a kangaroo?

Now think of what you will be doing tomorrow . . .

To get rid of that persistent kangaroo, you have to think of something else that is positive.

This trick makes the point that the brain can only understand a negative by turning it into a positive. In order to avoid something you have to know what it is you are avoiding, and keep your attention on it. You have to think of it to know what not to think of, just as you have to keep an object in view to avoid bumping into it. Whatever you resist, persists. This is one reason why giving up smoking is so difficult – you continually have to think about smoking in order to give it up.

Secondly, you must play an active part, so the outcome must be reasonably within your control. Outcomes that rely primarily on other people taking action are not well formed. If people do not respond the way you want, you are stuck. Concentrate instead on what you need to do to elicit those responses. So for example, instead of waiting for someone to make friends, think of what you could do to become friendly with them.

Think of your outcome as specifically as possible. What will you see, hear and feel? Imagine it through and describe it to yourself or write it down in terms of who, what, where, when, and how. The fuller the idea of what you want, the more your brain can rehearse it and notice opportunities to achieve it. In what context do you want it? Are there contexts where you do not want it?

How will you know that you have achieved your outcome? What is the sensory-based evidence that will let you know that you have what you want? What will you see, hear and feel when you have achieved it? Some outcomes are so open ended that they could take several lifetimes to achieve. You might also like to set a time limit on when you wish to have it.

Do you have the resources to initiate and maintain the outcome? What do you need? Do you already have it? If not, how are you going to get it? This is an issue that needs to be thoroughly explored. These resources may be internal, (specific skills, or positive states of mind), or external. If you find you need external resources, you may need to set a subsidiary outcome to get them.

The outcome needs to be an appropriate size. It could be too big, in which case it needs to be split into several smaller, more easily achievable outcomes. For example, you might set an outcome to be a top tennis player. This is obviously not going to happen by next week, as it is too vague and long term. It needs breaking down into smaller chunks, so ask yourself, 'What stops me from achieving this?'

This question will highlight some obvious problems. For example you do not have a good tennis racquet, and you need coaching from a professional player. Then convert these problems into outcomes by asking yourself, 'What do I want instead?' I need to buy a good racquet and find a coach. A problem is simply an outcome that is the wrong way up.

You may have to go through this process several times with a very big outcome before arriving at a reasonably sized and achievable first step. Even the longest journey starts with the first step (in the right direction of course).

On the other hand the outcome may seem too small and trivial to motivate you. For example, I might set out to tidy the workroom, a small and not very exciting task. To bring some energy to this, I need to forge a link with a larger, more important, more motivating outcome. So I ask myself, 'If I got this outcome, what would it do for me?' In this example, it might be a necessary step in order to create a working space for doing something else that is much more interesting. Having made that connection, I can tackle the small outcome with energy drawn from the larger one.

The final frame round choosing outcomes is ecology. No one exists in isolation; we are all part of larger systems, family, work, friendship networks, and society in general. You need to consider the consequences of achieving your outcome in the context of these wider relationships. Would there be any undesirable by-products? What would you have to give up, or take on, to achieve it?

For example, you might want more freelance work. This would take up more time, so you will spend less time with your family. Achieving a big contract might increase your workload to such an extent that you could not do the job adequately. Make sure your outcome is in harmony with you as a whole person. Outcomes are not about getting what you want at the expense of others. The most valuable and satisfying results are achieved by negotiating and co-operating to establish shared outcomes where everyone wins. This automatically takes care of the ecology issue.

These sorts of issues may make you revise your outcome, or change to another outcome that serves the same intention without having the undesirable by-products. The classic example of choosing an unecological outcome was King Midas, who wanted *everything* he touched to turn to gold. He soon found this was a distinct liability.

Outcomes Summary

You can remember this from the mnemonic **'POSERS'**, spelt out by the first letter of the key word for each step.

POSITIVE

Think of what you want rather than what you do not want.
Ask: 'What would I rather have?'
       'What do I really want?'

OWN PART

Think of what you will actively do that is within your control.
Ask: 'What will I be doing to achieve my outcome?'
       'How can I start and maintain it?'

SPECIFIC

Imagine the outcome as specifically as you can.
Ask: 'Who, where, when, what and how, specifically?'

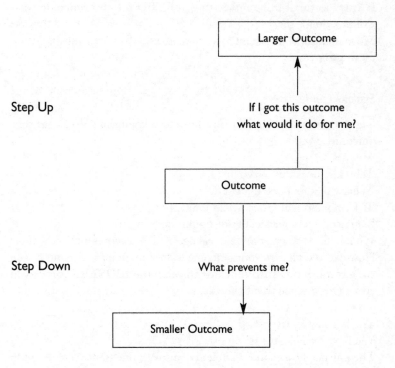

EVIDENCE

Think of the sensory-based evidence that will let you know you have
got what you want.
Ask: 'What will I see, hear and feel when I have it?'
         'How will I know that I have it?'

RESOURCES

Do you have adequate resources and choices to get your outcome?
Ask: 'What resources do I need to get the outcome?'

SIZE

Is the outcome the right size?
If it is too large ask, 'What prevents me from getting this?' and turn
the problems into other smaller outcomes. Make them sufficiently
clear and achievable.
If it is too small to be motivating, ask, 'If I got this outcome what
would it do for me?'
Move up until you relate it to an outcome that is sufficiently large and
motivating.

Ecology Frame

Check the consequences in your life and relationships if you got your
outcome.
Ask:
'Who else does this effect?'
'What would happen if I got it?'
'If I got it straight away, would I take it?'
Be sensitive to your feelings of doubt that start 'Yes, but . . .'
What considerations do these feelings of doubt represent?
How can you change your outcome to take them into account?
Now run this modified outcome through the **'POSERS'** process to
check that it is still well-formed.

The last step is, *take action*.
You have to make the first move.
The journey of a thousand miles begins with one step.
If the outcome is well-formed, it is achievable, motivating, and much
more likely to be compelling.

PRESENT STATE AND DESIRED STATE

One way of thinking about change in business, personal development, or education, is as a journey from a present state to a desired state. A problem is the difference between the two. By setting an outcome in the future, you have in a sense created a problem in the present, and conversely, every problem in the present can be changed into an outcome.

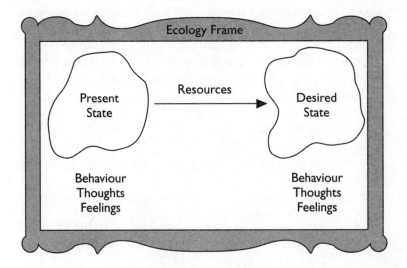

Your behaviour, thoughts and feelings will be different in the present state and in the desired state. To move from one to the other you need resources.

The energy for the journey comes from motivation. The desired state must be something we really want, or clearly connected to something we really want. We must also be committed to the outcome; reservations often show that ecology has not been taken fully into account. In short, we must want to make the journey, and believe the goal is achievable and worthwhile.

Skills, techniques, and resourceful states of mind are the means to achieve the goal. They may involve our physiology, nutrition, strength, and stamina. NLP skills are powerful resources to overcome barriers, resistance and interference.

COMMUNICATION

Communication is a multifaceted word that covers just about any interaction with others: casual conversation, persuading, teaching and negotiating.

What does 'communication' mean? The word is a static noun, but really communication is a cycle or loop that involves at least two people. You cannot communicate with a waxwork dummy; what you do is meaningless, it gets no response. When you communicate with another person, you perceive their response, and react with your own thoughts and feelings. Your ongoing behaviour is generated by your internal responses to what you see and hear. It is only by paying attention to the other person that you have any idea at all about what to say or do next. Your partner is responding to your behaviour in the same way.

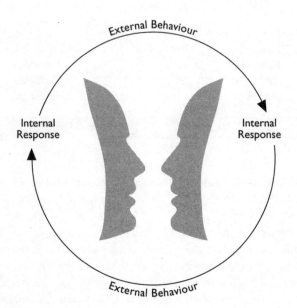

Enchanted Rings

You communicate with your words, with your voice quality and with your body: postures, gestures, expressions. You cannot *not* communicate. Some message is conveyed even if you say nothing and keep still. So communication involves a message that passes from one person to another. How do you know that the message you give is the message they receive? You have probably had the experience of making a neutral remark to someone, and being amazed at the meaning they read into it. How can you be sure the meaning they get is the meaning you intend?

There is an interesting exercise used in NLP training courses. You choose a simple sentence, for example, 'It's a nice day today', and three basic emotional messages you want to convey with it. You might choose to say it in a happy way, a menacing way, and a sarcastic way. You say your sentence in the three ways to another person, without telling her the three messages you wish to convey. She then tells you the emotional messages she actually got from your sentence. Sometimes what you intended matches what she perceived. Often it does not. You can then explore what you would have to do differently with your voice and body language to ensure the message she gets is the same as the message you send.

Communication is so much more than the words we say. These form only a small part of our expressiveness as human beings. Research shows that in a presentation before a group of people, 55 per cent of the impact is determined by your body language – posture, gestures and eye contact – 38 per cent by your tone of voice, and only 7 per cent by the content of your presentation. (Mehrabian and Ferris, 'Inference of Attitudes from Nonverbal Communication in Two Channels' in *The Journal of Counselling Psychology* Vol. 31, 1967, pp. 248–52.)

The exact figures will differ in different situations, and clearly body language and tonality make an enormous difference to the impact and meaning of what we say. It's not what we say, but how we say it that makes the difference. Margaret Thatcher spent a great deal of time and effort altering her voice quality. Tonality and body language determine whether the word 'Hello' is a simple recognition, a threat, a put down, or a delightful greeting. Actors do not really work with words, they are trained in tonality and body language. Any actor needs to be able to convey at least a dozen different shades of meaning with the word 'no'. All of us express many shades of meaning in everyday conversation and probably also have a dozen different ways to say 'no', only we do not consciously think about them.

If the words are the content of the message, then the postures gestures, expression, and voice tonality are the context in which the message is embedded, and together they make the meaning of the communication.

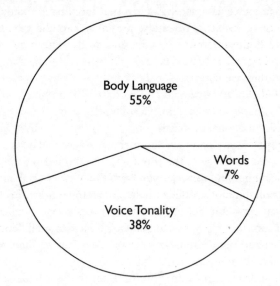

So there is no guarantee that the other person understands the meaning you are trying to communicate. The answer goes back to outcome, acuity and flexibility. You have an outcome for the communication. You notice what responses you are getting, and you keep changing what you do or say until you get the response you want.

To be an effective communicator, act on the principle that:

The meaning of the communication is the response that you get.

We constantly use our communication skills to influence people; all therapy, management and education involve influencing and communication skills. There is a paradox that while no-one would be interested in learning skills that are not effective, effective skills may be denigrated and labelled as manipulation. Manipulation carries a negative connotation that you are somehow forcing a person to do something against their best interests.

This is certainly not true of NLP, which has wisdom, choice and ecology built in at a deep level. NLP is the ability to respond effectively to others and to understand and respect their model of the world. Communication is a loop, what you do influences the other person, and what they do influences you; it cannot be otherwise. You can take responsibility for your part in the loop. You already influence others; the only choice is whether to be conscious or unconscious of the effects you create. The only question is, can you influence with integrity? Is the influence you are having in alignment with your values? NLP techniques are neutral. As with cars, how they are used and what they are used for depends on the skill and intentions of the person in the driver's seat.

RAPPORT

How do you get into the communication loop? How can you respect and appreciate another person's model of the world while keeping your own integrity? In education, therapy, counselling, business, selling and training, rapport or empathy is essential to establish an atmosphere of trust, confidence and participation, within which people can respond freely. What do we do to gain rapport with people, how do we create a relationship of trust and responsiveness, and how can we refine and extend this natural skill?

To get a practical rather than a theoretical answer, turn the question the other way round. How do you know when two people are in rapport? As you look around in restaurants, offices, any place where people meet and talk, how do you know which people have rapport and which do not?

Communication seems to flow when two people are in rapport, their bodies as well as their words match each other. What we say can create or destroy rapport, but that is only 7 per cent of the communication. Body language and tonality are more important. You may have noticed that people who are in rapport tend to mirror and match each other in posture, gesture and eye contact. It is like a dance, where partners respond and mirror each other's movements with movements of their own. They are engaged in a dance of mutual responsiveness. Their body language is complementary.

Have you ever found yourself enjoying a conversation with somebody and noticing that both your bodies have adopted the same posture? The deeper that rapport, the closer the match will tend to be. This skill would seem to be inborn, for newborn babies move in rhythm with the voices of the people around them. When people are not in rapport their bodies reflect it – whatever they are saying, their bodies will not be matching. They are not engaged in the dance and you can see it immediately.

Successful people create rapport, and rapport creates trust. You can create rapport with whoever you wish by consciously refining the natural rapport skills that you use every day. By matching and mirroring body language and tonality you can very quickly gain rapport with almost anyone. Matching eye contact is an obvious rapport skill and usually the only one that is consciously taught in English culture, which has a strong taboo against noticing body language consciously, and responding to it.

To create rapport join the other person's dance by matching their body language sensitively and with respect. This builds a bridge between you and their model of the world. Matching is not mimicry, which is noticeable, exaggerated and indiscriminate copying of another person's movements, and is usually considered offensive. You can match arm movements by small hand movements, body movements by your head movements. This is called 'cross over mirroring'. You can match distribution of the body weight, and basic posture. When people *are* like each other, they like each other. Matching breathing is a very powerful way of gaining rapport. You may already have observed that when two people are in deep rapport they breathe in unison.

These are the basic elements of rapport. But do not believe us. Notice what happens when you mirror others. Then notice what happens when you stop. Notice what people do who are in rapport. Start to be conscious of what you do naturally so you can refine it and choose when to do it.

Notice especially what happens when you mismatch. Some counsellors and therapists mirror and match unconsciously, almost compulsively. Mismatching is a very useful skill. The most elegant way to end a conversation is to disengage from the dance. And you cannot disengage from the dance if you have not been dancing in the first place. The most extreme mismatch of course is to turn your back.

Voice matching is another way that you can gain rapport. You can match tonality, speed, volume and rhythm of speech. This is like joining another person's song or music, you blend in and harmonize. You can use voice matching to gain rapport in a telephone conversation. Then you can also mismatch, changing the speed and tonality of your voice to end the conversation. This is a very useful skill. To close a telephone conversation naturally is sometimes very difficult.

There are only two limits to your ability to gain rapport: the degree to which you can perceive other people's postures, gestures and speech patterns, and the skill with which you can match them in the dance of rapport. The relationship will be a harmonious dance between your integrity, what you can do and believe wholeheartedly, and how far you are willing to build a bridge to another person's model of the world.

Notice how you feel when you match; you may well feel uncomfortable matching some people. There are certainly some behaviours you will not want to match directly. You would not match a breathing pattern that was much faster than was natural for you, nor would you match an asthmatic's breathing pattern. You could mirror both with small movements of your hand. A person's fidgety movements could be subtly mirrored by swaying your body. This is sometimes called cross matching, using some analogous behaviour rather than directly matching. If you are prepared to use these skills consciously, you can create rapport with whoever you choose. You do not have to like the other person to create rapport; you are simply building a bridge to understand them better. Creating rapport is one choice, and you will not know that it is effective or what results it has unless you *try it.*

So rapport is the total context round the verbal message. If the meaning of the communication is the response it elicits, gaining rapport is the ability to elicit responses.

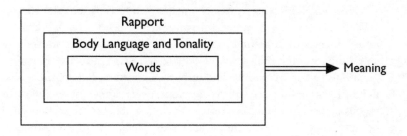

PACING AND LEADING

Rapport allows you to build a bridge to the other person: you have some point of understanding and contact. With that established, you can start to change your behaviour and they are likely to follow. You can lead them in another direction. The best teachers are those who establish rapport, and enter into the world of the learner, and so make it easier for the learner to enter into a greater understanding of their subject or skill. They get on well with their students, and the good relationship makes the task easier.

In NLP this is called pacing and leading. Pacing is establishing the bridge, through rapport and respect. Leading is changing your behaviour so the other person follows. Leading will not work without rapport. You cannot lead someone over a bridge without building it first. When I told my friend I was writing a book on Neuro-Linguistic Programming, I was not pacing him, so I could not lead him into an explanation of what I was writing about.

Keeping your own behaviour the same, and expecting other people to understand and pace you is one choice. Sometimes it will yield good results and sometimes it will not. By keeping your own behaviour constant you will get all sorts of different results and not all will be welcome. If you are prepared to change your behaviour to suit your outcome you are bound to have more success.

We pace all the time, to fit into different social situations, to put others at ease, and to feel at ease ourselves. We pace different cultures by respecting foreign customs. If you want to enter a high-class hotel, you wear a tie. You do not swear in front of the vicar. You go to an interview in suitable clothes if you are serious about wanting the job.

Pacing is a general rapport skill we use when discussing common interests, friends, work or hobbies. We pace emotions. When a loved one is sad, we use a sympathetic tone and manner, not a hearty shout of 'Cheer up!' This would probably make them feel worse. You mean well; that is you have a positive intention, but it does not work. A better choice would be first to mirror and match posture and use a gentle tonality that matches how they feel. Then gradually change and adjust to a more positive and resourceful posture. If the bridge is built, the other person will follow your lead. They will perceive unconsciously that you have respected their state, and be willing to follow if that is the way they want to go. This sort of emotional pacing and leading is a powerful tool in counselling and therapy.

With an angry person, match their anger a little below their level. If you go too far, there is a danger of escalation. Once you have matched, you can start to lead them down gradually into a calmer state by toning down your own behaviour. A sense of urgency can be paced and matched by voice tonality, speaking a little louder and quicker than usual.

You gain rapport by appreciating what people say. You do not have to agree with it. One very good way to do this is to eliminate the word 'but' from your vocabulary. Replace it with 'and'. 'But' can be a destructive word; it implies you have heard what is said . . . *but* . . . have some objections that discount it. 'And' is innocent. It simply adds to and expands what has been said already. Words have great power in themselves. You might consider making this change. But it could be difficult. But you will probably find it is worth it. And you will get more rapport.

People who share the same culture will tend to have common values and a common world view. Common interests, work, friends, hobbies, likes, dislikes and political persuasion will create some rapport. We get on naturally with people that share our basic values and beliefs.

Pacing and leading is a basic idea in NLP. It takes in rapport, and respect for the other person's model of the world. It assumes a positive intention, and is a powerful way of moving towards agreement or a shared outcome. In order to pace and lead successfully, you need to pay attention to the other person and be flexible enough in your own behaviour to respond to what you see and hear. NLP is the martial art of communication: graceful, enjoyable and very effective.

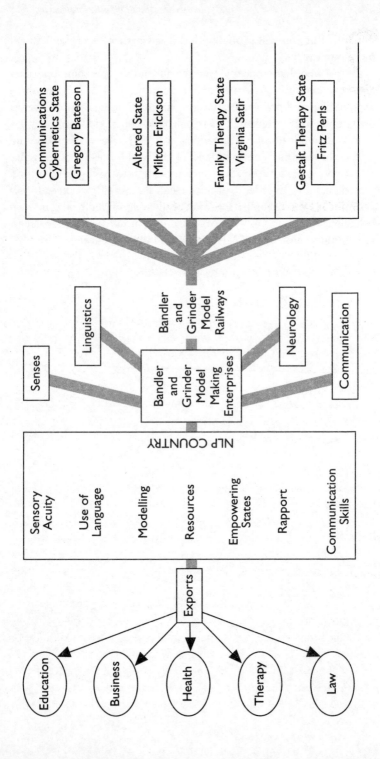

2

THE DOORS OF PERCEPTION

If the loop of communication has any beginning, it starts with our senses. As Aldous Huxley pointed out, the doors of perception are the senses, our eyes, nose, ears, mouth and skin, and these are our only points of contact with the world.

Even these points of contact are not what they seem. Take your eyes, for example, your 'windows on the world'. Well, they are not. Not windows at any rate, nor even a camera. Have you ever wondered why a camera can never catch the essence of the visual image that you see? The eye is much more intelligent than a camera. The individual receptors, the rods and cones of the retina, respond not to the light itself, but to changes or differences in the light.

Consider the apparently simple task of looking at one of these words. If your eye and the paper were perfectly still, the word would disappear as soon as each rod had fired in response to the initial black or white stimulus. In order to keep sending information about the shape of the letters, the eye flickers minutely and rapidly so that the rods at the boundary of black and white keep on being stimulated. In this way we continue to see the letter. The image is projected upside down onto the retina, coded into electrical impulses by the rods and cones and reassembled from these by the visual cortex of the brain. The resulting picture is then projected 'out there', but it is created deep inside the brain.

So we see through a complex series of active perceptual filters. The same is true of our other senses. The world we perceive is not the real world, the territory. It is a map made by our neurology. What we pay attention to in the map is further filtered through our beliefs, interests and preoccupations.

We can learn to allow our senses to serve us better. The ability to notice more, and make finer distinctions in all the senses can significantly enrich the quality of life, and is an essential skill in many work areas. A wine taster needs a very discriminating palate; a musician needs the ability to make fine auditory distinctions. A mason or woodcarver must be sensitive to the feel of his materials to release the figure imprisoned in the stone or wood. A painter must be sensitive to the nuances of colour and shape.

Training of this nature is not so much seeing more than others as knowing what to look for, learning to perceive the difference that makes the difference. The development of a rich awareness in each of our physical senses is sensory acuity, and an explicit goal of NLP training.

REPRESENTATIONAL SYSTEMS

Communication starts with our thoughts, and we use words, tonality and body language to convey them to the other person. And what are thoughts? There are many different scientific answers, yet everyone knows intimately what thinking is *for themselves*. One useful way of thinking about thinking is that we are using our senses internally.

When we think about what we see, hear and feel, we re-create these sights, sounds and feelings inwardly. We re-experience information in the sensory form in which we first perceived it. Sometimes we are aware of doing this, sometimes not. Can you remember where you went on your last holiday?

Now, how do you remember it? Maybe pictures of the place come into your mind. Perhaps you say the name or hear sounds. Or maybe you recall what you felt. Thinking is such an obvious, commonplace activity, we never give it a second thought. We tend to think about what we think about, not how we think about it. Also we assume that other people think in the same way as we do.

So one way we think is consciously or unconsciously remembering the sights, sounds, feelings, tastes and smells we have experienced. Through the medium of language we can even create varieties of sense experience without having had the actual experiences. Read the next paragraph as slowly as you comfortably can.

Take a moment to think about walking in a forest of pine trees. The trees tower above you, rising up on every side. You see the colours of the forest all around you and the sun makes leafy shadows and mosaics on the forest floor. You walk through a patch of sunlight that has broken through the cool ceiling of leaves above you. As you walk, you become aware of the stillness, broken only by the birds calling and the crunching sound of your feet as you tread on the debris of the forest floor. There is the occasional sharp crack as you snap a dried twig underfoot. You reach out and touch a tree trunk, feeling the roughness of the bark under your hand. As you gradually become aware of a gentle breeze stroking your face, you notice the aromatic smell of pine mingling with the more earthy smells of the forest. Wandering on, you remember that supper will be ready soon and it is one of your favourite meals. You can almost taste the food in your mouth in anticipation . . .

To make sense of that last paragraph, you went through those experiences in your mind, using your senses inwardly to represent the experience that was conjured up by the words. You probably created the scene sufficiently strongly to imagine the taste of food in an already imaginary situation. If you have ever walked in a pine forest, you may have remembered specific experiences from that occasion. If you have not, you may have constructed the experience from other similar experiences, or used material from television, films, books or similar sources. Your experience was a mosaic of memories and imagination. Much of our thinking is typically a mixture of these remembered and constructed sense impressions.

We use the same neurological pathways to represent experience inwardly as we do to experience it directly. The same neurons generate electrochemical charges which can be measured by electromyographic readings. Thought has direct physical effects, mind and body are one system. Take a moment to imagine eating your favourite fruit. The fruit may be imaginary, but the salivation is not.

We use our senses outwardly to perceive the world, and inwardly to 're-present' experience to ourselves. In NLP the ways we take in, store and code information in our minds – seeing, hearing, feeling, taste and smell – are known as representational systems.

The visual system, often abbreviated to 'V', can be used externally (e) when we are looking at the outside world (V^e), or internally (i) when we are mentally visualizing (V^i). In the same way, the auditory system (A), can be divided into hearing external sounds (A^e), or internal (A^i). The feeling sense is called the kinesthetic system (K). External kinesthetics (K^e), include tactile sensations like touch, temperature and moisture. Internal kinesthetics (K^i), include remembered sensations, emotions, and the inner feelings of balance and bodily awareness, known as the proprioceptive sense, which provide us with feedback about our movements. Without them we could not control our bodies in space with our eyes closed. The vestibular system is an important part of the kinesthetic system. It deals with our sense of balance, maintaining the equilibrium of our whole body in space. It is located in the complex series of canals in the inner ear. We have many metaphors about this system such as losing our balance, falling for somebody, or being put in a spin. The vestibular system is very influential and is often treated as a separate representational system.

Visual, auditory and kinesthetic are the primary representation systems used in Western cultures. The sense of taste, gustatory (G), and smell, olfactory (O), are not so important and are often included in the kinesthetic sense. They often serve as powerful and immediate links to the sights, sounds and pictures associated with them.

We use all three of the primary systems all the time although we are not equally aware of them all, and we tend to favour some over others. For example many people have an inner voice that runs in the auditory system creating an internal dialogue. They rehearse arguments, rehear speeches, make up replies and generally talk things over with themselves. This is, however, only one way of thinking.

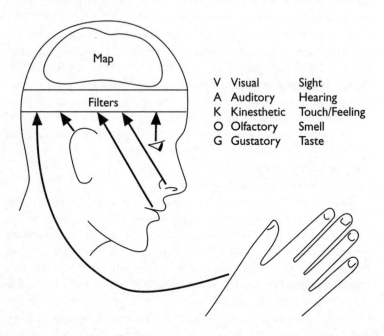

V	Visual	Sight
A	Auditory	Hearing
K	Kinesthetic	Touch/Feeling
O	Olfactory	Smell
G	Gustatory	Taste

Representational Systems

Representational systems are not mutually exclusive. It is possible to visualize a scene, have the associated feelings and hear the sounds simultaneously, although it may be difficult to pay attention to all three at the same time. Some parts of the thought process will be unconscious.

The more a person is absorbed in their inner world of sights, sounds and feelings, the less he or she will be able to pay attention to the external world. There is a story of a famous chess player in an international tournament who was so engrossed in the position he was seeing in his mind's eye that he had two full dinners in one evening. He had completely forgotten eating the first. Being 'lost in thought' is a very apt description. People experiencing strong inner emotions are also less vulnerable to external pain.

Our behaviour is generated from a mixture of internal and external sense experience. At any time we will be paying attention to different parts of our experience. While you read this book you will be focusing on the page and probably not aware of the feeling in your left foot . . . until I mentioned it . . .

As I type this, I am mostly aware of my internal dialogue pacing itself to my (very slow) rate of typing on the word processor. I will be distracted if I pay attention to outside sounds. Not being a very good typist, I look at the keys and feel them under my fingers as I type, so my visual and kinesthetic senses are being used outwardly. This would change if I stopped to visualize a scene I wanted to describe. There are some emergency signals that would get my immediate attention: a sudden pain, my name being called, the smell of smoke, or, if I am hungry, the smell of food.

PREFERRED REPRESENTATIONAL SYSTEMS

We use all our senses externally all the time, although we will pay attention to one sense more than another depending on what we are doing. In an art gallery we will use mostly our eyes, in a concert, our ears. What is surprising is that when we think, we tend to favour one, perhaps two representational systems regardless of what we are thinking about. We are able to use them all, and by the age of 11 or 12 we already have clear preferences.

Many people can make clear mental images and think mainly in pictures. Others find this viewpoint difficult. They may talk to themselves a good deal, while others base their actions mostly on their feel for a situation. When a person tends to use one internal sense habitually, this is called their preferred or primary system in NLP; they are likely to be more discriminating and able to make finer distinctions in this system than in the others.

This means some people are naturally better, or 'talented' at particular tasks or skills, they have learned to become more adept at using one or two internal senses and these have become smooth and practised, running without effort or awareness. Sometimes a representational system is not so well developed, and this makes certain skills more difficult. For example, music is a difficult art without the ability to hear sounds internally.

No system is better in an absolute sense than another, it depends what you want to do. Athletes need a well-developed kinesthetic awareness, and it is difficult to be a successful architect without a facility for making clear, constructed mental pictures. One skill shared by outstanding performers in any field is to be able to move easily through all the representational systems and use the most appropriate one for the task in hand.

Different psychotherapies show a representation system bias. The bodywork therapies are primarily kinesthetic; psychoanalysis is predominantly verbal and auditory. Art therapy and Jungian symbolism are examples of more visually based therapies.

LANGUAGE AND REPRESENTATIONAL SYSTEMS

We use language to communicate our thoughts so it is not surprising that the words we use reflect the way we think. John Grinder tells of the time when he and Richard Bandler were leaving a house to lead a Gestalt therapy group. Richard was laughing about someone who had said, 'I see what you are saying.'

'Think about it literally,' he said. 'What could they possibly mean?'

'Well,' said John, 'let's take it literally; suppose it means that people are making images of the meaning of the words that you use.'

This was an interesting idea. When they got to the group, they tried an entirely new procedure on the spur of the moment. They took green, yellow and red cards and had people go round the group and say their purpose for being there. People who used a lot of words and phrases to do with feelings got a yellow card. People who used a lot of words and phrases to do with hearing and sounds got green cards. Those who used words and phrases predominantly to do with seeing got red cards.

Then there was a very simple exercise. People with the same colour card were to sit down and talk together for five minutes. Then they sat down and talked to somebody with a different colour card. The differences they observed in rapport between people were profound. People with the same colour card were getting on much better. Grinder and Bandler thought this was fascinating and suggestive.

PREDICATES

We use words to describe our thoughts, so our choice of words will indicate which representational system we are using. Consider three people who have just read the same book.

The first might point out that he *saw* a lot in it, the examples were well chosen to *illustrate* the subject and it was written in a *sparkling* style.

The second might object to the *tone* of the book; it had a *shrill* prose style. In fact, he cannot *tune* in to the author's ideas at all, and he would like to *tell* him so.

The third feels the book dealt with a *weighty* subject in a *balanced* way. He liked the way the author *touched* on all the key topics, and he *grasped* the new ideas easily. He felt in sympathy with the author.

They all read the same book. You will notice that each person expressed themselves about the same book in a different way. Regardless of what they thought about it, *how* they thought about it was different. One was thinking in *pictures,* the second in *sounds* and the third in *feelings.* These sensory-based words, adjectives, adverbs and verbs, are called *predicates* in NLP literature. Habitual use of one kind of predicate will indicate a person's preferred representational system.

It is possible to find out the preferred system of the writer of any book by paying attention to the language that he or she uses. (Except for NLP books, where the writers may take a rather more calculated approach to the words they use . . .) Great literature always has a rich and varied mix of predicates, using all the representational systems equally, hence its universal appeal.

Words such as 'comprehend', 'understand', 'think' and 'process' are not sensory-based, and so are neutral in terms of representational systems. Academic treatises tend to use them in preference to sensory-based words, perhaps as an unconscious recognition that sensory-based words are more personal to the writer and reader and so less 'objective'. However, neutral words will be translated differently by the kinesthetic, auditory or visual readers, and give rise to many academic arguments, often over the meaning of the words. Everyone thinks they are right.

You may like to become aware over the coming weeks what sort of words you favour in normal conversation. It is also fascinating to listen to others and discover what sort of sensory-based language they prefer. Those of you who prefer to think in pictures may like to see if you can identify the colourful language patterns of the people around you. If you think kinesthetically, you could get in touch with the way people put themselves over, and if you think in sounds, we would ask you to listen carefully and tune in to how different people talk.

There are important implications for gaining rapport. The secret of good communication is not so much what you say, but how you say it. To create rapport, match predicates with the other person. You will be speaking their language, and presenting ideas in just the way they think about them. Your ability to do this will depend on two things. Firstly your sensory acuity in noticing, hearing or picking up other people's language patterns. And secondly, having an adequate vocabulary of words in that representational system to respond. Conversations will not all be in one system of course, but matching language does wonders for rapport.

You are more likely to gain rapport with a person who thinks in the same way as you, and you discover this by listening to the words he or she uses, regardless of whether you agree with them or not. You might be on the same wavelength, or you might see eye to eye. Then again you might get a solid understanding.

It is a good idea to use a good mix of predicates when you address a group of people. Let the visualizers see what you are saying. Let the auditory thinkers hear you loud and clear, and put yourself over so that the kinesthetic thinkers in the audience can grasp your meaning. Otherwise why should they listen to you? You risk two thirds of your audience not following your talk if you confine yourself to explaining in one representational system.

LEAD SYSTEM

Just as we have a preferred representational system for our conscious thinking, so we also have a preferred means of bringing information into our conscious thoughts. A complete memory would contain all the sights, sounds, feelings, tastes and smells of the original experience, and we prefer to go to one of these to recall it. Think back again to your holiday.

What came first . . . ?

A picture, sound or feeling?

This is the lead system, the internal sense that we use as a handle to reach back to a memory. It is how the information reaches conscious mind. For example, I may remember my holiday and start to be conscious of the feelings of relaxation I experienced, but the way it comes to mind initially might be as a picture. Here my lead system is visual and my preferred system is kinesthetic.

The lead system is rather like a computer's start-up program – unobtrusive, but necessary for the computer to work at all. It is sometimes called the input system, as it supplies the material to think about consciously.

Most people have a preferred input system, and it need not be the same as their primary system. A person may have a different lead system for different types of experience. For example, they may use pictures to get in touch with painful experiences, and sounds to take them back to pleasant ones.

Occasionally a person may not be able to bring one of the representational systems into consciousness. For example, a person may say he does not see any mental pictures. While this is true for him in his reality, it is actually impossible, or he would be unable to recognize people, or describe objects. He is simply not conscious of the pictures he is seeing internally. If this unconscious system is generating painful images, he may feel bad without knowing why. This is often how jealousy is generated.

SYNESTHESIAS, OVERLAP AND TRANSLATION

Have you seen but a white lily grow?
Before rude hands have touched it?
Have you marked but the fall of the snow,
Before the soil has smirched it?
Have you felt the wool of beaver,
Or swan's down, ever?
Have you smelt of the bud of the briar
Or the nard in the fire,
Have you tasted the bag of the bee?

O so white, O so soft,
O so sweet is she.

Ben Jonson 1572–1637

The richness and range of our thoughts depends on our ability to link and move from one way of thinking to another. So if my lead system is auditory, and my preferred system is visual, I will tend to remember a person through the sound of their voice and then think about them in pictures. From there I might get a feeling for the person.

So we take information in from one sense, but represent it internally with another. Sounds can conjure up visual memories or abstract visual imagery. We talk of tone colour in music, and of warm sounds, and also of loud colours. An immediate and unconscious link across the senses is called a *synesthesia*. A person's lead to preferred system will usually be their strong, typical synesthesia pattern.

Synesthesias form an important part of the way we think and some are so pervasive and widespread that they seem to be wired into our brain at birth. For example, colours are usually linked to moods: red for anger and blue for tranquillity. In fact both blood pressure and pulse rate increase slightly in a predominantly red environment, and decrease if the surroundings are mostly blue. There are studies that show that people experience blue rooms as colder than yellow rooms, even when they are actually slightly warmer. Music makes extensive use of synesthesias; how high a note is set visually on the stave relates to how high it sounds, and there are a number of composers who associate certain musical sounds with definite colours.

Synesthesias happen automatically. Sometimes we want to link internal senses in a purposeful way, for example to gain access to a whole representation system that is out of conscious awareness.

Suppose a person has great difficulty visualizing. First you could ask her to go back to a happy, comfortable memory, perhaps a time by the sea. Invite her to hear the sound of the sea internally, and the sound of any conversation that took place. Holding this in mind, she might overlap to feeling the wind on her face, the warmth of the sun on her skin, and the sand between her toes. From here it is a short step for her to see an image of the sand beneath her feet, or see the sun in the sky. This technique of overlapping can bring back a full memory: pictures, sounds and feelings.

Just as a translation from one language to another preserves the meaning but totally changes the form, so experiences can be translated between internal senses. For example, you might see a very untidy room, get an uncomfortable feeling and want to do something about it. The sight of the same room might leave a friend feeling unaffected and he would be at a loss to understand why you feel so bad. He might label you as oversensitive because he cannot enter into your world of experience. He might understand how you feel if you told him it was like having itching powder in his bed. Translating into sound, you might compare it to the discomfort of hearing an instrument played out of tune. This analogy would strike a chord with any musician; you would at last be speaking his language.

EYE ACCESSING CUES

It is easy to know if a person is thinking in pictures, sounds or feelings. There are visible changes in our bodies when we think in different ways. The way we think affects our bodies, and how we use our bodies affects the way we think.

What is the first thing you see as you walk through the front door of your home?

To answer that question you probably looked up and to your left. Looking up and left is how most right-handed people remember images.

Now, really get in touch with how it would feel to have velvet next to your skin.

Here you probably looked down and to your right, which is the way the majority of people get in touch with their feelings.

We move our eyes in different directions in a systematic way depending on how we are thinking. Neurological studies have shown that eye movement both laterally and vertically seems to be associated with activating different parts of the brain. These movements are called lateral eye movements (LEM) in neurological literature. In NLP they are called eye accessing cues because they are the visual cues that let us know how people are accessing information. There is some innate neurological connection between eye movements and representational systems, for the same patterns occur worldwide (with the exception of the Basque region of Spain).

When we visualize something from our past experience our eyes tend to move up and to our left. When constructing a picture from words or trying to 'imagine' something we have never seen, our eyes move up and to our right. The eyes move across to our left for remembered sounds and across to our right for constructed sounds.

When accessing feelings, the eyes will typically go down to our right. When talking to ourselves, the eyes will usually go down left. Defocusing the eyes and staring straight ahead, 'looking into the distance', also shows visualization.

Visualization

Visual-constructed images

Visual-remembered images

Constructed sounds

Remembered sounds

**Kinesthetic
(Feelings and bodily
sensations)**

**Auditory Digital
(Internal dialogue)**

NB: This is as you look at another person

Most right-handed people have the pattern of eye movements shown in the diagram. They may be reversed for left-handed people, who may look right for remembered images and sounds, and left for constructed images and sounds. Eye accessing cues are consistent for a person even if they contradict this model. For example, a left-handed person may look down to his left for feelings and down to his right for internal dialogue. However, he will do this consistently and not mix the accessing cues randomly. There are always exceptions – look carefully before applying these general rules to anybody. The answer is not the generalization, but the person in front of you.

Although it is possible to move your eyes consciously in any direction while thinking, accessing a particular representation system is generally much easier if you are using the appropriate natural eye movements. They are ways of fine tuning the brain to think in a particular way. If you want to remember something you saw yesterday, it is easiest to look up to your left or stare straight ahead. It is difficult to remember images while looking down.

We are not normally conscious of our lateral eye movements and there is no reason why we should be, but 'looking' for information in the right place is a very useful skill.

Accessing cues allow us to know how another person is thinking, and an important part of NLP training involves becoming aware of other people's eye accessing cues. One way to do this is to ask different sorts of questions and notice the eye movements, not the replies. For example, if I ask, 'What colour is your lounge carpet?' you would have to visualize the lounge to give the answer regardless of the colour.

You might like to try out the following exercise with a friend. Sit down in a quiet place, ask her the following questions and watch her eye accessing cues. Make a note of them if you want to. Tell her to keep her answers brief or just nod when she has the answer. When you have finished, change places and answer the questions yourself. This is nothing to do with trying to catch her out to prove a point, only simple curiosity about how we think.

QUESTIONS THAT WOULD NECESSARILY INVOLVE VISUAL
MEMORIES TO GET AN ANSWER WOULD BE:

What colour is your front door?
What do you see on your journey to the nearest shop?
How do the stripes go round a tiger's body?
How tall is the building you live in?
Which of your friends has the longest hair?

THESE ANSWERS WOULD INVOLVE VISUAL CONSTRUCTION
TO GIVE AN ANSWER:

What would your bedroom look like with pink-spotted wallpaper?
If a map is upside down, which direction is southeast?
Imagine a purple triangle inside a red square.
How do you spell your Christian name backwards?

TO ACCESS AUDITORY MEMORY YOU MIGHT ASK:

Can you hear your favourite piece of music in your mind?
Which door slams loudest in your house?
What is the sound of the engaged tone on the telephone?
Is the third note in the national anthem higher or lower than the
second note?
Can you hear the dawn chorus in your mind?

QUESTIONS FOR AUDITORY CONSTRUCTION:

How loud would it be if ten people shouted at once?
What would your voice sound like underwater?
Think of your favourite tune played at double speed.
What sound would a piano make if it fell off the top of a ten-storey
building?
What would the scream of a mandrake sound like?
What would a chainsaw sound like in a corrugated iron shed?

QUESTIONS TO START INTERNAL DIALOGUE:

What tone of voice do you use when you talk to yourself?
Recite a nursery rhyme silently.
When you talk to yourself, where does the sound come from?
What do you say to yourself when things go wrong?

QUESTIONS FOR THE KINESTHETIC SENSE
(INCLUDING SMELL AND TASTE):

What does it feel like to put on wet socks?
What is it like to put your foot into a cold swimming pool?
What is it like to feel wool next to the skin?
Which is warmer now, your left hand or your right hand?
What is it like to settle down in a nice hot bath?
How do you feel after a good meal?
Think of the smell of ammonia.
What is it like to taste a spoonful of very salty soup?

The thought process is what matters, not the actual answers. It is not even necessary to get verbal replies. Some questions can be thought of in different ways. For example, to find out the number of sides of a 50 pence piece, you might visualize the coin and count the sides, or alternatively, you might count them by mentally feeling round the edge. So if you ask a question that should evoke visualization, and the accessing cues are different, this is a tribute to the person's flexibility and creativity. It does not mean that the patterns are wrong necessarily, or the person is 'wrong'. If in doubt, ask, 'What were you thinking then?'

Eye accessing cues happen very quickly, and you need to be observant to see them all. They will show the sequence of representational systems that a person uses to answer these questions. For example, in the auditory question about the loudest slamming door, a person might visualize each door, mentally feel himself slamming it and then hear the sound. He might have to do this several times before being able to give an answer. Usually a person will go to their lead system first to answer a question. Someone who leads visually will typically make a picture of the various situations in the auditory and feeling questions before hearing the sound or having the feeling.

OTHER ACCESSING CUES

Eye movements are not the only accessing cues, although they are probably the easiest to notice. As the body and mind are inseparable, how we think always shows somewhere, if you know where to look. In particular, it shows in breathing patterns, skin colour and posture.

A person who is thinking in visual images will generally speak more quickly and at a higher pitch than someone who is not. Images happen fast in the brain and you have to speak fast to keep up with them. Breathing will be higher in the chest and more shallow. There is often an increase in muscle tension, particularly in the shoulders, the head will be up, and the face will be paler than it is normally.

People who are thinking in sounds breathe evenly over the whole chest area. There are often small rhythmic movements of the body and the voice tonality is clear, expressive and resonant. The head is well balanced on the shoulders or slightly at an angle as if listening to something.

People who are talking to themselves will often lean their head to one side, resting it on their hand or fist. This is known as a 'telephone position' because it looks as if they are speaking on an invisible telephone. Some people repeat what they have just heard under their breath. You will be able to see their lips move.

Kinesthetic accessing is characterized by deep breathing low in the stomach area, often accompanied by muscle relaxation. With the head down, the voice will have a deeper tonality, and the person will typically speak slowly, with long pauses. Rodin's famous sculpture of 'The Thinker' is undoubtedly thinking kinesthetically.

Movements and gestures will also tell you how a person is thinking. Many people will point to the sense organ that they are using internally: they will point to their ears while listening to sounds inside their head, point to the eyes if visualizing, or to the abdomen if they are feeling something strongly. These signs will not tell you what a person is thinking about, only how he or she is thinking it. This is body language at a much more refined and subtle level than it is normally interpreted.

The idea of representational systems is a very useful way of understanding how different people think, and reading accessing cues is an invaluable skill for anyone who wants to communicate better with others. For therapists and educators it is essential. Therapists can begin to know how their clients are thinking, and discover how they might change it. Educators can discover what ways of thinking work best for a particular subject and teach those precise skills.

There have been many theories of psychological types based both on physiology and ways of thinking. NLP suggests another possibility. Habitual ways of thinking leave their mark on the body. These characteristic postures, gestures and breathing patterns will become habitual in individuals who think predominantly in one way. In other words, a person who speaks quickly in a high tonality, who breathes fairly rapidly high in the chest, and who is tense in the shoulder area is likely to be someone who thinks mostly in pictures. A person who speaks slowly, with a deep voice, breathing deeply as he or she does so, will probably rely on their feelings to a large extent.

A conversation between a person thinking visually and a person thinking in feelings can be a very frustrating experience for both sides. The visual thinker will be tapping his foot in impatience, while the kinesthetic person literally 'can't see' why the other has to go so quickly. Whoever has the ability to adapt to the other person's way of thinking will get better results.

However, do remember that these generalizations must all be checked against observation and experience. NLP is emphatically not another way to pigeonhole people into types. To say that someone is a visual type is no more useful than saying he has red hair. If it blinds you to what he is doing in the here and now, it is worse than useless, and just another way of creating stereotypes.

There can be a great temptation to categorize yourself and others in terms of primary representation system. To make this error is to fall into the trap that has beset psychology: invent a set of categories and then cram people into them whether they fit or not. People are always richer than generalizations about them. NLP provides a rich enough set of models to fit what people actually do rather than try to make the people fit the stereotypes.

SUBMODALITIES

So far we have talked about three main ways of thinking – in sounds, in pictures and in feelings – but this is only a first step. If you wanted to describe a picture you have seen, there is a lot of detail you could add. Was it in colour or black and white? Was it a moving-film strip, or still? Was it far away or near? These sorts of distinctions can be made regardless of what is in the picture. Similarly you could describe a sound as high or low pitched, near or far, loud or soft. A feeling could be heavy or light, sharp or dull, light or intense. So having established the general way we think, the next step is to be much more precise within that system.

Make yourself comfortable and think back to a pleasant memory. Examine any picture you have of it. Are you seeing it as if through your own eyes (associated), or are you seeing it as if from somewhere else (dissociated)? For example, if you see yourself in the picture, you must be dissociated. Is it in colour? Is it a movie or a slide? Is it a three-dimensional image or is it flat like a photograph? As you continue to look at the picture you may make other descriptions of it as well.

Next pay attention to any sounds that are associated with that memory. Are they loud or soft? Near or far? Where do they come from?

Finally pay attention to any feelings or sensations that are a part of that memory. Where do you feel them? Are they hard or soft? Light or heavy? Hot or cold?

These distinctions are known as submodalities in NLP literature.

If representational systems are modalities – ways of experiencing the world – then submodalities are the building blocks of the senses, how each, picture, sound or feeling is composed.

People have used NLP ideas throughout the ages. NLP did not spring into being when the name was invented. The ancient Greeks talked about sense experience, and Aristotle talked about submodalities in all but name when he referred to the qualities of the senses.

Here is a list of the most common submodality distinctions:

VISUAL

Associated (seen through own eyes), or dissociated (looking on at self)
Colour or black and white
Framed or unbounded
Depth (two or three dimensional)
Location (e.g. to left or right, up or down)
Distance of self from picture
Brightness
Contrast
Clarity (blurred or focused)
Movement (like a film or a slide show)
Speed (faster or slower than usual)
Number (split screen or multiple images)
Size

AUDITORY

Stereo or mono
Words or sounds
Volume (loud or soft)
Tone (soft or harsh)
Timbre (fullness of sound)
Location of sound
Distance from sound source
Duration
Continuous or discontinuous
Speed (faster or slower than usual)
Clarity (clear or muffled)

KINESTHETIC

Location
Intensity

Pressure (hard or soft)
Extent (how big)
Texture (rough or smooth)
Weight (light or heavy)
Temperature
Duration (how long it lasts)
Shape

These are some of the most common submodality distinctions that people make, not an exhaustive list. Some submodalities are discontinuous or digital; like a light switch, on or off, an experience has to be one or the other. An example would be associated or dissociated; a picture cannot be both at the same time. Most submodalities vary continuously, as if controlled by a dimmer switch. They form a sort of sliding scale, e.g. clarity, brightness or volume. Analogue is the word used to describe these qualities that can vary continuously between limits.

Many of these submodalities are enshrined in the phrases we use, and if you look to the list at the end of this chapter, you may see them in a new light or they may strike you differently, for they speak volumes about the ways our minds work. Submodalities can be thought of as the most fundamental operating code of the human brain. It is simply not possible to think any thought or recall any experience without it having a submodality structure. It is easy to be unaware of the submodality structure of experience until you put your conscious attention on it.

The most interesting aspect of submodalities is what happens when you change them. Some may be changed with impunity and make no difference. Others may be crucial to a particular memory, and changing them changes the whole way we feel about the experience. Typically the impact and meaning of a memory or thought is more a function of a few critical submodalities than it is of the content.

Once an event has happened, it is finished and we can never go back and change it. After that, we are not responding to the event any more, but to our memory of the event, which can be changed.

Try this experiment. Go back to your pleasant experience. Make sure you are associated in the picture, seeing it as through your own eyes. Experience what this is like. Next dissociate. Step outside it and view the person who looks and sounds very like you. This will almost certainly change how you feel about the experience. Dissociating from a memory robs it of its emotional force. A pleasant memory will lose its pleasure, an unpleasant one, its pain. When dealing with trauma, it is important to dissociate from the emotional pain first, otherwise the whole episode may be completely blocked out of consciousness and be difficult if not impossible to think about. Dissociating first puts the feelings at a safe distance so they can be dealt with. This is the basis of the phobia cure set out in Chapter 8. The next time your brain conjures up a painful scene, dissociate from it. To enjoy pleasant memories to the full, make sure you are associated. You can change the way you think. This is one essential piece of information for the unwritten Brain Users' Manual.

Try this experiment in changing how you think and discover which submodalities are most critical for you.

Think back to a specific situation of emotional significance that you can remember well. First become aware of the visual part of the memory. Imagine yourself turning the brightness control up and down, just as you would on a TV. Notice what difference it makes to your experience when you do this. What brightness do you prefer? Finally put it back how it was originally.

Next bring the image closer, then push it far away. What difference does this make and which do you prefer? Put it back how it was.

Now, if it has colour, make it black and white. If it was black and white give it colour. What is the difference and which is better? Put it back.

Next, does it have movement? If so, slow it right down until it is at a standstill. Then try speeding it up. Notice your preference and put it back.

Finally try changing from associated to dissociated and back.

Some or all of these changes will have a profound impact on how you feel about that memory. You may like to leave the memory with the submodalities at the values you like best. You may not like the default values your brain has given you. Do you remember choosing them?

Now, carry on your experiment with the other visual submodalities and observe what happens. Do the same for the auditory and kinesthetic parts of the memory.

For most people an experience will be most intense and memorable if it is big, bright, colourful, close and associated. If this is so for you, then make sure you store your good memories like this. By contrast, make your unpleasant memories small, dark, black and white, far away and dissociate from them. In both cases the content of the memory stays the same; it is how we remember it that has changed. Bad things happen and have consequences that we have to live with, but they need not haunt us. Their power to make us feel bad in the here and now is derived from the way we think about them. The crucial distinction to make is between the actual event at the time, and the meaning and power we give it by the way we remember it.

Perhaps you have an internal voice that nags you.

Slow it down.

Now speed it up.

Experiment with changing the tone.

Which side does it come from?

What happens when you change it to the other side?

What happens if you make it louder?

Or softer?

Talking to yourself can be made a real pleasure.

The voice may not even be your own. If it is not, ask it what is it doing inside your head.

Changing submodalities is a matter of personal experience, difficult to convey in words. Theory is arguable, experience is convincing. You can be the director of your own mental film show and decide how you want to think, rather than be at the mercy of the representations that seem to arise of their own accord. Like television in summer, the brain shows a lot of repeats, many of which are old, and not very good films. You do not have to watch them.

Emotions come from somewhere, although their cause may be out of conscious awareness. Also, emotions themselves are a kinesthetic representation and have weight, location and intensity; they have submodalities which can be changed. Feelings are not entirely involuntary and you can go a long way towards choosing the feelings you want. Emotions make excellent servants, but tyrannical masters.

Representational systems, accessing cues and submodalities are some of the essential building blocks of the structure of our subjective experience. It is no wonder that people make different maps of the world. They will have different lead and preferred representational systems, different synesthesias, and code their memories with different submodalities. When finally we use language to communicate, it is a wonder we understand each other as well as we do.

Examples of Sensory-Based Words and Phrases

VISUAL

Look, picture, focus, imagination, insight, scene, blank, visualize, perspective, shine, reflect, clarify, examine, eye, focus, foresee, illusion, illustrate, notice, outlook, reveal, preview, see, show, survey, vision, watch, reveal, hazy, dark.

AUDITORY

Say, accent, rhythm, loud, tone, resonate, sound, monotonous, deaf, ring, ask, accent, audible, clear, discuss, proclaim, remark, listen, ring, shout, speechless, vocal, tell, silence, dissonant, harmonious, shrill, quiet, dumb.

KINESTHETIC

Touch, handle, contact, push, rub, solid, warm, cold, rough, tackle, push, pressure, sensitive, stress, tangible, tension, touch, concrete, gentle, grasp, hold, scrape, solid, suffer, heavy, smooth.

NEUTRAL

Decide, think, remember, know, meditate, recognize, attend, understand, evaluate, process, decide, learn, motivate, change, conscious, consider.

OLFACTORY

Scented, stale, fishy, nosy, fragrant, smoky, fresh.

GUSTATORY

Sour, flavour, bitter, taste, salty, juicy, sweet.

VISUAL PHRASES

I see what you mean.
I am looking closely at the idea.
We see eye to eye.
I have a hazy notion.
He has a blind spot.
Show me what you mean.
You'll look back on this and laugh.
This will shed some light on the matter.
It colours his view of life.
It appears to me.

Beyond a shadow of doubt.
Taking a dim view.
The future looks bright.
The solution flashed before his eyes.
Mind's eye.
Sight for sore eyes.

AUDITORY PHRASES

On the same wavelength.
Living in harmony.
That's all Greek to me.
A lot of mumbo jumbo.
Turn a deaf ear.
Rings a bell.
Calling the tune.
Music to my ears.
Word for word.
Unheard-of.
Clearly expressed.
Give an audience.
Hold your tongue.
In a manner of speaking.
Loud and clear.

KINESTHETIC PHRASES

I will get in touch with you.
I can grasp that idea.
Hold on a second.
I feel it in my bones.
A warm-hearted man.
A cool customer.
Thick skinned.
Scratch the surface.
I can't put my finger on it.
Going to pieces.
Control youself.
Firm foundation.
Heated argument.
Not following the discussion.
Smooth operator.

OLFACTORY AND GUSTATORY PHRASES

Smell a rat.
A fishy situation.
A bitter pill.
Fresh as a daisy.
A taste for the good life.
A sweet person.
An acid comment.

3

PHYSIOLOGICAL STATES AND EMOTIONAL FREEDOM

When people are emotionally and physically at a low ebb, we often say that they are in 'an awful state'. In the same way, we recognize that to make the most of a challenge, we must be 'in the right state of mind'. What is a state of mind? Quite simply it is all the thoughts, emotions, and physiology that we express at that moment; the mental pictures, sounds, feelings, and all the patterns of physical posture and breathing. Mind and body are completely interconnected, so our thoughts immediately influence our physiology, and vice versa.

Our state of mind changes continually, and this is one of the few things about it we can rely on. When you change state, the whole world out there changes too. (Or seems to.) We are usually more conscious of our emotional state than of our physiology, posture, gesture and breathing patterns. In fact, emotions are often considered to be beyond conscious control; they are the visible tip of the iceberg. We do not see the whole physiology and thought process that lies underneath and supports the emotions. These are the submerged nine tenths of the iceberg. To try to influence the emotions without changing state is as futile as trying to make the iceberg disappear by sawing the top off it. More will simply surface, unless you spend an inordinate amount of energy holding it underwater, and this is what we often do, with drugs or willpower. For us, the mind leads, and the body follows obediently. Thus habitual emotions can be stamped onto a person's face and posture, because the person does not notice how the emotions mould his or her physiology.

Try this experiment. Take a moment to think of some enjoyable experience, a time when you felt really good. When you have thought of one, think yourself back into that experience. Spend a minute or two re-experiencing it as fully as you can.

As you enjoy these pleasant feelings, look around you, notice what you see and what sounds you are hearing as you re-live this memory.

Notice how you feel. When you are ready, return to the present.

Notice the impact this has on your present state, especially your posture and your breathing. Past experiences are not gone forever; they can help you feel good in the present. Although the sights and the sounds of the past are gone, when we mentally re-create them the actual feeling is still as real and as tangible as it was then. So regardless of what you were feeling before you read this paragraph, you have just put yourself in a more resourceful state.

Now, by contrast, think back to a slightly uncomfortable past experience. When one comes to mind, imagine yourself back in it again.

Back in that situation, what do you see?

What are you hearing?

Notice how you feel.

Do not stay with this experience for very long; return to the present and notice the effect this has had on you. Become aware of how you feel after this experience compared with how you felt after the previous one. Notice too your different posture and breathing pattern.

Now change your emotional state. Do some kind of physical activity, move your body and switch your attention from the memory to something completely different. Look out of the window, jump up and down, run to the other side of the room and touch the wall, or bend down and touch your toes. Pay attention to the physical sensations of moving and to what you sense in the here and now.

This is known as changing state or breaking state in NLP terms, and is worth doing whenever you notice yourself feeling negative or unresourceful. Whenever you remember unpleasant memories and access unresourceful states, your entire body takes up these negative states and holds them as patterns of muscle tone, posture, and breathing. These physically stored memories can contaminate your future experiences for minutes or hours. We all know what it is like to 'get out of bed on the wrong side'. People who suffer depression have unconsciously mastered the ability to maintain an unresourceful state for long periods. Others have mastered the ability to change their emotional state at will, creating for themselves an emotional freedom that transforms the quality of their lives. They fully experience the emotional ups and downs of life, but they learn, move on, and do not dwell on emotional pain unnecessarily.

As we go through life we continually move through different emotional states, sometimes quickly, sometimes more gradually. For example, you may be feeling quite low and a friend telephones with some good news. Your spirits lighten. Or maybe it is a bright sunny day and you open your mail to find an unexpectedly large bill. Mental clouds can cover a real sun.

We can influence our states, rather than simply react to what happens on the outside. In the last few minutes, you have felt good, then uncomfortable, then . . . however you feel now. And nothing has actually happened in the outside world. You have done this all yourself.

ELICITATION

Elicitation is the word used in NLP to describe the process of guiding someone into a particular state. This is an everyday skill under a different label, for we are all greatly practised in putting people into different moods, or bringing them out of moods. We do it all the time by our words, tonality and gestures. Sometimes, however, we do not elicit what we want. How many times have you heard a phrase like, 'What's the matter with him, all I said was . . .'

The simplest way to elicit an emotional state is to ask the person to remember a past time when he was experiencing that emotion. The more expressive you are, the more expressiveness you will elicit. If your voice tone, words, facial expression and body posture match the response you are asking for, you are more likely to get it.

All your efforts get results. If you are trying to put someone in a calm resourceful state, it is useless talking in a loud, fast tone of voice, breathing quickly and shallowly, and making lots of fidgety movements. Despite your soothing words, the other person will become more anxious. You need to do what you say. So if you want to lead someone into a confident state, you ask him to remember a particular time when he was confident. You speak clearly, in a confident tone of voice, breathe evenly, with your head up, and your posture erect. You act 'confident'. If your words are not congruent with your body language and voice tone, he will tend to follow the nonverbal message.

It is important too that the person remembers the experience as if inside it, not watching dissociated from the outside. Being associated in the situation will bring back the feelings more fully. Imagine watching someone else eating your favourite fruit. Now imagine yourself eating the fruit. Which is the more tasteful experience? To elicit your own states, put yourself back in the experience as fully and as vividly as possible.

CALIBRATION

Calibration is the NLP word that means recognizing when people are in different states. This is a skill that we all have and use in our everyday lives, and one that is well worth developing and refining.

You distinguish the subtly different expressions as others experience different memories, and different states. For example, when someone remembers a frightening experience his lips may become thinner, his skin paler and his breathing more shallow. Whereas when he is remembering a pleasurable experience, his lips are more likely to be fuller, the skin colour more flushed and breathing deeper, with softening of the facial muscles.

Often our calibration is so poor that we only notice someone is upset when he starts to cry. We rely too much on people telling us verbally how they feel, instead of using our eyes and ears. We do not want to calibrate from a punch on the nose to know that a person is angry, nor do we want to hallucinate all sorts of possibilities from a twitch of an eyebrow.

There is an exercise in NLP training that you may like to try with a friend. Ask your friend to think of a person he likes very much. As he does this, notice his eye position, and angle of his head. Also notice his breathing: is it deep or shallow, fast or slow, high or low? Notice too the differences in facial muscle tone, skin colour, lip size and tone of voice. Pay attention to these subtle signs that are normally disregarded. They are the outward expression of inner thoughts. They *are* those thoughts in the physical dimension.

Now ask your friend to think of someone he dislikes. Notice the difference in these signs. Ask your friend to think of one, then the other, until you are sure you can detect some differences in his physiology. In NLP terms, you have now calibrated these two states of mind. You know what they look like. Ask your friend to think of one of the people, but without telling you which one. You will know which one it is by reading the physical cues you have already identified.

It seems as if you are mind reading . . .

So we can refine our skills. Mostly we calibrate unconsciously. For example if you ask a loved one whether he or she would like to go out for a meal, you will know intuitively, immediately, before they open their mouth what the answer will be. The 'yes' or 'no' is the very last step in the thought process. We cannot help but respond with body, mind and language so deeply are the three connected.

You may have had the experience of talking to someone and getting an intuition that he or she was lying. You had probably calibrated this unconsciously, and you got the feeling without knowing why. The more you practise calibration, the better you will become. Some differences between states will be slight, some will be unmistakable. As you practise, subtle changes will become easier to detect. The changes, no matter how small, were always there. As your senses become sharper, you will detect them.

ANCHORS

Emotional states have a powerful and pervasive influence on thinking and behaviour. After eliciting and calibrating these states, how can we use them to become more resourceful in the present? We need some way of making them consistently available and stabilizing them in the here and now.

Imagine the impact on your life if you could switch on your high-performance states at will. Top performers in politics, sports, the arts and business must be able to be resourceful in the moment. The actor must be able to commit himself to the role when the curtain goes up, not an hour before, or half way through the second act. This is the bottom line of professionalism.

It is just as important to be able to switch off. The actor must be able to drop his role when the curtain falls. Many people in business become highly motivated, achieve great things, yet burn themselves out and become unhappy, lose their family life, or in extreme cases, suffer a coronary. Managing our states needs balance and wisdom.

We each have a personal history that is rich in different emotional states. To re-experience them, we need a trigger, some association in the present to elicit the original experience. Our minds naturally link experiences, it is the way we give meaning to what we do. Sometimes these associations are very enjoyable; for example, a favourite piece of music that brings back a pleasant memory. Every time you hear that particular tune, it evokes those pleasant feelings. And every time it does that, it strengthens the association.

A stimulus which is linked to and triggers a physiological state is called an *anchor* in NLP. Other examples of naturally occurring positive anchors would be favourite photographs, evocative smells, or a loved one's special expression or voice tone.

Anchors are usually external. An alarm clock rings and it is time to get up. The school bell signals the end of playtime. These are auditory anchors. A red traffic light means stop. A nod of the head means yes. These are visual anchors. And the smell of newly laid tar might take you back as if by magic to a childhood scene where you first smelt it. Advertisers try to make their brand name an anchor for a particular commodity.

An anchor is anything that accesses an emotional state, and they are so obvious and widespread that we hardly notice them. How are anchors created? In one of two ways. First by repetition. If you see repeated instances of red being associated with danger, it will become anchored. This is simple learning: red means danger. Secondly, and much more important, anchors can be set in a single instance if the emotion is strong and the timing is right. Repetition is only needed if there is no emotional involvement. Think back to when you were at *school* (that's a powerful anchor in itself), and found that something interesting and exciting was easy to learn. Facts that did not interest you needed a lot of repetition. The less emotionally involved you are, the more repetitions are needed to learn the association.

Most associations are very useful. They form habits and we could not function without them. If you are a driver you already have an association between a green light turning to red and moving your feet in a certain way on the pedals. This is not an operation you want to have to think about consciously every time, and if you do not make that association, you are not likely to survive for very long on the roads.

Other associations, while useful, may be less pleasant. The sight of a police car in your rear-view driving mirror is quite likely to start you wondering about the state of your car, and what speed you are travelling at.

Other associations are not useful. Many people associate speaking in public with anxiety and mild panic attacks. The thought of an examination makes many people feel nervous and uncertain. Words can act as anchors. The word 'test' is an anchor for most schoolchildren to feel anxious and not able to give of their best.

In extreme cases an external stimulus can trigger a very powerful negative state. This is the realm of phobias. For example, people who suffer from claustrophobia have learnt a very powerful association between being in a confined space and feeling panic, and they always make that association.

Many people's lives are unnecessarily limited by fears from their past history that have not yet been re-evaluated. Our minds cannot help making associations. Are the ones you have made and are making, enjoyable, useful and empowering?

We *can* choose the associations we want to make. You can take whatever experiences in life you find most difficult or most challenging, and decide in advance what physiological state you would like to be in to meet them. For any situation you are unhappy about, you can create a new association and therefore a new response by using anchors.

This is done in two stages. First, you choose the emotional state you want, then you associate it with a stimulus or anchor so that you can bring it to mind whenever you want it. Sportsmen use lucky mascots to harness their skill and stamina. You will often see sportsmen going through small ritual movements that serve the same purpose.

Using your resourceful states through anchors is one of the most effective ways to change your own and other people's behaviour. If you go into a situation in a more resourceful state than you did in the past, your behaviour is bound to change for the better. Resourceful states are the key to peak performance. When you change what you do, other people's behaviour will also change. Your whole experience of the situation will be different.

Cautionary note. The change techniques in this chapter and throughout this book are very powerful, and this power comes mainly from the skill of the person who uses them. A carpenter can make superb furniture with precision tools; the same tools in the hands of an apprentice will not get the same results. Similarly it takes practice and work to get the best sound from a fine musical instrument.

In the course of training many people in these skills, we have seen the pitfalls in applying these techniques for the first time. We strongly recommend that you practise these techniques in a safe context, like an NLP training seminar, until you are confident, and your skill levels are high enough.

RESOURCE ANCHORING

Here are the steps for transferring positive emotional resources from past experiences to the present situations where you want them to be available. You may want to get together with a friend and ask him or her to guide you through these steps.

Take some comfortable position in a chair, or stand where you can consider the process in an uninvolved way. Think of some specific situation in which you would like to be different, feel different and respond differently. Then choose a particular emotional state, from the many different ones you have experienced in your life, that you would most like to have available to you in that situation. It can be any resourceful state – confidence, humour, courage, persistence, creativity – whatever comes intuitively to mind as being most appropriate. When you are clear about the resource you want, begin to find one specific occasion in your life when you felt that resource. Take your time, noticing which examples come to your mind and choose whichever one is most clear and intense.

If you have chosen a resource, and it is difficult to remember a time when you experienced it, then imagine somebody you know, or even a fictitious character from a film or book. What would it be like, being them, experiencing this resource? Remember that although the character may not be real, your feelings are, and these are what count.

When you have a specific instance in mind, real or imaginary, you are ready to go to the next step, which is to choose the anchors that will bring this resource to mind when you want it.

First, your kinesthetic anchor: some feeling you can associate to your chosen resource. Touching your thumb and finger together or making a fist in a particular way works well as a kinesthetic anchor. I see a very common one on the squash court when players touch the side wall to bring back a confident feeling if their game is going badly.

It is important that the anchor is unique and not part of your ongoing behaviour. You want a distinctive anchor that does not occur all the time, and so does not get associated with other states and behaviours. Also you want the anchor to be discreet; something you can do without being conspicuous. Standing on your head might work well as a confidence anchor, but would get you a reputation for eccentricity if you were to use it to help you make after dinner speeches.

Next, the auditory anchor. This can be a word or phrase that you say to yourself internally. It does not matter which word or phrase you use as long as it is in tune with the feeling. The way you say it, the particular voice tone you use, will have as much impact as the word or phrase itself. Make it distinctive and memorable. For example, if 'confidence' is the resource state that you want to anchor, then you might say to yourself, 'I am feeling more and more confident,' or simply, 'Confidence!' Use a confident voice tone. Make sure the resource really is appropriate to the problem situation.

Now the visual anchor. You might choose a symbol, or you can remember what you were seeing when you did feel confident. As long as the image you choose is distinctive, and helps to evoke the feeling, then it will work.

When you have chosen an anchor in each representation system, the next step is to relive those feelings of confidence by vividly re-creating the resource situation. Step forward or change chairs as you associate fully into the experience. Putting different emotional states in actual different physical locations helps to separate them cleanly.

In your imagination, go back now to the specific resource state you have chosen . . .

Remember where you were and what you were doing . . .

As that becomes clearer, imagine that you are right back in it now and that you are seeing what you were seeing . . .

You can begin to hear whatever sounds you were hearing and start to re-experience those feelings that were so strong a part of that experience . . .

Take some time and enjoy reliving that experience as fully as possible . . .

To really get back in touch with your full body sense of your resource state it often helps to act out your activities in that moment again. You may want to put your body into that same position, doing the same things that you were doing (only if appropriate) . . .

When those feelings have come to a peak and start to diminish, physically move back to your uninvolved position. You have now found out how best to recreate your resourceful state and how long it takes to do so.

Now you are ready to anchor the resources. Step into your place for the resource state and re-experience it again. As it reaches its peak, see your image, make your gesture and say your words. You must connect your anchors to the resource state as it is coming to its peak.

The timing is critical. If you connect them after the peak, you would anchor going out of the state, which is not what you want. The sequence of anchors is not critical, use the order that works best for you, or fire them simultaneously. Sometime after your resourceful feelings have peaked, you will need to step out and change state before you are ready to test the anchor.

Use all three anchors in the same way and the same sequence and notice the extent to which you do indeed access your resourceful state. If you are not satisfied, go back and repeat the anchoring process to strengthen the association between your anchors and your resourceful state. You may need to repeat this a few times and this is worth it to be able to have that state when you need it.

Lastly, think of a future situation where you are likely to want that resourceful state. What can you use as a signal to let you know you need that resource? Find the first thing that you see, hear or feel that lets you know that you are in that situation. The signal can be external or internal. For example, a particular expression on somebody's face or their voice tone would be an external signal. Starting an internal dialogue would be an internal signal. Being aware that you have a choice about how you feel is a resource state in itself. It will also interrupt the habitual, anchored response. It is worth anchoring this awareness to the signal. The signal then acts as a reminder that you can choose your feelings.

After a time, if you keep using the anchor, the signal itself will become an anchor for you to feel resourceful. The trigger that used to make you feel bad now becomes one that makes you feel strong and resourceful. Here is a summary of the basic steps of the process.

Anchors need to be:
  Timed just as the state is reaching its peak
  Unique and distinctive
  Easy to repeat exactly
  Linked to a state that is cleanly and completely re-experienced.

Anchoring Resourceful States Summary
1. Identify the situation where you want to be more resourceful.
2. Identify the particular resource you want, e.g. confidence.
3. Check the resource really is appropriate by asking, 'If I could have this resource here, would I really take it?' If yes, proceed. If no, go back to 2.
4. Find an occasion in your life when you had that resource.

5. Select the anchors you are going to use in each of the three main representation systems; something you see, hear and feel.
6. Step into another location and in your imagination put yourself fully back into the experience of that resourceful state. Re-experience it again. When it has peaked, change state and step out of it.
7. Re-experience your resource state and, as it comes up to peak, connect the three anchors. Hold the state for as long as you want, then change state.
8. Test the association by firing the anchors and confirming that you do indeed go into the state. If you are not satisfied, repeat step 7.
9. Identify the signal that lets you know you are in a problem situation where you want to use your resource. This signal will remind you to use your anchor.

You can now use these anchors to summon your resource state whenever you wish. Remember to experiment with this or any other NLP technique to find the way that works best for you. Keep your outcome in mind, (feeling more resourceful), and play with the technique until you succeed. Some people find that simply making their gesture ('firing' their kinesthetic anchor) is enough to produce the resource state. Others want to continue using all three anchors.

You can use this process to anchor different resources. Some people anchor a different resource on each finger. Other people connect many different resource states to the same anchor to produce a very powerful resource anchor. This technique of adding different resources to the same anchor is known as *stacking resources*.

Anchoring and using your resourceful states is a skill, and like all skills, becomes easier and more effective the more you use it. Some people find it works dramatically the very first time. Others find they need to practise to build their competence at doing it as well as their confidence that it does indeed make a difference. Remember the learning model. If anchoring is new to you, congratulations on passing from unconscious incompetence to conscious incompetence. Enjoy this stage as you become consciously competent.

Resource anchoring is a technique for increasing emotional choice. This culture, unlike some, believes that emotional states are involuntary, and created by external circumstances or other people. The universe may deal us a mixed hand of cards, but we can choose how and when to play them. As Aldous Huxley said, 'Experience is not what happens to you, it is what you do with what happens to you.'

CHAINING ANCHORS

Anchors can be chained so that one leads to another. Each anchor provides a link in the chain and triggers the next one, just as the electrical impulse flows from nerve to nerve in our body. In a sense, anchors are a mirror on the outside of how we create a new neural pathway in our nervous system between an initial trigger and a new response. Chaining anchors allows us to move through a sequence of different states easily and automatically. Chaining is particularly useful if the problem state is strong and the resource state is too far away to reach in one stage.

For example, think of a situation where you feel frustrated. Can you identify the consistent signal that triggers this feeling?

A tone of voice in your internal dialogue?

A particular sensation?

Something you see?

It can often seem that the world is conspiring against you, but you can control how you react to the conspiracy. And the feeling of frustration is not going to change the outside world. When you have this internal signal, decide which state you would like to move on to. Curiosity perhaps? And from there maybe to creativity?

To set up your chain, think back to a time when you were intensely curious, and anchor it, perhaps kinesthetically, by a touch on your hand. Break state, and then think yourself back to a time when you were in a very creative state and anchor that, perhaps with a touch on another place on your hand.

Next, take yourself back to a frustrating experience, and as soon as you get the frustration signal, fire your anchor for curiosity, and as the feeling of curiosity is peaking, touch your anchor for creativity.

This establishes a neural network of associations that moves easily from frustration through curiosity to creativity. Practise it as many times as you wish so that the connection becomes automatic.

Once you can elicit, calibrate and anchor different emotional states, you have a tremendously powerful tool for counselling and therapy. You and your clients have quick and easy access to any emotional state. Anchoring can be used to assist clients to make changes remarkably quickly, and can be done in any system, visual, auditory or kinesthetic.

COLLAPSING ANCHORS

Now what would happen if you tried to feel hot and cold at the same time? What happens when you mix yellow and blue? What happens if you fire two opposite anchors at once? You feel warm or green. To collapse anchors, you anchor an unwanted negative state (call it cold or blue), and a positive state (call it hot or yellow), and fire the anchors simultaneously. After a short period of confusion, the negative state is changed, and a new and different state comes into being. You can use this technique of collapsing anchors with a friend or client. Here is an outline of the steps; make sure you establish and maintain rapport throughout.

Collapse Anchors Summary
1. Identify the problem state and a powerful positive state the person would rather have available.
2. Elicit the positive state, and calibrate the physiology so you can distinguish it. Break state: have the client change to some other state by directing their attention elsewhere and asking him to move.
3. Elicit the desired state again, and anchor it with a particular touch and/or word or phrase, then break state again.
4. Test the positive anchor to make sure it is established. Fire the anchor by applying the same touch on the same spot and/or saying the appropriate words. Be sure that you do indeed see the physiology of the desired state. If you do not, repeat steps 1 to 3 to make the association stronger. When you have established a positive anchor for the desired state, break state.
5. Identify the negative state or experience, and repeat steps 2 to 4 using the negative state, and anchor it with a particular touch on a different spot. Break state. This establishes an anchor for the problem state.
6. Take the person through each state in turn, using the anchors alternately, saying something like, 'So there are some times when you have felt "blue" (fire negative anchor) and in these situations you would really rather feel "yellow" (fire positive anchor).' Repeat this a number of times without breaking state between them.
7. When you are ready, lead in with some appropriate words such as, 'Notice any changes you become aware of' and fire both anchors at the same time. Watch the person's physiology carefully. You will probably see signs of change and confusion. Remove the negative anchor before the positive anchor.

8. Test your work either by asking him to access the problem state or by firing the negative anchor. You should see the person go into a state somewhere between the two (different shades of green), or a new and different state, or into the positive state. If you are still getting the negative state, find out what other resource the person needs. Anchor that on the same spot as the first positive resource and then go on from step 6.

9. Finally, ask the person to think of a situation in the near future where they might have expected to feel negative, and ask him to run through it in his imagination while you notice his state. Listen as he describes it. If you are not happy with his state or if he is still unhappy about the prospect, find out what other resources are needed, and anchor those on the same spot as the first positive resource, and then go on from step 6. Collapse anchors will not work unless the positive state is stronger than the negative, and you may have to stack positive resources on one anchor to achieve this.

One way of thinking about what is happening is that the nervous system is trying to engage two mutually incompatible states at the same time. It cannot, so it does something different. The old pattern is broken and new ones are created. This explains the confusion that often happens when the two anchors are collapsed. Anchors allow experiences to be available by consciously using the natural processes that we normally use unconsciously. We anchor ourselves all the time, usually in a completely haphazard way. Instead, we can be much more selective about what anchors we respond to.

CHANGE PERSONAL HISTORY

Human experience only exists in the present moment. The past exists as memories and to remember these we have to re-experience them in some way in the present. The future exists as expectations or fantasies, again created in the present. Anchoring enables us to increase our emotional freedom by escaping from the tyranny of past negative experiences and creating a more positive future.

Change Personal History is a technique for re-evaluating troublesome memories in the light of present knowledge. We all have a rich personal history of past experiences that exist as memories in the present. While what *actually* happened (whatever that was, for human memories are fallible) cannot be changed, we can change its meaning for us in the present, and therefore its effect on our behaviour.

For example, the feeling of jealousy is almost always generated not from what actually happened, but from constructed images of what we believe happened. We then feel bad in response to those images. The images are real enough to cause some extreme reactions, even though they never happened.

If past experiences were very traumatic or very intense, so that even to think about them causes pain, then the phobia cure in Chapter 8 is a better technique to use. It is designed for dealing with very intense negative emotional experiences.

Change Personal History is useful when problem feelings or behaviour keep recurring. The 'Why do I keep doing this?' type of feeling. The first step in using this technique with a client or friend is, of course, to establish and maintain rapport.

Change Personal History Summary

1. Identify the negative state, elicit it, calibrate to it, anchor it and then break state.
2. Hold the negative anchor and ask the person to go back and think of a time when he had similar feelings. Continue until you reach the earliest experience the person can remember. Release the anchor, break state, and bring the client fully back to the present.
3. Ask the client, in the light of what he now knows, to think of what resource he would have needed in those past situations for them to have been satisfying rather than problematic experiences. He will probably identify the resource with a word or phrase like, 'security', 'being loved' or 'understanding'. The resource must come from within the person, and be under his control. Having other people in the situation behave differently would not allow the person to learn anything new. He can elicit different responses from the other people involved, only if he himself is different.
4. Elicit and anchor a specific and full experience of the necessary resource state, and test this positive anchor.
5. Holding the positive anchor, take the person back again to the earliest experience. Invite him to watch himself from the outside (dissociated) with this new resource and notice how it changes his experience. Then invite him to step inside the situation (associated) with the resource (you are still holding the anchor) and run the

experience through as if it were happening again. Ask him to notice the other people's responses in the situation, now he has this new resource. Invite him to imagine what he would be like from their point of view, so he can get a sense of how they perceive this new behaviour. If he is dissatisfied at any stage, go back to step 4, identify and stack other resources to bring to the earlier situation. When the person is satisfied, experiences the situation as different and can learn from it, remove the anchor and break state.

6. Test the change without using any anchors by asking the client to remember the past experience and notice how those memories have changed. Pay attention to his physiology. If there are signs of the negative state go back to step 4 and stack more resources.

FUTURE PACING

Experiencing a situation in advance is called future pacing in NLP, and is the final step in many NLP techniques. You step into the future in imagination with the new resources you have, and experience in advance how you wish it to be. For example, the future pace in Change Personal History is to ask the person to imagine the next time the problem situation is likely to recur. As he does this, you calibrate to see if there is any sign of a slip back into the negative state. If there is, then you know there is more work to be done.

Future pacing tests if your work is effective. It is the nearest you can get to being in the problem situation. However, the real test of any change is the next time the person encounters the problem for real. Insights and changes can easily get anchored to the psychological consulting room. Learning gets anchored to the classroom, and business plans to the board room. The real world is the real test.

Secondly, future pacing is a form of mental rehearsal. Mental preparation and practice is a consistent pattern that is found in all top performers: actors, musicians, salesmen, and particularly sportsmen. Whole training programmes are built around this one element. Mental rehearsal is practice in the imagination, and since the body and mind form one system, it prepares and primes the body for the actual situation.

Giving the brain strong positive images of success programs it to think in those terms, and makes success more likely. Expectations are self-fulfilling prophecies. These ideas of future pacing and mental rehearsal can be used to learn from every day, and to generate new behaviour. You might like to run through the following steps each night before going to sleep.

As you review the day, choose something you did very well, and something you are not so happy with. See both scenes again, rehear the sounds, experience them again in an associated way. Then step out of them and ask yourself, 'What could I have done differently?' What were the choice points in these experiences? How could the good experiences become even better? You may well identify some other choices you could have made in the not so good experience.

Now replay the experiences fully, but with you behaving differently. What does this look like? How does it sound? Check your feelings. This little ritual will build in choices. You may identify a signal in the not so good experience that will alert you the next time it happens, to use another choice that you have already mentally rehearsed.

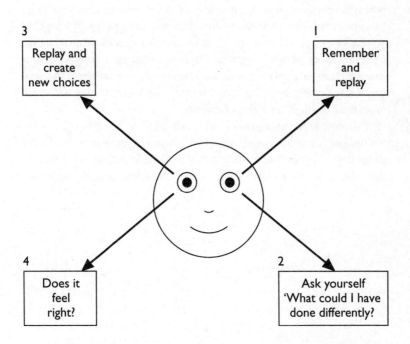

You can use this type of technique for generating entirely new behaviour, or for changing and improving something you already do.

NEW BEHAVIOUR GENERATOR

This is the more general technique to use if there is some new behaviour you want, or one that you would like to change or improve. For example, you may want to improve at your favourite sport. Watch yourself in your imagination behaving the way you would like to, hitting the tennis serve just right for example. If this is difficult, watch a role model doing the behaviour. Take the director's chair of the inner film. Be Steven Spielberg in your imagination. Watch the scene as it unfolds before your inner eye. Stay dissociated as you listen to, and edit the soundtrack. You are the star as well as the director. If there are any other people involved, notice their responses to what you are doing.

Direct the scene and edit the soundtrack until you are completely satisfied, then step inside that image of yourself and run it through as though you are doing it. As you do this, pay particular attention to both your feelings, and the responses of the people around you. Does this new behaviour represent your values and your personal integrity?

If it does not feel right, go back to the director's chair and change the film before stepping back into it. When you are happy with your imagined performance, identify an internal or external signal that you can use to trigger this behaviour. Mentally rehearse noticing the signal and going through the new behaviour.

The new behaviour generator is a simple but powerful technique to use in your personal and professional development. Every experience becomes an opportunity for learning. The more you do this, the faster you move towards becoming the person you really want to be.

4

No man is an island entire unto himself

John Donne

LOOPS AND SYSTEMS

Communication can be treated as simple cause and effect. Isolate one interaction, treat it as a cause, and analyse the effect it has without considering further influences. We often talk as if this is what happens, but it is clearly a great simplification.

The laws of cause and effect work for inanimate objects; if one billiard ball collides with another, you can predict with a fair amount of accuracy the final resting place of each. After the initial collision they no longer influence each other.

Living systems are another matter. If I kick a dog, I could calculate the force and momentum of my foot and work out exactly how far the dog should travel in a particular direction, given its size and weight. The reality would be a bit different – if I were to be foolish enough to kick a dog, it might turn round and bite my leg. The dog's final resting place is very unlikely to be anything to do with Newton's laws of motion.

Human relationships are complex – many things happen simultaneously. You cannot predict exactly what will occur, because one person's response influences the other person's communication. The relationship is a loop; we are continuously responding to feedback in order to know what to do next. Focusing on only one side of the loop is like trying to understand tennis by studying only one end of the court. You could spend a lifetime figuring out how hitting the ball 'causes' it to come back, and the laws that determine what the next shot must be. Our conscious mind is limited and can never see the whole loop of communication, only small parts of it.

The content and the context of a communication combine to make the meaning. The context is the total setting, the whole system that enfolds it. What does one piece of a jigsaw mean? Nothing in itself; it depends where it goes in the total picture, where it fits and what relationship it has to the other pieces.

What does a musical note mean? Very little on its own, it depends how it relates to the notes around it, how high or low it is, and how long it lasts. The same note can sound quite different if the notes around it change.

There are two main ways of understanding experience and events. You can focus on the content, information. What is this piece? What is it called? What does it look like? How is it like others? Most education is like this; jigsaw pieces can be interesting and beautiful to study in isolation, but you only get a one-dimensional understanding. Understanding in depth needs another viewpoint: relationship or context. What does the piece mean? How does it relate to others? Where does it fit into the system?

Our inner world of beliefs, thoughts, representational systems and submodalities also form a system. Changing one can have widespread effects and will generate other changes, as you will have discovered when you experimented with changing the submodalities of your experience.

A few well-chosen words at just the right time can transform a person's life. Changing one small piece of a memory can alter your whole state of mind. This is what happens when you deal with systems – one small push in the right direction can generate profound change, and you have to know where to push. Trying is useless. You can try really hard to feel better and finish feeling worse. Trying is like attempting to force a door inwards, you can waste a lot of energy before you realize it actually opens outwards.

When we act to achieve our goals, we need to check that there are no inner reservations or doubts. We need also to pay attention to the outer ecology and appreciate the effect our goals will have on our wider system of relationships.

So the results of our actions come back to us in a loop. Communication is a relationship, not a one-way passage of information. You cannot be a teacher without a student, or a seller without a buyer, a counsellor without a client. Acting wholeheartedly with wisdom means appreciating the relationships and interactions between ourselves and others. The balance and relationship between parts of our mind will be a mirror of the balance and relationships we have with the outside world. NLP thinking is in terms of systems. For example Gregory Bateson, one of the most influential figures in the development of NLP, applied cybernetic or systems thinking to biology, evolution and psychology, while Virginia Satir, the world-famous family therapist, and also one of the original models for NLP, treated a family as a balanced system of relationships, not a collection of individuals with problems to be fixed. Each person was a valuable part. She helped the family to achieve a better and healthier balance, and her art lay in knowing exactly where to intervene and exactly which person needed to change so that all the relationships improved. As with a kaleidoscope, you cannot change one piece without

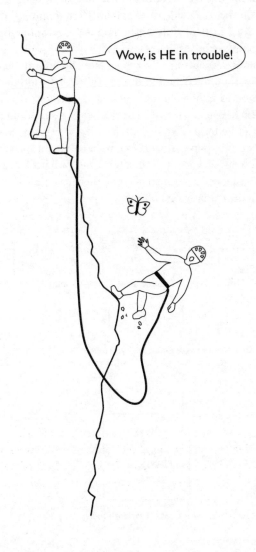

changing the whole pattern. But, which bit do you change to create the pattern you want? This is the art of effective therapy.

The best way to change others is to change yourself. Then you change your relationships and other people must change too. Sometimes we spend a lot of time on one level trying to change somebody, while on another level behaving in a way that exactly reinforces what they are doing. Richard Bandler calls this the 'Go away . . . *closer* . . .' pattern.

There is a nice metaphor from physics known as the Butterfly Effect. In theory, the movement of a butterfly's wing can change the weather on the other side of the globe, for it might just disturb the air pressure at a critical time and place. In a complex system a small change can have a huge effect.

So not all elements in a system are equally important. Some can be changed with little effect, but others will have a widespread influence. If you want to induce changes in your pulse, appetite, life span and growth rate, you need only tamper with a small gland called the pituitary at the base of your skull. It is the body's nearest equivalent to a master control panel. It works in the same way a thermostat controls a central heating system. You can set the radiators individually, but the thermostat controls them all. The thermostat is on a higher logical level than the radiators it controls.

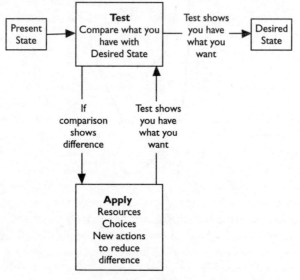

Learning Model

NLP identifies and uses the successful elements that different psychologies have in common. The human brain has the same structure the world over, and has generated all the different psychological theories, so they are bound to share some basic patterns. Because NLP takes patterns across the whole field, it is on a different logical level. A book about how to make maps is on a different level to the various books of maps, even though it is another book.

LEARNING LOOPS

We learn from our mistakes, much more than from our successes. They give us useful feedback, and we spend a lot more time thinking about them. We rarely get something right first time, unless it is very simple, and even then there will be room for improvement. We learn by a series of successive approximations. We do what we can (the present state) and compare that to what we want (desired state). We use this as feedback to act again and reduce the difference between what we want, and what we are getting. Slowly we approach our goal. This comparison drives our learning at every level through conscious incompetence to unconscious competence.

This is a general model of the way to become more effective at anything you do. You compare what you have with what you want, and act to reduce the mismatch. Then you compare again. The comparison will be based on your values: what is important to you in that situation. For example, in checking over these pages, I have to decide whether they are good enough or whether they need rewriting. My values are clarity of meaning (from the reader's viewpoint, not mine), correctness of grammar and the flow of the words.

I also need to decide on my evidence procedure. How will I know that it meets my values? If I have no evidence procedure I could go round and round the loop forever, because I will never know when to stop. This is a trap for authors who spend years correcting their manuscript to get it perfect and never publish at all. Evidence in my example would involve putting the text through the spell checker initially, then showing it to friends whose advice I value and getting their feedback. I would make alterations based on that feedback.

The model is known as the TOTE model, which stands for Test – Operate – Test – Exit. The comparison is the Test. The Operation is where you apply your resources. Test by comparing again and Exit from the loop when your evidence procedure tells you your outcome has been achieved. How successful you are will depend on the number of choices of operations you have: your flexibility of behaviour, or requisite variety, a term from cybernetics. So the journey from present state to desired state is not even a zig-zag after all, but a spiral.

There will probably be smaller loops like this going on within the larger one: smaller outcomes that you need to achieve the main one. The whole system fits together like a collection of Chinese boxes. In this model of learning, mistakes are useful, for they are results you do not want in this context. They can be used as feedback to get closer to your goal.

Children are taught many subjects at school and forget most of them. They are not usually taught how to learn. Learning to learn is a higher-level skill than learning any particular material. NLP deals with how to become a better learner, regardless of the subject. The quickest and most effective way to learn is to use what happens naturally, and easily. Learning and change is often thought to be a slow, painful process. This is not true. There are slow and painful ways of learning and changing, but using NLP is not one of them.

Robert Dilts has developed a technique for converting what could be looked on as failure into feedback, and learning from it. It is easiest with another person taking you through the following steps.

FAILURE TO FEEDBACK

1. What is the problem attitude or belief? Are all your Do-It-Yourself projects ending in ignominy? Are your attempts at cooking good news for the local take-away restaurants? In what area are you getting unwanted results? Do you believe that you cannot do something, or are not very good at it?

   As you think about the problem, what is your physiology and eye accessing position? Thinking about failure will usually involve a bad feeling, pictures of specific times you failed, and perhaps some internal voice reprimanding you, all at the same time. You cannot deal with them all together. You need to find out what is happening internally in each of the representational systems separately.

2. Look down right and get in touch with the feeling. What is the feeling by itself trying to do for you? What is its positive intention? To motivate you perhaps? Or protect you?

Look down left. Is there a message in the words taken in isolation that could be helpful?

Look up left and see the pictures of the memories. Is there something new you can learn from them? Start to get a more realistic perspective on the problem. You are capable of more than this. Notice how there are positive resources mixed in with the memories of the problem. Relate the words, pictures and feelings to the desired goal. How can they help you achieve it?

3. Identify a positive, resourceful experience to come, something you are sure you can achieve in the future. This need not be something momentous. Identify the main visual, auditory and kinesthetic submodalities of the way you think about this experience. Anchor the experience kinesthetically by touch. Check that when you fire the anchor, you access the resource experience. This is a reference experience of what you know you can achieve.

4. Look up and right and construct a picture of a desired goal or attitude that takes into account what you have learned from the feelings, pictures and words associated with the problem belief. Check that it is in harmony with your personality and relationships. Be sure there is a clear connection between the memories and the positive goal or attitude. You may want to modify the goal with what you learned from looking at the memories.

5. Make the submodalities of the desired goal the same as those of the positive reference experience, hold the anchor for the reference experience as you do this. The entire process will enable you to learn from what is past and free your expectation of the future from the grip of past failure. You will be thinking about your goal with submodalities of positive anticipation.

LEVELS OF LEARNING

Learning at the simplest level is trial and error with or without guidance. You learn to make the best choice available, the 'right' answer. This may take one trial, or many trials. You learn to write, to spell, that red traffic lights mean stop. You start from unconscious incompetence and progress to conscious competence by going through the learning loop.

Once a response becomes a habit, you stop learning. Theoretically, you could act differently, but in practice you do not. Habits are extremely useful, they streamline the parts of our lives we do not want to think about. How tedious to decide how to do up your shoelaces every morning. Definitely not an area to engage your creativity. But there is an art to deciding what parts of your life you want to turn over to habit, and what parts of your life you want to continue to learn from and have choice about. This is a key question of balance.

This question actually takes you up a level. You can look at the skills you have learned, and choose between them, or create new choices that will fulfil the same intention. Now you can learn to be a better learner, by choosing how you are going to learn.

The poor man who was granted three wishes in the fairy story obviously did not know about levels of learning. If he had known, instead of using his last wish to restore the status quo, he would have wished for three more wishes.

Children learn at school that $4 + 4 = 8$. At one level this is simple learning. You do not need to understand, just remember. There is an automatic association; it has been anchored. Left at this level, this would mean that $3 + 5$ cannot make 8 because $4 + 4$ do. Obviously learning mathematics this way is useless. Unless you connect your ideas to a higher level, they remain limited to a particular context. True learning involves learning other ways of doing what you can do already. You learn that 1 and 7 make 8 and so do 2 and 6. Then you can go up a level and understand the rules behind these answers. Knowing what you want, you can find different creative ways of satisfying it. Some people will change what they want rather than what they are doing to get it. They give up trying to get 8 because they are determined to use $3 + 4$, and it will not work out. Others may always use $4 + 4$ to make 8, never anything else.

The so-called 'hidden curriculum' of schools is an example of higher-level learning. Regardless of what is learnt, how is it learnt? Nobody consciously teaches the values of the hidden curriculum it is the school as a context, and has a greater influence on children's behaviour than the formal lessons. If children never learn that there are any other ways to learn than passively, by repetition, in a peer group, and from someone in authority, they are in an analogous position at a higher level to the child who learns that $4 + 4$ is the only way to make 8.

A still higher level of learning results in a profound change in the way we think about ourselves and the world. It involves understanding the relationships and paradoxes of the different ways we learn to learn.

Gregory Bateson tells an interesting story in his book *Steps to the Ecology of Mind* about the time he was involved in studying the communication patterns of dolphins at the Marine Research Institute in Hawaii. He would watch the trainers teach the dolphins to do tricks for a paying audience. On the first day, when the dolphin did something unusual, such as jumping out from the water, the trainer blew a whistle and threw the dolphin a fish as a reward. Every time the dolphin behaved that way, the trainer would blow the whistle and throw the dolphin a fish. Very soon the dolphin learned that this behaviour guaranteed a fish; it would repeat it more and more and come to expect the reward.

The next day the dolphin would come out and do its jump, expecting a fish, but none was forthcoming. The dolphin would repeat its jump fruitlessly for some time, then in annoyance do something else such as rolling over. The trainer then blew the whistle and threw the dolphin a fish. The dolphin then repeated this new trick, and was rewarded with fish. No fish for yesterday's trick, only for something new. This pattern was repeated for 14 days. The dolphin would come out and do the trick it had learned the day before for some time to no avail. When it did something new, it was rewarded. This was probably very frustrating for the dolphin. On the fifteenth day however, it suddenly appeared to learn the rules of the game. It went wild and put on an amazing show, including eight new unusual behaviours, four of which had never been observed in the species before. The dolphin had moved up a learning level. It seemed to understand not only how to generate new behaviours, but the rules about how and when to generate them.

One further point: during the 14 days Bateson saw the trainer throwing unearned fish for the dolphin outside the training context. When he questioned this, the trainer replied, 'That is to keep my relationship with him. If I do not have a good relationship, he is not going to bother about learning anything.'

DESCRIPTIONS OF REALITY

To learn the most from any situation or experience, you will need to gather information from as many points of view as possible. Each representational system gives a different way of describing reality. New ideas emerge from these different descriptions as white light emerges when you combine the colours of the rainbow. You cannot function with just one representational system. You need at least two: one to take in the information, and another to interpret it in a different way.

In the same way any single person's viewpoint will have blind spots caused by their their habitual ways of perceiving the world, their perceptual filters. By developing the skill of seeing the world from other people's points of view we have a way of seeing through our own blind spots, in the way that we ask a friend for advice and a different viewpoint if we are stuck. How can we shift our perceptions to get outside our own limited world view?

TRIPLE DESCRIPTION

There is a minimum of three ways we can look at our experience. In the most recent work by John Grinder and Judith DeLozier they are called first, second and third perceptual positions. Firstly, you can look at the world completely from your own point of view, your own reality within yourself, in a completely associated way, and not take anyone else's point of view into account. You simply think, 'How does this affect me?' Think back and concentrate on a time when you were intensely aware of what you thought, regardless of anyone else in the situation. This is called 'first position' (and you have just experienced it as you concentrated on your own reality, regardless of the instance you selected).

Secondly, you can consider how it would look, feel and sound from another person's point of view. It is obvious that the same situation or behaviour can mean different things to different people, so it is essential to appreciate another person's point of view and ask, 'How would this appear to them?' This is called 'second position', often known as empathy. If you are in conflict with another person, you need to appreciate how they feel about what you are doing. The stronger the rapport you have with the other person, the better you will be able to appreciate their reality, and the more skilled you will be at achieving second position.

Thirdly, you can have the experience of seeing the world from an outside point of view, as if you are a completely independent observer, someone with no personal involvement in the situation. Ask, 'How would this look to someone who is not involved?' This gives you an objective viewpoint and is known as 'third position'. It is on a different level to the other two, but it is not superior. Third position is different from being dissociated. For third position to be useful you need to be in a strong, resourceful state. You take an objective and resourceful view of your own behaviour so you can evaluate and generate some useful choices in any difficult situation. Being able to take a third position view of a problem is a very useful skill and can save you a lot of the stress and trouble that results from hasty actions. All three positions are equally important; the point is to be able to move between them freely. Someone stuck in first position will be an egoistical monster, while someone habitually in second will be unduly influenced by other people's views. Someone habitually in third will be a detached observer of life.

The idea of triple description is just one aspect of the approach taken by John Grinder and Judith DeLozier in their book *Turtles All the Way Down* to describe NLP in a simpler way. The approach is known as the 'new code' of NLP, and focuses on achieving a wise balance between conscious and unconscious processes.

We all spend time in these three positions, we do them naturally, and they help us to understand any situation or outcome better. The ability to move cleanly between them, consciously or unconsciously, is necessary to act with wisdom, and to appreciate the wonderful complexity of our relationships. The differences you see when you look at the world in different ways are what give it richness and what gives you choice. First, second and third positions are an explicit recognition that the map is not the territory. There are many different maps.

The idea is to be aware of difference, rather than try to impose uniformity. It is the difference and the tension between these different ways of looking at the world that is important. Excitement and invention comes from seeing things in a different way. Sameness breeds boredom, mediocrity and struggle. In biological evolution it is the species that are the same that come into conflict and struggle to survive. Wars erupt when people want exactly the same scarce resources. Wisdom comes from balance, and you cannot balance unless there are different forces to be balanced.

ROBERT DILTS' UNIFIED FIELD OF NLP

Robert Dilts has built a simple, elegant model for thinking about personal change, learning and communication that brings together these ideas of context, relationship, levels of learning and perceptual position. It also forms a context for thinking about the techniques of NLP, and gives a framework for organizing and gathering information, so you can identify the best point to intervene to make the desired change. We do not change in bits and pieces, but organically. The question is, exactly where does the butterfly have to move its wings? Where to push to make a difference?

Learning and change can take place at different levels.

1. Spiritual
This is the deepest level, where we consider and act out the great metaphysical questions. Why are we here? What is our purpose? The spiritual level guides and shapes our lives, and underpins our existence. Any change at this level has profound repercussions on all other levels, as St Paul found on the road to Damascus. In one sense it contains everything we are and do, and yet is none of those things.

2. Identity
This is my basic sense of self, my core values and mission in life.

3. Beliefs
The various ideas we think are true, and use as a basis for daily action. Beliefs can be both permissions and limitations.

4. Capability
These are the groups or sets of behaviours, general skills and strategies that we use in our life.

5. Behaviour
The specific actions we carry out, regardless of our capability.

6. Environment
What we react to, our surroundings and the other people we meet.

To take an example of a salesman thinking about his work at these different levels:

Environment: This neighbourhood is a good area for my work in selling.
Behaviour: I made that sale today.
Capability: I can sell this product to people.
Belief: If I do well at sales, I could be promoted.
Identity: I am a good salesman.

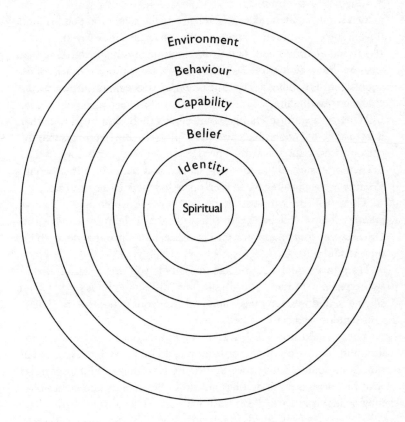

Neurological Levels

This is an example of success. The model can equally well be applied to problems. For example, I might misspell a word. I could put this down to the environment: the noise distracted me. I could leave it at the level of behaviour. I got this one word wrong. I could generalize and question my capability with words. I could start to believe I need to do more work to improve, or I could call my identity into question by thinking I am stupid.

Behaviour is often taken as evidence of identity or capability, and this is how confidence and competence are destroyed in the classroom. Getting a sum wrong does not mean you are stupid or that you are poor at maths. To think this is to confuse logical levels, equivalent to thinking a 'No Smoking' sign in a cinema applies to the characters in the film.

When you want to change yourself or others, you need to gather information, the noticeable parts of the problem, the symptoms that the person is uncomfortable with. This is the present state. Less obvious than the symptoms are the underlying causes that maintain the problem. What does the person have to keep doing to maintain the problem?

There will be a desired state, an outcome which is the goal of change. There will be the resources that will help to achieve this outcome. There are also side effects of reaching the outcome, both for oneself and others.

From this model it is possible to see how you can be embroiled in two types of conflict. You might have difficulty choosing between staying in and watching television and going out to the theatre. This is a straightforward clash of behaviours.

There could be a clash where something becomes good on one level but bad on another. For example, a child may be very good at drama in school, but believe that doing it will make him unpopular with his classmates, so he does not do it. Behaviours and capabilities may be highly rewarded, yet clash with one's beliefs or identity.

The way we view time is important. A problem may have to do with a past trauma, which has continuing repercussions in the present. A phobia would be an example, but there are many others, less dramatic, where difficult and unhappy times in the past affect our quality of life in the present. Many therapies think of present problems as determined by past events. While we are influenced by, and create our personal history, the past can be used as a resource rather than as a limitation. The Change Personal History technique has already been described. It re-evaluates the past in terms of present knowledge. We are not trapped forever to repeat past mistakes.

On the other hand, hopes and fears for the future can paralyse you in the present. This can range from worrying about giving an after dinner speech on Wednesday week, to important questions of personal and financial security in the future. And there is the present moment when all our personal history and possible futures converge. You can imagine your life on a line through time, stretching from distant past to distant future, and see how the present and desired state, identity, belief, capability, behaviour and environment all relate to your personal history and possible future.

Our total personality is like a hologram, a three-dimensional image created by beams of light. Any piece of the hologram will give you the whole image. You can change small elements like submodalities and watch the effect ripple upwards, or work from the top downwards by changing an important belief. The best way will become apparent as you gather information about the present and desired states.

Change on a lower level will not necessarily cause any change on higher levels. A change in environment is unlikely to change my beliefs. How I behave may change some beliefs about myself. However change in belief will definitely change how I behave. Change at a high level will always affect the lower levels. It will be more pervasive and lasting. So if you want to change behaviour, work with capability or belief. If there is a lack of capability, work with beliefs. Beliefs select capabilities which select behaviours, which in turn directly build our environment. A supportive environment is important, a hostile environment can make any change difficult.

It is difficult to make a change at the level of identity or beyond without the beliefs and capabilities to support you. Nor is it enough for a businessman to believe he can be a top manager – he needs to back his belief up with work. Beliefs without capabilities and behaviours to back them up are castles built on sand.

The unified field is a way of putting together the different parts of NLP in a framework made up from the ideas of neurological levels, time and perceptual position. You can use it to understand the balance and relationship of the different elements in yourself and others. The key is balance. Problems arise from a lack of balance, and the unified field enables you to identify which elements have assumed too great an importance, and which are absent or too weak.

For example, a person may put too much emphasis on past time and pay undue attention to past events, letting these influence her life, and devalue the present and the future. Another person might spend too much time in first position, and not take other people's viewpoints into account. Others may pay a lot of attention to behaviour and environment, and not enough to their identity and beliefs. The unified field framework gives you a way of identifying an imbalance, as a necessary first step to finding ways of achieving a healthier balance. For therapists it is invaluable as a diagnostic tool to let you know which of the many techniques to use. This is a rich model and we leave you to think of the many different ways you can use it.

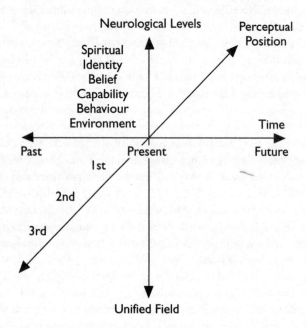

BELIEFS

> 'I can't believe that!' said Alice.
> 'Can't you?' the Queen said in a pitying tone. 'Try again: draw a
> long breath, and shut your eyes.'
> Alice laughed. 'There's no use trying,' she said. 'One can't believe
> impossible things.'
> 'I dare say you haven't had much practice,' said the Queen. 'When
> I was your age, I always did it for half an hour a day. Why,
> sometimes I've believed as many as six impossible things before
> breakfast.'
>
> *Alice Through the Looking Glass*, Lewis Carroll

Our beliefs strongly influence our behaviour. They motivate us and
shape what we do. It is difficult to learn anything without believing it
will be pleasant and to our advantage. What are beliefs? How are they
formed, and how do we maintain them?

Beliefs are our guiding principles, the inner maps we use to make
sense of the world. They give stability and continuity. Shared beliefs
give a deeper sense of rapport and community than shared work.

We all share some basic beliefs that the physical world confirms
every day. We believe in the laws of nature. We do not walk off the
tops of buildings, or need to test anew each day that fire burns. We
also have many beliefs about ourselves and the sort of world we live in
that are not so clearly defined. People are not so consistent and
immutable as the force of gravity.

Beliefs come from many sources – upbringing, modelling of
significant others, past traumas and repetitive experiences. We build
beliefs by generalizing from our experience of the world and other
people. How do we know what experiences to generalize from? Some
beliefs come to us ready made from the culture and environment we
are born into. The expectations of the significant people around us
in childhood instil beliefs. High expectations (providing they are
realistic) build competence. Low expectations instil incompetence. We
believe what we are told about ourselves when we are young because
we have no way of testing, and these beliefs may persist unmodified
by our later achievements.

When we believe something, we act as if it is true. This makes it
difficult to disprove; beliefs act as strong perceptual filters. Events are
interpreted in terms of the belief, and exceptions prove the rule. What
we do maintains and reinforces what we believe. Beliefs are not

just maps of what has happened, but blueprints for future actions.

Studies have been done where a group of children have been divided into two groups of equal IQ. Teachers were told that one group had a high IQ and were expected to do better than the second group. Although the only difference between the two groups was the teachers' expectation (a belief), the 'high IQ' group got much better results than the second group when tested later. This type of self-fulfilling prophecy is sometimes known as the Pygmalion effect.

A similar kind of self-fulfilling prophecy is the placebo effect, well known in medicine. Patients will improve if they *believe* they are being given an effective drug, even when they are actually being given placebos, inert substances with no proven medical effect. The belief effects the cure. Drugs are not always necessary, but belief in recovery always is. Studies consistently show that about 30 per cent of patients respond to placebos.

In one study a doctor gave an injection of distilled water to a number of patients with bleeding peptic ulcers, telling them that it was a wonder drug and it would cure them. Seventy per cent of the patients showed excellent results which lasted over a year.

Positive beliefs are permissions that turn on our capabilities. Beliefs create results. There is a saying, 'Whether you believe you can or you can't do something . . . You're right.'

Limiting beliefs usually centre round, 'I can't . . .' Regard this phrase as simply a statement of fact that is valid for the present moment only. For example to say, 'I can't juggle' means I can (not juggle). It is very easy not to juggle. Anyone can do it. Believing that 'I can't' is a description of your capability now and in the future, instead of being a description of your behaviour now, will program your brain to fail, and this will prevent you finding out your true capability. Negative beliefs have no basis in experience.

A good metaphor for the effect of limiting beliefs is the way a frog's eye works. A frog will see most things in its immediate environment, but it only interprets things that move and have a particular shape and configuration as food. This is a very efficient way of providing the frog with food such as flies. However, because only moving black objects are recognized as food, a frog will starve to death in a box of dead flies. So perceptual filters that are too narrow and too efficient can starve us of good experiences, even when we are surrounded by exciting possibilities, because they are not recognized as such.

The best way to find out what you are capable of is to pretend you can do it. Act 'as if' you can. What you can't do, you *won't*. If it really is impossible, don't worry, you'll find that out. (And be sure to set up appropriate safety measures if necessary.) As long as you believe it is impossible, you will actually never find out if it is possible or not.

We are not born with beliefs as we are with eye colour. They change and develop. We think of ourselves differently, we marry, divorce, change friendships and act differently because our beliefs change.

Beliefs can be a matter of choice. You can drop beliefs that limit you and build beliefs that will make your life more fun and more successful. Positive beliefs allow you to find out what could be true and how capable you are. They are permissions to explore and play in the world of possibility. What beliefs are worth having that will enable and support you in your goals? Think of some of the beliefs you have about yourself. Are they useful? Are they permissions or barriers? We all have core beliefs about love, and what is important in life. We have many others about our possibilities and happiness that we have created, and can change. An essential part of being successful is having beliefs that allow you to be successful. Empowering beliefs will not guarantee you success every time, but they keep you resourceful and capable of succeeding in the end.

There have been some studies at Stanford University on 'Self Efficacy Expectation', or how behaviour changes to match a new belief. The study was about how well people think they do something, compared to how well they actually do it. A variety of tasks were used, from mathematics to snake handling.

At first, beliefs and performance matched, people performed as they thought they would. Then the researchers set about building the subjects' belief in themselves by setting goals, arranging demonstrations, and giving them expert coaching. Expectations rose, but performance typically dropped because they were trying out new techniques. There was a point of maximum difference between what they believed they could do, and what they were actually achieving. If the subjects stuck to the task, their performance would rise to meet their expectations. If they became discouraged, it dropped to its initial level.

Think for a moment of three beliefs that have limited you. Go ahead and write them down.

Now, in your mind, look into a huge, ugly mirror. Imagine how your life will be in five years if you continue to act as if these limiting beliefs were true. How will your life be in ten years? In twenty?

Take a moment to clear your mind. Stand up, walk around or take a few deep breaths. Now think of three new beliefs that would empower you, that would truly enhance the quality of your life. You can stop for a few seconds to write these down now.

In your mind, look into a big, friendly mirror. Imagine yourself acting as if these new beliefs were really true. How will your life be in five years now? In ten years? In twenty?

Changing beliefs allows behaviour to change, and it changes quickest if you are given a capability or strategy to accomplish the task. You can also change a person's belief through changing their behaviour, but this is not so reliable. Some people are never convinced by repeated experiences. They see only disconnected coincidences.

Beliefs are an important part of our personality, yet they are expressed in extraordinarily simple terms: if I do this . . . then that will happen. I can . . . I can't . . . And these are translated into: I must . . . I should . . . I must not . . . The words become compelling. How do these words gain their power over us? Language is an essential part of the process we use to understand the world and express our beliefs. In the next chapter we take a closer look at the *linguistic* part of Neuro-Linguistic Programming.

5

WORDS AND MEANINGS

'But "glory" doesn't mean "a nice knock-down argument",' Alice
objected.
'When I use a word,' Humpty Dumpty said in a rather scornful
tone, 'it means just what I choose it to mean – neither more nor
less.'
'The question is,' said Alice, 'whether you can make words mean
different things.'
'The question is,' said Humpty Dumpty, 'which is to be master –
that's all.'

Alice Through the Looking Glass, Lewis Carroll

This is a chapter about the power of language. It is about making
sure you say what you mean, understanding as clearly as possible what
other people mean and enabling people to understand what they
mean. It is about re-connecting language with experience.

Words are cheap, the saying goes, they cost nothing, yet they have
power to evoke images, sounds and feelings in the listener or reader
as every poet and advertising copywriter knows. They can start or
break up relationships, sever diplomatic relations, provoke fights
and wars.

Words can put us into good or bad states, they are anchors for a
complex series of experiences. So the only answer to the question
'What does a word *really* mean?' is 'To whom?' Language is a tool of
communication and, as such, words mean what people agree they
mean. It is a shared way to communicate about sense experience.
Without it there would be no basis for society as we know it.

We rely on the intuitions of native speakers of the same language,
and on the fact that our sense experience is sufficiently similar for
our maps to have many features in common. Without these, all

conversations would be hopeless and we would all be Humpty Dumpty communicators.

But . . . we do not all share exactly the same map.

We each experience the world in a unique way. Words are inherently meaningless, as becomes clear when you listen to a foreign language that you do not understand. We give words meaning through their anchored associations to objects and experiences throughout our life. We do not all see the same objects or have the same experiences. The fact that other people do have different maps and meanings adds richness and variety to life. We are likely to agree on the meaning of the words 'treacle tart' for we have shared the same sight, smell and taste of it. But we will argue far into the night over the meaning of such abstract words as 'respect', 'love' and 'politics'. The possibilities for confusion are immense. These words particularly, are like Rorschach ink blots, meaning different things to different people. This is without even considering such things as lapses of attention, lack of rapport, clarity of presentation or mutual inability to understand certain ideas. How do we know we understand someone? By giving their words meaning. Our meaning. Not their meaning. And there is no guarantee that the two meanings are the same. How do we make sense of the words we hear? How do we choose words to express ourselves? And how do words structure our experiences? This gets to the heart of the linguistic part of NLP.

Two people who say they like listening to music may find they have very little in common when they discover one is fond of Wagner's operas, while the other listens to hard rock. If I tell a friend I spent the day relaxing, he might picture me sitting in an armchair watching television all afternoon. If I actually had a game of squash and a long walk in the park, he may think I am crazy. He may also wonder how the same word, *relaxation*, can be used to mean two such different things. No great issues are at stake in this example. Most of the time our meanings are sufficiently close for an adequate understanding. There are also instances when it is very important to communicate very precisely, for example in intimate relationships or in business agreements. You will want to be sure the other person shares your meaning, you will want to know as exactly as possible what a person means in her map and you will want her to be clear about what she means.

Words mean different things depending on your point of view.

THINKING OUT LOUD

Language is a powerful filter on our individual experience. It is part of the culture we are born into and cannot change. It channels our thoughts in particular directions, making it easy to think in some ways and difficult to think in others. Our language makes fine distinctions in some areas and not in others, depending on what is important in the culture. For example, we have dozens of words for a hamburger and over 50 differently named models of car. The world is as rich and varied as we wish to make it, and the language we inherit plays a crucial part in directing out attention to some parts of it and not others.

    Our thoughts are not determined by our language. While we can and do think in words, our thoughts are also a mixture of mental pictures, sounds and feelings. Knowing a language is knowing how to translate these into words. The question we want to explore here is, what happens to our thoughts as we clothe them in language, and how faithfully are they preserved when our listeners undress them? Language, of course, has its own ambiguities. For example, we particularly enjoyed the newspaper article headed: 'Census gives facts on men broken down by age, sex and occupation.' Leaving these sorts of examples aside, words have different meaning to different people, because no two people have had the same experiences.

Words are anchors for sense experience, but the experience is not the reality, and the word is not the experience. Language is thus two removes from reality. To argue about the real meaning of a word is rather like arguing that one menu tastes better than another because you prefer the food that is printed on it. People who learn another language nearly always report a radical change in the way they think about the world.

MAKING SENSE OF WORDS – THE META MODEL

Good communicators exploit the strengths and the weaknesses of language. The ability to use language with precision is essential to any professional communicator. To be able to use the precise words that will have meaning in the other person's map, and to determine precisely what a person means by the words he or she uses, are invaluable communication skills.

NLP has a very useful map of how language operates which will save you from Humpty Dumpty communicators, and will make sure you do not become one yourself. This map of language is known as the Meta Model in NLP literature. The word 'meta' comes from the Greek, and means over and beyond, or on a different level. The Meta Model uses language to clarify language, preventing you from deluding yourself that you understand what words mean; it reconnects language with experience.

The Meta Model was one of the first patterns developed by John Grinder and Richard Bandler. They noticed that two outstanding therapists, Fritz Perls and Virginia Satir, tended to use certain types of question when they were gathering information.

John and Richard set out to develop their insights about language, change and perception, and found they also had to create a vocabulary to describe them. They thought a great failure of therapeutic training in the middle of the 1970s was that a person could get an academic education, start practising therapy and then have to re-invent the wheel, because there was no vocabulary for passing on the wisdom of the last generation to the new psychotherapists.

This all changed in 1975 with the appearance of *The Structure of Magic 1*, published by Science and Behaviour Books. It describes the Meta Model in detail, and contains much of the material John and Richard had obtained from modelling Fritz Perls and Virginia Satir. Now people could benefit from the experience of gifted psychotherapists who had spent many years discovering what did and did not work. The book is dedicated to Virginia Satir.

SAYING IT ALL – THE DEEP STRUCTURE

To understand the Meta Model, which is a tool for gaining a fuller understanding of what people say, we need to look at how thoughts are translated into words. Language can never do justice to the speed, variety and sensitivity of our thinking. It can only be an

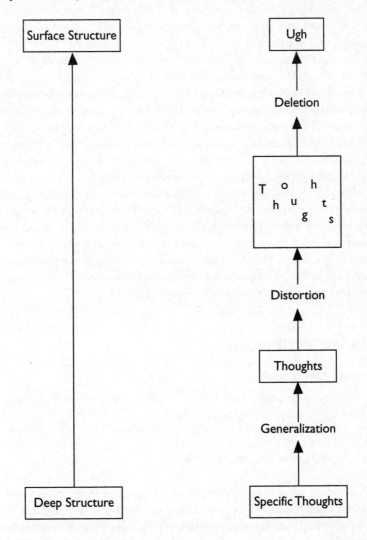

To go from the deep structure, we generalize, change and leave out part of our ideas when we speak to others.

approximation. A speaker will have a complete and full idea of what he wishes to say; this is called the deep structure in NLP. The deep structure is not conscious. Language exists at a very deep level in our neurology. We shorten this deep structure to talk clearly and what we actually say is called the surface structure. If we did not shorten this deep structure, conversation would be terribly long-winded and pedantic. Someone who asks you the way to the nearest hospital is not going to thank you for giving him a reply involving transformational grammar.

In order to go from the deep structure to the surface structure, we unconsciously do three things.

Firstly, we will select only some of the information available in the deep structure. A great deal will be left out.

Secondly, we will give a simplified version which will inevitably distort the meaning.

Thirdly, we will generalize. Spelling out all the possible exceptions and conditions would make a conversation very tedious.

The Meta Model is a series of questions that seek to reverse and unravel the deletions and distortions and generalizations of language. These questions aim to fill in the missing information, reshape the structure and elicit specific information to make sense of the communication. It is worth bearing in mind that none of the following patterns are good or bad in themselves. It depends on the context in which they are used and the consequences of using them.

UNSPECIFIED NOUNS

Consider the sentence:

The seven-year-old girl, Lara, fell over a cushion in the living room and bruised her right hand on a wooden chair.

And:

The child had an accident.

Both these sentences mean the same thing, yet the first has much more specific information. We can reach the second sentence from the first in easy stages by leaving out or generalizing the specific nouns. Also, both sentences are perfectly good English. Good grammar is no guarantee of clarity. Many people are adept at speaking at length in excellent English and leaving you none the wiser afterwards.

The active subject of a sentence can be deleted by using the passive voice, saying for example, 'The house was built.' rather than 'X built the house.' Just because you leave out the builders in the sentence does not mean the house sprang up by itself. The builders still exist. This type of deletion can imply a view of the world where you are a helpless spectator, and events just happen with no one responsible for them.

So when you hear the sentence, 'The house was built,' you can ask for the missing information. '*Who built the house?*'

Other examples where the nouns are not specified are:

'They are out to get me.' '*Who is?*'
'It's a matter of opinion.' '*What is?*'
'The neighbourhood has been ruined.' '*Who ruined it?*'
'Pets are a nuisance.' '*What pets?*'

The next gem comes from a two-year-old when asked what happened to a bar of chocolate that was on the table.

'If people leave chocolate around, people eat it.' '*Which people?*'

Unspecified Nouns are clarified by asking: 'Who or what specifically . . .?'

UNSPECIFIED VERBS

Alice was too much puzzled to say anything so after a minute Humpty Dumpty began again. 'They've a temper, some of them – particularly verbs, they're the proudest – adjectives you can do anything with, but not verbs – however I can manage the whole lot! Impenetrability! That's what I say!'

Alice Through the Looking Glass, Lewis Carroll

Sometimes a verb will not be specified, for example:

'He travelled to Paris.'
'She hurt herself.'
'She helped me.'
'I am trying to remember it.'
'Go and learn this for next week.'

It could be important to know *how* these things were done. We want the adverb. So, how did he travel? How did she hurt herself? How did she help you? How are you trying to remember it? (What specifically are you trying to remember anyway?) How am I to learn this?

Unspecified Verbs are clarified by asking:
'How specifically . . .?'

COMPARISONS

The next two examples of missing information are similar and often found together: judgements and comparisons. Advertisements are an excellent source of both patterns.

New, improved Fluffo washing powder is better.

There is a comparison being made here, but this is not made clear. Something cannot be better in isolation. Better than what? Better than it was before? Better than its competitors Buffo and Duffo? Better than using treacle instead of washing powder?

Any sentence that uses words like 'best', 'better', 'worse', or 'worst' is making a comparison. You can only make a comparison if you have something to compare with. If that is missing, you will have to ask what it is.

Another example would be:

I handled that meeting badly.

Badly compared with what? How you might have handled it? How Joe Bloggs would have handled it? How superman might have handled it?

Very often the deleted half of the comparison is unrealistic. If you compare yourself with superman or superwoman, note how badly you come off in the comparison, and then delete the standard of comparison. All you are left with is a feeling of inadequacy, and nothing you can do about it.

Comparisons are clarified by asking:
'Compared with what . . .?'

JUDGEMENTS

Judgements are closely allied to comparisons. If Fluffo is 'quite simply the best washing powder money can buy', it would be interesting to know whose opinion this is. The managing director of Fluffo? An opinion poll? Joe Bloggs?

Judgements need not involve comparisons, although they often do. If someone says, 'I'm a selfish person,' you might ask, *'Who says?'* If the answer is, 'I do!' then you might ask, *'By what standard do you judge yourself to be a selfish person?'*

So it is useful to know who is making a judgement. It might come from a childhood memory. Also, what are the reasons for the judgement? Are they good reasons? Are they your reasons or have they been imposed on you? Has their date stamp expired now that you are an adult?

Judgements often creep in on the coat tails of adverbs. Consider this:

'Obviously, the man is an ideal candidate.'
'To whom is it obvious?'

Very often adverbs ending in -ly will delete the person who is making the judgement. *Clearly,* if you can paraphrase that sentence into the form 'It is obvious . . .' then there is a deletion. It must be obvious to somebody. (And who was it clear to?)

Judgements are clarified by asking: 'Who is making this judgement, and on what grounds are they making it?'

NOMINALIZATIONS

The next pattern is when a verb describing an ongoing process has been turned into a noun. This is called a nominalization by linguists. Read the following sentence and think about what it might mean:

Teaching and discipline, applied with *respect* and *firmness,* are *essentials* in the *process* of *education.*

A perfectly grammatical sentence containing a nominalization (in italics) in virtually every other word. If a noun cannot be seen, heard, touched, smelt or tasted, in short, if it cannot be put in a wheelbarrow, it is a nominalization.

There is nothing wrong with nominalizations – they can be very useful – but they hide the biggest differences between people's maps of the world.

Take 'education', for example. Who is educating whom, and what is the knowledge that is passing between them?

Or 'respect'. Who is respecting whom, and how are they doing it?

'Memory' is an interesting example. What does it mean to say you have a bad memory? To find out, you might ask what specific information you have trouble memorizing, and how you go about memorizing it. Inside every nominalization you will find one or more missing nouns (in a manner of speaking) and an unspecified verb.

A verb involves action or an ongoing process. This is lost if it is nominalized and changed into a static noun. Someone who thinks he has a bad memory is stuck if he thinks about it in the same way as having a bad back. He is helpless. As George Orwell said, 'If thought corrupts language, language can also corrupt thought.' To come to believe that the external world is patterned by the way we talk about it is even worse than eating the menu – it is eating the printing ink on the menu. Words can be combined and manipulated in ways that have nothing to do with sensory experience. I can say pigs can fly, but this does not make it true. To think so is to believe in magic.

Nominalizations are the dragons of the Meta Model. They cause no trouble as long as you do not think they actually exist. They delete so much information that there is scarcely anything left. Medical conditions and diseases are interesting examples of nominalizations and this may explain why parents often feel they are helpless and lack choices. By turning processes into things, nominalizations may be the single most misleading language pattern.

A Nominalization is clarified by turning it into a verb and asking for the missing information: 'Who is nominalizing about what, and how they are doing it?'

MODAL OPERATORS OF POSSIBILITY

There are rules of conduct beyond which we believe we cannot or must not go. Words like 'cannot' and, 'must not' are known as modal operators in linguistics – they set limits governed by unspoken rules.

There are two main types of modal operators: modal operators of necessity and modal operators of possibility.

Modal operators of possibility are the stronger of the two. These are 'can' and 'cannot', 'possible' and 'impossible'. They define (in the speaker's map) what is considered possible. Obviously (I hope you recognize a judgement here – *obvious to whom?*) there are laws of nature. Pigs cannot fly, man cannot live without oxygen. However, limits set by a person's beliefs are quite different. 'I just couldn't refuse,' or 'I am the way I am. I can't change' or, 'It's impossible to tell them the truth.'

There is no problem if a person thinks he has some capabilities, (unless this is obviously untrue or defies the laws of nature); it is 'cannot' that is limiting. 'I can't' is often taken as an absolute state of incompetence, not amenable to change.

Fritz Perls, the originator of Gestalt therapy, used to respond to clients who said, 'I can't . . .' by saying, 'Don't say I can't, say I won't!' This rather ferocious reframe immediately shifts the client's stuck state to a state of being able to at least acknowledge the possibility of choice.

A clearer question (and one less likely to break rapport) is, *'What would happen if you did?'* or, *'What stops you?'* or, *'How do you stop youself?'* When someone says he can't do something, he has set up an outcome and then put it out of reach. The question, 'What stops you?' puts the emphasis on the outcome again and sets to work to identify the barriers as a first step to getting past them.

Teachers and therapists work with changing these sorts of limitations and the first step is to question the modal operator. Teachers come up against this every day when students say they can't understand or always get work wrong. Therapists help clients to break through their limitations.

If a person says, 'I can't relax', she must have some idea of what relaxation is like or how does she know she is not doing it? Take the positive goal (what you could do), and discover what is preventing it being realized (what stops you), or carefully examine the consequences (what would happen if you did). It is these consequences and barriers that have been deleted. And on critical examination they may turn out to be less formidable than you think.

Modal Operators of Possibility – 'I can't' – are clarified by asking: 'What would happen if you did . . .?' or, 'What prevents you . . .?'

MODAL OPERATORS OF NECESSITY

Modal operators of necessity involve a need and are indicated by the use of words like, 'should' and 'should not', 'must' and 'must not', 'ought' and 'ought not'. There is some rule of conduct operating, but the rule is not explicit. What are the consequences, real or imagined, of breaking the rule? These are brought into the open by asking, *'What would happen if you did, or did not, do this?'*

'I must always put other people first.'
'What would happen if you did not?'

'I must not talk in class.'
'What would happen if you did?'

'I ought to learn these Meta Model categories.'
'What would happen if you did not?'

'You shouldn't talk to those people.'
'What would happen if you did?'

'You should wash your hands before meals.'
'What would happen if you did not?'

Once these consequences and reasons are made explicit they can be thought over and critically evaluated, otherwise they just limit choice and behaviour.

Rules of conduct are obviously important and society survives on a code of morals, but there is a world of difference between 'You should be honest in your business dealings' and, 'You should go to the cinema more often.' Should and shouldn't often attract moral judgements they do not deserve.

Discoveries are only made by asking, *'What would happen if . . .?'* . . . I kept sailing west? . . . I could travel at the speed of light? . . . I allowed penicillin to grow? . . . The earth went round the sun? This question is the basis of the scientific method.

Education can easily become a ghastly minefield of modal operators, comparisons and judgements. The whole concept of standards and testing and what children should or should not be able to do is so vague as to be useless, or worse, so restricting as to be crushing.

If I tell a child, 'You should be able to do this,' I am only stating my belief. I cannot sensibly answer the reasonable question, 'What would happen if I don't?'

As far as capabilities are concerned, it is very much easier to think in terms of what a person can or cannot do than what he or she should and should not be able to do.

Using 'should' on the level of capabilities is usually taken as a rebuke; you ought to be able to do something, but cannot, so a quite unnecessary feeling of failure is introduced. Using 'should' in this way either on yourself or others is an excellent way of conjuring up instant guilt (because a rule is broken), by creating an artificial gap between expectation and reality. Is the expectation realistic? Is the rule a useful or appropriate one? 'Should' is often an angry blaming response from someone who is not directly admitting his anger nor his expectations, nor is he taking responsibility for them.

Modal Operators of Necessity – 'I mustn't/I have to' – are clarified by asking: 'What would happen if you did/didn't . . .?'

UNIVERSAL QUANTIFIERS

A generalization is when one example is taken as the representative of a number of different possibilities. If we did not generalize, we would have to do things over and over again, and to think of all possible exceptions and qualifications would be too time consuming. We sort our knowledge into general categories, but we gain knowledge in the first place by comparing and evaluating difference, and it is important to continue sorting for difference, so generalizations can be changed if necessary. There are times when we need to be specific and thinking in genera-lizations is woolly and inaccurate. Each case needs to be taken on its merits. There is a danger of not seeing the trees for the wood if a whole diverse chunk of experience is lumped together under one heading.

Being willing to admit exceptions allows you to be more realistic. Decisions do not have to be all or nothing. The person who thinks he is always right is a bigger menace than one who thinks he is always wrong. At worst, this can mean prejudice, narrow-mindedness and discrimination. Generalizations are linguistic fluff that clogs the works of clear communication.

Generalizations are made by taking a few instances as representing a whole group, so they usually contain generalized nouns and unspecified verbs. Many of these Meta Model categories overlap. The vaguer the statement, the more likely it is to include several patterns.

Generalizations are usually expressed by words like 'all', 'every', 'always', 'never' and 'none'. These words admit no exceptions, and are known as universal quantifiers. In some cases they are absent but implied, e.g. 'I think computers are a waste of time', or 'Pop music is rubbish.'

Some other examples would be:

'Indian food tastes terrible.'
'All generalizations are wrong.'
'Houses are too expensive.'
'Actors are interesting people.'

Universal quantifiers are paradoxically limiting. Extending a statement to cover all possibilities, or deny all possibilities, makes an exception difficult to spot. A perceptual filter or self-fulfilling prophecy is created – you will see and hear what you expect to see and hear.

Universal quantifiers are not always wrong. They can be factual: night always follows day, and apples never fall upwards. There is a big difference between this sort of statement and one like, 'I never do anything right.' For someone to believe this, he must notice only the times when he was wrong, and forget or discount all the times he was right. No-one can consistently get everything wrong. Such perfection does not exist. He has limited his world by the way he talks about it.

Successful and confident people tend to generalize the opposite way. They believe they usually do things right, except in isolated instances. In other words, they believe they have the capability.

For example, to question the universal quantifier in *'I NEVER do anything right!'*, seek the exception: *'You NEVER do anything right?'* *'Can you think of any time that you did do something right?'*

Richard Bandler tells the story of a client who came to him for therapy about a lack of self-confidence (a nominalization). He started by asking her, 'Was there ever a time when you have been self-confident?'

'No.'

'You mean to say you have never in your whole life been self-confident?'

'That's right.'

'Not even on one occasion?'

'No.'

'You're sure?'

'Oh, absolutely!'

The second way you can question this kind of generalization is by exaggerating to bring out its absurdity. So in reply to, 'I'll never be able to understand NLP,' you might say, 'You're right. It's obviously much too difficult for you to understand. Why not give up now? It's hopeless; the rest of your life isn't long enough to master it.'

This will usually bring a response on the lines of, 'Alright, alright, I'm not that stupid.'

If you do question the generalization by exaggerating forcibly enough, the person who made it will often end up defending the opposite view. You feed back its absurdity. He will become more moderate if you occupy his extreme position more forcefully than he does.

Universal Quantifiers are questioned by asking for a counter example: 'Has there ever been a time when . . .?'

COMPLEX EQUIVALENCE

A *complex equivalence* is when two statements are linked in such a way that they are taken to mean the same thing, for example, 'You are not smiling . . . you are not enjoying yourself.'

Another example would be, 'If you don't look at me when I'm talking to you, then you are not paying attention.' This accusation is often levelled at others by predominantly visual thinkers, who need to look up at the speaker to understand what he is saying. A person who thinks more kinesthetically will want to look down to process what he hears. This, to a visual person, is not paying attention, because if *he* were to look down, *he* could not pay attention. He has generalized his own experience to include everyone else and has forgotten that people think in different ways.

Complex Equivalences can be questioned by asking: 'How does this mean that?'

PRESUPPOSITIONS

We all have beliefs and expectations from our personal experience; it is impossible to live without them. Since we have to make some assumptions, they might as well be ones that allow us freedom, choice and fun in the world, rather than ones that limit us. You often get what you expect to get.

Basic assumptions that limit choice may need to be brought out into the open. They are often disguised as 'why' questions. 'Why can't you look after me properly?' presupposes that you do not look after the person properly. If you attempt to answer the question directly, you are lost before you begin.

'Are you going to wear your green or your red pyjamas to go to bed?' is an example of the trick of offering choice in one area, only if the more important presupposition is accepted, in this case, going to bed. It can be challenged by asking, *'What leads you to believe that I am going to bed?'*

Sentences containing the words 'since', 'when' and 'if' usually contain a presupposition, and so does anything after such verbs as 'realize', 'be aware' or 'ignore', e.g. 'Realize why we place so much importance on the individual.'

Other examples of presuppositions are:

'When you get smart, you'll understand this.' (*You are not smart.*)
'You're not going to tell me another lie?' (*You have told me a lie already.*)
'Why don't you smile more?' (*You don't smile enough.*)
'You are as stupid as your father.' (*Your father is stupid.*)
'I will try hard at this work.' (*This work is difficult.*)
'My dog has a cockney accent.' (*My dog can talk.*)

A presupposition is bound to have other Meta Model patterns that will need sorting out. (So you think I do not smile enough? How much is enough? In what circumstances do you expect me to smile?)

Presuppositions can be brought into the open by asking: 'What leads you to believe that . . .?' and filling in the presupposition.

CAUSE AND EFFECT

'You just make me feel bad. I can't help it.' The English language encourages thinking in terms of cause and effect. Active subjects typically do things to passive objects, but this is a gross simplification. There is a danger of thinking of people as billiard balls, following the laws of cause and effect. 'The sunshine makes the flowers grow' is a shorthand way of expressing an extremely complex relationship. Thinking in causes explains nothing but simply invites the question, 'How?'

Even so, there is a world of difference between saying, 'The wind made the tree bend' and 'You made me feel angry.' To believe that someone else is responsible for your emotional state is to give them a sort of psychic power over you they do not have.

Examples of this sort of distortion would be:

'You bore me.' (*You make me feel bored.*)
'I'm glad because you've gone away.' (*You going away makes me feel glad.*)
'The weather gets me down.' (*The weather makes me feel down.*)

One person does not have direct control over another person's emotional state. Thinking that you can force people to experience different states of mind, or that other people can force you into different moods is very limiting, and causes a great deal of distress. Being responsible for the feelings of others is a heavy burden. You will have to take exaggerated and unnecessary care in what you say and do. With cause and effect patterns you become either the victim or the nursemaid of others.

The word 'but' very often implies cause and effect by introducing a reason why a person feels compelled not to do something:

'I would help you but I'm too tired.'
'I would take a vacation, but the firm would fall to pieces without me.'

There are two levels to questioning cause and effect. One response is to simply ask how exactly one thing causes the other. A description of how this happens will often open up new choices of how to respond. However, this still leaves the fundamental cause and effect belief intact, a belief that is very strongly rooted in our culture, namely that other people have power over, and are responsible for, our internal emotional states. However, we really do generate our own feelings. No one else can do it for us. We respond and are responsible. To think other people are responsible for our feelings is to inhabit a billiard ball, inanimate universe. The feelings we generate in response to other people's actions are often the result of a synesthesia. We hear or see something and respond with a feeling. It seems as if the link is automatic.

The Meta Model question that will address the basic cause–effect assumption of a statement like 'He *makes* me feel angry' is, 'How exactly do you *make* yourself feel angry at what he says?' This builds in the idea that the person has some choice in his or her emotional response.

It is not easy to assume responsibility for one's own feelings, so use this type of question only when you have very good rapport. It can be very challenging.

> **Cause and Effect can be questioned by asking: 'How exactly does this cause that?' or 'What would have to happen for this not to be caused by that?'**
> **To question the Cause and Effect belief, ask: 'How exactly do you make yourself feel or respond like that to what you saw or heard?'**

MIND READING

A person mind reads when he presumes to know, without direct evidence, what another is thinking or feeling. We do it often. It is sometimes an intuitive response to some non-verbal clues that we have noticed on an unconscious level. Often it is pure hallucination, or what we ourselves would think or feel in that situation: we project our own unconscious thoughts and feelings, and experience them as coming from the other person. It is always the miser who experiences other people as mean. People who mind read usually feel they are right, but this does not guarantee they are. Why guess when you can ask?

There are two main types of mind reading. In the first type a person presumes to know what another is thinking. Examples:

'George is unhappy.'
'I could tell she did not like the present I gave her.'
'I know what makes him tick.'
'He was angry but he wouldn't admit it.'

There needs to be good sensory-based evidence for attributing thoughts, feelings and opinions to others. You might say, 'George is depressed,' but it might be more useful to say, 'George is looking down to his right, his face muscles are slack and his breathing is shallow. The corners of his mouth are turned down and his shoulders are slumped.'

The second type of mind reading is a mirror of the first and gives other people the power to read your mind. This can then be used to blame them for not understanding you when you think they should.

For example:

'If you liked me you would know what I wanted.'
'Can't you see how I feel?'
'I'm upset you did not consider my feelings.'
'You should know that I like that.'

A person using this pattern will not communicate clearly to others what she wants; the others are presumed to know anyway. This can lead to some first class quarrels.

The way to question mind reading is to ask how specifically do they know what you were thinking. Or, in projected mind reading, how specifically were you supposed to know how they felt.

When you seek to clarify mind reading by asking, *'How do you know?'*, the answer is usually some belief or generalization. For example:

'George does not care about me any more.'
'How do you know that George does not care about you any more?'
'Because he never does what I say.'

So in the speaker's model of the world, 'doing what I say' equals 'caring for me'. This is a questionable assumption to say the least. It is a complex equivalence and invites the questions, 'How exactly does caring about someone mean doing what they say? If you care about someone, do you always do what they say?'

Mind Reading is questioned by asking: 'How exactly do you know . . .?'

The Meta Model reconnects language with experiences, and can be used for:

1. Gathering information.
2. Clarifying meanings.
3. Identifying limitations.
4. Opening up choices.

The Meta Model is an extremely powerful tool in business, therapy and education. The basic presupposition behind it is that people make different models of the world and you cannot assume that you know what words mean.

Firstly, it enables you to gather high-quality information when it is important to understand exactly what people mean. If a client comes to a therapist complaining of depression, the therapist needs to find out, *in the client's model*, what this means, rather than assuming (quite wrongly) that he knows exactly what the client means.

In business, money can be wasted if a manager misunderstands instructions. How many times do you hear the sad cry, 'But I thought you meant . . .'

When a student says he always gets geometry problems wrong, you can find out if there was ever a time he got one right, and also, precisely how he manages to get geometry problems wrong so consistently.

There are no 'why?' questions in the Meta Model. 'Why' questions have little value, at best they get justifications or long explanations which do nothing to change the situation.

Secondly, the Meta Model clarifies meanings. It gives a systematic framework for asking, 'What exactly do you mean?'

Thirdly, the Meta Model gives choices. Beliefs, universals, nominalizations and rules all set limits. And the limits exist in the words, not in the world. Questioning and finding out the consequences or exceptions can open up large areas of life. Limiting beliefs are identified and changed.

Which Meta Model pattern you question will depend on the context of the communication and your outcome. Consider the following sentence:

'Why don't these awful people stop always trying to help me, it makes me even angrier; I know I should keep my temper, but I can't.'

This contains mind reading and presupposition (they are trying to annoy me), cause and effect (makes), universal quantifiers (always), judgements (awful), comparisons (angrier), modal operators of possibility and necessity (should, can't), unspecified verbs (trying and help), nominalization (temper) and unspecified nouns (people, it).

In this sort of example, the mind reading, presuppositions and causality fuel all the others. Sorting these out would be the first step towards change. The nominalization, unspecified verbs and unspecified nouns are the least important. The rest, generalizations, universal quantifiers, judgements, comparisons and modal operators, come somewhere in the middle. A more general strategy would be to specify the key nouns, then the key verbs, then sort out the distortions with a priority override if any modal operators come up. Remember that you can never specify all the deletions. Practise with the Meta Model and you will start to get a feel for what is important to question.

The Meta Model is a powerful way of gathering information, clarifying meanings and identifying limits in a person's thinking. It is particularly useful to get the desired state of someone who is dissatisfied. What would he rather have? Where would he rather be? How would he rather be feeling? Questions are also interventions. A good question can take a person's mind in a completely new direction and change his life. For example, ask yourself frequently, 'What is the most useful question to ask now?'

There is also a very real danger of getting too much information when you use the Meta Model. You need to ask yourself, 'Do I really need to know this? 'What is my outcome?' It is important only to use these Meta Model questions within a context of rapport and a mutually agreed outcome. Repeated questions can be experienced as aggressive, and the challenges need not be so direct. Rather than asking, 'How specifically do you know that?' you might say, 'I'm curious to know exactly how you knew that?' Or, 'I don't exactly

META MODEL PATTERN	QUESTION
Deletions	
Unspecified Noun	'Who or what specifically . . .?'
Unspecified Verb	'How specifically is this happening?'
Comparison	'Compared with what?'
Judgement	'Who says . . .?'
Nominalization	'How is this being done?'
Generalizations	
Modal Operator of Possibility	'What prevents you . . .?'
Modal Operator of Necessity	'What would happen if you did/didn't . . .?'
Universal Quantifier	'Always? Never? Everyone?'
Distortions	
Complex Equivalence	'How does this mean that?'
Presupposition	'What leads you to believe that . . .?'
Cause and Effect	'How exactly do you *make yourself* do this . . .?'
Mind Reading	'How do you know . . .?'

understand how you know that.' Conversations do not have to be cross examinations. You can use polite and soft voice tones to soften the question.

Robert Dilts tells how he was in a linguistics class at the University of Santa Cruz in the early 1970s, where John Grinder taught the Meta Model in one two-hour period. It was on a Thursday when he turned the class loose to practise the Meta Model. The following Tuesday half the class came in looking extremely dejected. They had alienated their lovers, their teachers and their friends, cutting them to pieces with the Meta Model. Rapport is the first step in any NLP pattern. Used without sensitivity and rapport, the Meta Model becomes Meta Mayhem, Meta Muddle and Meta Misery.

You can often ask a question elegantly and precisely. For example a person might say, (*looking* up), 'My job just isn't working out.' You might reply, 'I wonder how you would *see* your job if it was OK?'

One very useful way to use the Meta Model is to use it on your own internal dialogue. This can have more effect than attending years of seminars about how to think clearly.

A good strategy for learning to use the Meta Model is to pick one or two categories, and spend a week simply noticing examples in everyday conversation. The next week pick some different categories. As you become more familiar and practised at seeing the patterns, you might construct a silent question in your mind. Finally, when you have an idea of the patterns and the questions you could start to use them in appropriate situations.

The Meta Model also relates to the logical levels. Think about the statement:

'I can't do that here.'

'*I*' is the person's identity.
'*can't*' relates to their belief.
'*do*' expresses their capability.
'*that*' indicates a behaviour.
'*here*' is the environment.

You could challenge this statement on a number of grounds. One way of starting would be to think about which logical level you want to work on. Also, the person may give you a clue about what is the most important part of the statement by tonally emphasizing one of the words. This is known as tonal marking.

If he says, 'I *can't* do that here' then you could go for the modal operator by asking, 'What prevents you?'

If he says, 'I can't do *that* here', you might ask, 'What specifically?'

Noticing what words a person emphasizes through voice tone or body language is one way of knowing which Meta Model pattern to question. Another strategy would be to listen to the person talking for a few minutes and notice which category he uses the most. This is likely to indicate where his thinking is limited and a question there could be the best way to start.

In an everyday context, the Meta Model gives you a systematic way of gathering information, when you need to know more precisely what a person means. It is a skill that is well worth learning.

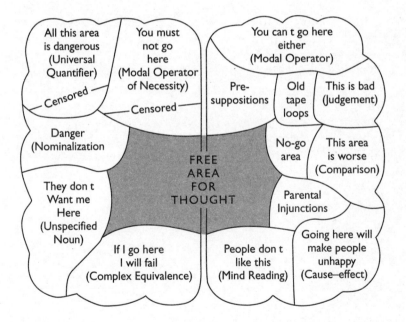

Language can limit our world

'Would you tell me, please,' said Alice, 'what that means?' 'Now you talk like a reasonable child,' said Humpty Dumpty, looking very much pleased. 'I meant by "impenetrability" that we've had enough of that subject, and it would be just as well if you'd mention what you mean to do next, as I suppose you don't intend to stop here all the rest of your life.'

Alice Through the Looking Glass, Lewis Carroll

6

UPTIME AND DOWNTIME

So far we have concentrated on the importance of sensory acuity, keeping the senses open and noticing the responses of people around you. This state of tuning the senses to the outside world is known as *Uptime* in NLP terms. However, there are also states that take us deeper into our own mind, our own reality.

Break off from this book for a moment and remember a time when you were deep in thought . . .

You probably had to go deep in thought to remember. You would have focused inwards, feeling, seeing and hearing inwardly. This is a state we are all familiar with. The more deeply you go in, the less you are aware of outside stimuli; deep in thought is a good description of this state, known as *Downtime* in NLP. Accessing cues take you into downtime. Whenever you ask anyone to go inside to visualize, hear sounds and have feelings, you are asking him to go into downtime. Downtime is where you go to daydream, to plan, to fantasize and create possibilities.

In practice we are seldom completely in uptime or downtime; our everyday consciousness is a mixture of partly internal and partly external awareness. We turn the senses outwards or inwards depending on the circumstances we are in.

It is useful to think of mental states as tools for doing different things. Playing a game of chess involves a radically different state of mind to eating. There is no such thing as a wrong state of mind, but there are consequences. These could be catastrophic, if, for example, you try to cross a busy street in the state of mind you use to go to sleep – uptime is most definitely the best state to use for crossing the road – or laughable, if you try to say a tongue twister while in the state of mind brought on by too much alcohol. Often you do not do something well because you are not in the right state. You will not

play a good game of tennis if you are in the state of mind you use to
play chess.

VAKOG	VAKOG
Internal	External
Attention in ←————————→	Attention out
Downtime	Uptime
Daydream	Sport
Trance	Driving a car

You can access unconscious resources directly by inducing and
using a type of downtime known as trance. In trance you become
deeply involved in a limited focus of attention. It is an altered state
from your habitual state of consciousness. Everybody's experience of
trance will be different, because everybody starts from a different
normal state, dominated by their preferred representational systems.

Most of the work on trance and altered states has been done in a
psychotherapy setting, for all therapies use trance to some extent.
They all access unconscious resources in different ways. Anyone free-
associating on an analyst's couch is well into downtime, and so is
someone who is role playing in Gestalt therapy. Hypnotherapy uses
trance explicitly.

A person goes into therapy because he has run out of conscious
resources. He is stuck. He does not know what he needs or where to
find it. Trance offers an opportunity to resolve the problem because it
bypasses the conscious mind and makes unconscious resources
available. Most change takes place at the unconscious level and work
their way up. The conscious mind is not needed to initiate changes
and often does not notice them anyway. The ultimate goal of any
therapy is for the client to become resourceful again in his or her own
right. Everyone has a rich personal history, filled with experience and
resources that can be drawn on. It contains all the material needed to
make changes, if only you can get at it.

One of the reasons that we use such a small part of our possible
mental capacity could be that our education system places so much
emphasis on external testing, standardized achievements and
meeting other people's goals. We get little training in utilizing our
unique internal abilities. Most of our individuality is unconscious.
Trance is the ideal state of mind to explore and recover our unique
internal resources.

THE MILTON MODEL

'That's a great deal to make one word mean,' Alice said in a thoughtful tone.

'When I make a word do a lot of work like that,' said Humpty Dumpty, 'I always pay it extra.'

Alice Through the Looking Glass, Lewis Carroll

Gregory Bateson was enthusiastic about *The Structure of Magic 1*, which contained the Meta Model. He saw great potential in the ideas. He told John and Richard, 'There's a strange old guy down in Phoenix, Arizona. A brilliant therapist, but nobody knows what he's doing, or how he does it. Why don't you go and find out?' Bateson had known this 'strange old guy', Milton Erickson, for 15 years, and he set up an appointment for them to meet Erickson.

John and Richard worked with Milton Erickson in 1974 when he was widely regarded as the foremost practitioner of hypnotherapy. He was the founding president of the American Society for Clinical Hypnosis, and travelled extensively giving seminars and lectures as well as working in private practice. He had a world-wide reputation as a sensitive and successful therapist, and was famous for his acute observation of non-verbal behaviour. John and Richard's study gave rise to two books. *Patterns of Hypnotic Techniques of Milton H. Erickson Volume 1* was published by Meta Publications in 1975. *Volume 2*, co-written with Judith DeLozier, followed in 1977. The books are as much about their perceptual filters as Erickson's methods, although Erickson did say that the books were a far better explanation of his work than he himself could have given. And that was a fine compliment.

John Grinder has said that Erickson was the single most important model that he ever built, because Erickson opened the doorway not just to a different reality, but to a whole different class of realities. His work with trance and altered states was astonishing, and John's thinking underwent a profound rebalancing.

NLP underwent a rebalancing too. The Meta Model was about precise meanings. Erickson used language in artfully vague ways so that his clients could take the meaning that was most appropriate for them. He induced and utilized trance states, enabling individuals to overcome problems and discover their resources. This way of using language became known as the Milton Model, as a complement and contrast to the exactness of the Meta Model.

The Milton Model is a way of using language to induce and

maintain trance in order to contact the hidden resources of our personality. It follows the way the mind works naturally. Trance is a state where you are highly motivated to learn from your unconscious in an inner directed way. It is not a passive state, nor are you under another's influence. There is co-operation between client and therapist, the client's responses letting the therapist know what to do next.

Erickson's work was based on a number of ideas shared by many sensitive and successful therapists. These are now presuppositions of NLP. He respected the client's unconscious mind. He assumed there was a positive intention behind even the most bizarre behaviour, and that individuals make the best choices available to them at the time. He worked to give them more choices. He also assumed that at some level, individuals already have all the resources they need to make changes.

The Milton Model is a way of using language to:

1. Pace and lead the person's reality.
2. Distract and utilize the conscious mind.
3. Access the unconscious and resources.

PACING AND LEADING

Milton Erickson was masterful at gaining rapport. He respected and accepted his clients' reality. He assumed that resistance was due to lack of rapport. To him, all responses were valid and could be used. To Erickson, there were no resistant clients, only inflexible therapists.

To pace someone's reality, to tune into their world, all you need do is to simply describe their ongoing sensory experience: what they must be feeling, hearing and seeing. It will be easy and natural for them to follow what you are saying. How you talk is important. You will best induce a peaceful inward state by speaking slowly, using a soft tonality and pacing your speech to the person's breathing.

Gradually suggestions are introduced to lead them gracefully into downtime by directing their attention inwards. Everything is described in general terms so it accurately reflects the person's experience. You would not say, 'Now you will close your eyes and feel comfortable and go into a trance.' Instead you might say, 'It's easy to close your eyes whenever you wish to feel more comfortable . . . many people find it easy and comfortable to go into a trance.' These sort of general comments cover any response, while gently introducing the trance behaviour.

A loop is set up. As the client's attention is constantly focused and riveted on a few stimuli, he goes deeper into downtime. His experiences become more subjective, and these are fed back by the therapist to deepen the trance. You do not tell a person what to do, you draw his attention to what is there. How can you possibly know what a person is thinking? You cannot. There is an art to using language in ways that are vague enough for the client to make an appropriate meaning. It is a case not so much of telling him what to think, but of not distracting him from the trance state.

These sort of suggestions will be most effective if the transitions between sentences are smooth. For example, you might say something like, 'As you see the coloured wallpaper in front of you . . . the patterns of light on the walls . . . while you become aware of your breathing . . . the rise and fall of your chest . . . the comfort of the chair . . . the weight of your feet on the floor . . . and you can hear the sounds of, the children playing outside . . . while you listen to the sound of my voice and begin to wonder . . . how far you have entered trance . . . already.'

Notice the words 'and', 'while' and 'as' in the example as they smoothly link the flow of suggestions, while you mention something that is occurring (the sound of your voice) and link it to something that you want to occur (going into trance).

Not using transitions makes jumpy sentences. They will be detached from each other. Then they are less effective. I hope this is clear. Writing is like speech. Smooth or staccato. Which do you prefer?

A person in a trance is usually still, the eyes are usually closed, the pulse is slower and the face relaxed. The blinking and swallowing reflexes are normally slower or absent, and the breathing rate is slower. There is a feeling of comfort and relaxation. The therapist will either use a prearranged signal to bring the client out of trance, or lead them out by what he says, or the person may spontaneously return to normal consciousness if his unconscious thinks this is appropriate.

THE SEARCH FOR MEANING

The Meta Model keeps you in uptime. You do not have to go inside your mind searching for the meaning of what you hear; you ask the speaker to spell it out specifically. The Meta Model recovers information that has been deleted, distorted or generalized. The Milton Model is the mirror image of the Meta Model; it is a way of constructing sentences rife with deletions, distortions and generalizations. The listener must fill in the details and actively search for the meaning of what he hears from his own experience. In other words you provide context with as little content as possible. You give him the frame and leave him to choose the picture to put in it. When the listener provides the content, this ensures he makes the most relevant and immediate meaning from what you say.

Imagine being told that in the past you have had an important experience. You are not told what it was, you must search back through time and select an experience that seems most relevant to you now. This is done at an unconscious level, our conscious mind is much too slow for the task.

So a sentence like, 'People can make learnings,' is going to evoke ideas about what specific learnings I can make, and if I am working on a particular problem those learnings are bound to relate to questions I am pondering. We make this kind of search all the time to make sense of what others tell us, and it is utilized to the full in trance. All that matters is the meaning that the client makes; the therapist need not know.

It is easy to make up artfully vague instructions so that a person can pick an appropriate experience and learn from it. Ask him to pick some important experience in his past, and go through it again in all internal senses to learn something new from it. Then ask his unconscious to use this learning in future contexts where it could be useful.

DISTRACTION AND UTILIZATION OF THE CONSCIOUS MIND

An important part of the Milton Model is leaving out information, and so keeping the conscious mind busy filling the gaps from its store of memories. Have you ever had the experience of reading a vague question and trying to work out what it could mean?

Nominalizations delete a great deal of information. As you sit with a *feeling* of *ease* and *comfort*, your *understanding* of the *potential* of this sort of *language* is growing, for every *nominalization* in this sentence is in italics. The less that is mentioned specifically, the less risk of a clash with the other person's experience.

Verbs are left unspecified. As you *think* of the last time you heard someone *communicate* using unspecified verbs, you might *remember* the feeling of confusion you *experienced*, and how you have to *search* for your own meaning to make sense of this sentence.

In the same way noun phrases can be generalized or left out completely. It is well known that *people* can read *books* and make *changes*. (Well known by whom? Which people, what books and how will they make these changes? And what will they change from, and what will they change to?)

Judgements can be used. 'It is really good to see how relaxed you are.'

Comparisons also have deletions. 'It is better to go into a deeper trance.'

Both comparisons and judgements are good ways of delivering presuppositions. These are powerful ways of inducing and utilizing trance. You presuppose what you do not want questioned. For example:

'You may wonder when you will go into a trance.' Or, 'Would you like to enter trance now or later?' (You will go into a trance, the only question is when.)

'I wonder if you realize how relaxed you are?' (You are relaxed.)

'When your hand rises that will be the signal you have been waiting for.' (Your hand will rise and you are waiting for a signal.)

'You can relax while your unconscious learns.' (Your unconscious is learning.)

'Can you enjoy relaxing and not having to remember?' (You are relaxed and will not remember.)

Transitions (and, as, when, during, while) to link statements are a mild form of cause and effect. A stronger form is to use the word 'make', e.g. 'Looking at that picture will make you go into a trance.'

I am sure you are curious to know how mind reading can be woven into this model of using language. It must not be too specific, or it may not fit. General statements about what the person may be thinking act to pace and then lead their experience. For example, 'You might wonder what trance will be like,' or, 'You are beginning to wonder about some of the things I am saying to you.'

Universal quantifiers are used too. Examples are: 'You can learn from *every* situation,' and, 'Don't you realize the unconscious always has a purpose?'

Modal operators of possibility are also useful. 'You can't understand how looking at that light puts you deeper into trance.' This also presupposes that looking at the light does deepen the trance.

'You can't open your eyes,' would be too direct a suggestion, and invites the person to disprove the statement.

'You can relax easily in that chair,' is a different example. To say you *can* do something gives permission without forcing any action. Typically people will respond to the suggestion by doing the permitted behaviour. At the very least, they will have to think about it.

LEFT AND RIGHT BRAIN HEMISPHERES

How does the brain process language and how does it deal with these artfully vague forms of language? The front part of the brain, the cerebrum, is divided into two halves or hemispheres. Information passes between them through the connecting tissue, the corpus callosum.

Experiments which measured the activity in both hemispheres for different tasks have shown they have different but complementary functions. The left hemisphere is commonly known as the dominant hemisphere and deals with language. It processes information in an analytical, rational way. The right side, known as the non-dominant hemisphere deals with information in a more holistic and intuitive way. It also seems to be more involved in melody, visualization and tasks involving comparison and gradual change.

This specialization of the hemispheres holds true for over 90 per cent of the population. For a small minority (usually left-handed people) it is reversed and the right hemisphere deals with language. Some people have these functions scattered over both hemispheres.

There is evidence that the non-dominant hemisphere also has language abilities, mostly simple meanings and childish grammar. The dominant hemisphere has been identified with the conscious mind, and the non-dominant with the unconscious, but this is too simple. It is useful to think of our left brain dealing with our conscious understanding of language and the right brain dealing with simple meanings, in an innocent way below our level of awareness.

Milton Model patterns distract the conscious mind by keeping the dominant hemisphere overloaded. Milton Erickson could speak in such a complex and multi-layered way that all the seven plus or minus two chunks of conscious attention were engaged searching for possible meanings and sorting out ambiguities. There are many ways of using language to confuse and distract the left hemisphere.

Ambiguity is one such method. What you say can be soundly ambiguous. Like the last sentence. Does 'soundly' here mean definitely or phonetically? Hear, it means the latter, and it's a good example of one word carrying two meanings. Another example would be, 'When you experience insecurity . . . (In security?)'

There are many words that have different meanings but sound the same . . . there/they're . . . nose/knows. It is difficult to right/write phonological ambiguity.

Another form of ambiguity is called syntactic, for example 'Fascinating people can be difficult.' Does this mean the people are fascinating, or is it difficult to fascinate people? This sort of ambiguity is constructed by using a verb plus 'ing' and making a sentence where it is not clear whether it serves as an adjective or a verb.

A third type is called punctuation ambiguity. As you read this sentence is an example of punctuation ambiguity. Two sentences run together that begin and end with the same word(s). I hope you can hear you are reading this book. All these forms of language take some time to sort out and they fully engage the left hemisphere.

ACCESSING THE UNCONSCIOUS AND RESOURCES

The right hemisphere is sensitive to voice tone, volume and direction of sound: all those aspects that can change gradually rather than the actual words which are separate from each other. It is sensitive to the context of the message, rather than the verbal content. As the right hemisphere is capable of understanding simple language forms, simple messages that are given some special emphasis will go to the right brain. Such messages will bypass the left brain, and will seldom be consciously recognized.

There are many ways to give this sort of emphasis. You can mark out portions of what you say with different voice tones or gestures. This can be used to mark out instructions or questions for unconscious attention. In books this is done by using *italics*. When an author wishes to *please* you and wants you to *read* something on *this* page, a particular *sentence*, very *carefully*, he will mark it out in italics.

Did you *get* the message embedded in *it* ?

In the same way words can be marked out in a particular voice tone for special attention to form a command that is embedded in the speech. Erickson, who was confined to a wheelchair for part of his life, was adept at moving his head to make parts of what he said come from different directions. For example, 'Remember you don't have to *close your eyes* to go into a trance.' He would mark out the embedded command by moving his head when he said those words in italics. Marking out important words with voice and gesture is an extension of what we do naturally all the time in normal conversation.

There is a good analogy with music. Musicians mark out important notes in the flow of the music in various ways to make a tune. The listener may not notice this consciously if the notes are far apart and the intervening material is diverting, but it all adds to his pleasure and appreciation. He does not need to be aware of the performer's device.

You can embed questions in longer sentences in the same way. 'I wonder if you know *which of your hands is warmer than the other?*' This also contains a presupposition. It is not a direct question, but it will typically result in the person checking his hands for warmth. I wonder if you fully appreciate what a gentle and elegant way to gather information this pattern is?

There is an interesting pattern known as *quotes*. You can say anything if you first set up a context where it is not really you saying it. The easiest way to do this is by telling a story where someone says the message you want to convey, and mark it out in some way from the rest of the story.

I am reminded of a time when we did a seminar on these patterns. One of the participants came up to us afterwards, and we asked him during the course of the conversation if he had heard of the quotes pattern. He said, 'Yes. It was funny how that happened. I was walking down a street a couple of weeks ago and a complete stranger came up to me and said, *"Isn't this quotes pattern interesting?"*'

Negatives fit into these patterns. Negatives exist only in language, not experience. Negative commands work just like positive commands. The unconscious mind does not process the linguistic negative and simply disregards it. A parent or teacher who tells a child not to do something is ensuring the child will do it again. Tell a tightrope walker, 'Be careful!' not 'Don't *slip!*'

What you resist persists because it still has your attention. This being so, we would not want you to consider how much better and more effective your communication would be if it were phrased positively . . .

The last pattern we will deal with here is called *conversational postulates*.

These are questions that literally only require a yes/no answer, yet actually draw a response. For example, 'Can you take out the garbage?' is not a literal request about your physical capability to do this task, but a request to do so. Other examples are:

'Is the door still open?' (Shut the door.)
'Is the table set?' (Set the table.)

These patterns are used all the time in normal conversation and we all respond to them. If you know about them, you can be more selective where you use them, and have more choice about whether you react to them. Because these patterns are so common, John Grinder and Richard Bandler would contradict each other in public seminars. One would say, 'There is no such thing as hypnosis,' the other, 'No! everything is hypnosis.' If hypnosis is just another word for multi-layered, influential communication, it may be that we are all hypnotists and we are constantly moving in and out of trance . . . now . . .

METAPHOR

The word metaphor is used in NLP in a general way to cover any story or figure of speech implying a comparison. It includes simple comparisons or similes, and longer stories, allegories and parables. Metaphors communicate indirectly. Simple metaphors make simple comparisons: as white as a sheet, as pretty as a picture, as thick as two short planks. Many of these sayings become cliches, but a good simple metaphor can illuminate the unknown by relating it to what you already know.

Complex metaphors are stories with many levels of meaning. Telling a story elegantly distracts the conscious mind and activates an unconscious search for meaning and resources. As such, it is an excellent way of communicating with someone in a trance. Erickson made extensive use of metaphors with his clients.

The unconscious appreciates *relationships*. Dreams make use of imagery and metaphor; one thing stands for another because they have some feature in common. To create a successful metaphor, one that will point the way towards resolving a problem, the relationships between the elements of the story need to be the same as the relationships between the elements of the problem. Then the metaphor will resonate in the unconscious and mobilize the resources there. The unconscious gets the message and starts to make the necessary changes.

Creating a metaphor is like composing music, and metaphors affect us in the same way music does. A tune consists of notes in a relationship, it can be transposed higher or lower and will still be the same tune, provided the notes still have the same relationships to each other, the same distances between them, as they had in the original tune. At a deeper level, these notes combine to make chords, and a sequence of chords will have certain relationships to each other. Musical rhythm is how long different notes last relative to each other. Music is meaningful in a different way to language. It goes straight to the unconscious; the left brain has nothing to catch on to.

Allegro con brio

'Once upon a time . . .'

Creating a metaphor is like composing music.

Like good music, good stories must create expectation and then satisfy it in some way consistent with the style of the composition. The 'with a bound he was free' type of solutions are not allowed.

Fairy tales are metaphors. 'Once upon a time . . .' locates them in inner time. The information that follows is not useful real-world information, but inner-world process information. Story-telling is an age-old art. Stories entertain, give knowledge, express truths, give hints of possibilities and potential beyond habitual ways of acting.

Creating a Metaphor

Story telling needs the skills of the Milton Model and more. Pacing and leading, synesthesias, anchoring, trance and smooth transitions are all needed to make a good story. The plot must be (psycho)logical and match the listener's experience.

To create a helpful story, first examine the person's present state and desired state. A metaphor will be a story of the journey from one to the other.

Present State ————————————————➤ Desired State

'Once upon a time . . .'   '. . . and they
                                            lived happily ever after.'

Sort out the elements of both states, the people, the places, the objects, activities, time, not forgetting the representational systems and submodalities of the various elements.

Next, choose an appropriate context for the story, one that will interest the other person, and replace all the elements in the problem with different elements, but hold the relationships the same. Plot the story so that it has the same form as the present state and leads through a connecting strategy to a resolution (the desired state). The story-line beguiles the left brain and the message goes to the unconscious.

Perhaps I can illustrate this process with an example, even though the printed word loses tonality, congruity and the Milton Model patterns of the storyteller. I would not, of course, try to tell a metaphor that was relevant to you, the reader. This is an example of the process of making a metaphor.

Once I was working with a person who was expressing concern about the lack of balance in his life. He was finding it difficult to decide the important issues in the present, and was worried about devoting a lot of energy to some projects and little to others. Some of his enterprises seemed ill-prepared to him, and others overprepared.

This reminded me of when I was a young boy. I was learning to play the guitar and sometimes I was allowed to stay up late to entertain guests by playing to them over supper. My father was a film actor and many household names used to eat and talk far into the night about all sorts of subjects at those parties. I used to enjoy these times and I got to meet many interesting people.

One night, one of my father's guests was a fine actor, renowned for his skill both in films and on the stage. He was a particular hero of mine, and I enjoyed listening to him talk.

Late in the evening, another guest asked him the secret of his extraordinary skill. 'Well,' said the actor, 'funnily enough I learned a lot by asking someone the very same question in my youth. As a boy, I loved the circus – it was colourful, noisy, extravagant and exciting. I imagined I was out there in the ring under the lights, acknowledging the roar of the crowd. It felt marvellous. One of my heroes was a tight-rope walker in a famous travelling circus company; he had extraordinary balance and grace on the high wire. I made friends with him one summer, I was fascinated by his skill and the aura of danger about him, he rarely used a safety net. One afternoon in late summer, I was sad, for the circus was going to leave our town the next day. I sought out my friend and we talked into the dusk. At that time, all I wanted was to be like him; I wanted to join a circus. I asked him what was the secret of his skill.

"First," he said, "I see each walk as the most important one of my life, the last one I will do, I want it to be the best. I plan each walk very carefully. Many things in my life I do from habit, but this is not one of them. I am careful what I wear, what I eat, how I look. I mentally rehearse each walk as a success before I do it, what I will see, what I will hear, how I will feel. This way I will get no unpleasant surprises. I also put myself in place of the audience, and imagine what they will see, hear and feel. I do all my thinking beforehand, down on the ground. When I am up on the wire I clear my mind and put all my attention out."

'This was not exactly what I wanted to hear at the time, although strangely enough, I *always remember* what he said.

"You think I don't lose my *balance?*" he asked me.

"I've never seen you lose your balance," I replied.

"You're wrong," he said. "I am always losing my balance. I simply control it within the bounds I set myself. I couldn't walk the rope unless I lost my balance all the time, first to one side and then to the other. Balance is not something you have like the clowns have a false nose; it is the state of controlled movement to and fro. When I have finished my walk, I review it to see if there is anything I can learn from it. Then I forget it completely."

'I apply the same principles to my acting,' said my hero.

Finally we would like to leave you with a story from *The Magus*, by John Fowles. This lovely story says a lot about NLP, but remember, it's only one way of talking about it. We leave it to echo in your unconscious.

THE PRINCE AND THE MAGICIAN

Once upon a time there was a young prince who believed in all things but three. He did not believe in princesses, he did not believe in islands, he did not believe in God. His father, the king, told him that such things did not exist. As there were no princesses or islands in his father's domains, and no sign of God, the young prince believed his father.

But then, one day, the prince ran away from his palace. He came to the next land. There, to his astonishment, from every coast he saw islands, and on these islands, strange and troubling creatures whom he dared not name. As he was searching for a boat, a man in full evening dress approached him along the shore.

'Are those real islands?' asked the young prince.

'Of course they are real islands,' said the man in evening dress.

'And those strange and troubling creatures?'

'They are all genuine and authentic princesses.'

'Then God also must exist!' cried the prince.

'I am God,' replied the man in full evening dress, with a bow.

The young prince returned home as quickly as he could.

'So you are back,' said his father, the king.

'I have seen islands, I have seen princesses, I have seen God,' said the prince reproachfully.

The king was unmoved.

'Neither real islands, nor real princesses, nor a real God, exist.'

'I saw them!'

'Tell me how God was dressed.'

'God was in full evening dress.'

'Were the sleeves of his coat rolled back?'

The prince remembered that they had been. The king smiled.

'That is the uniform of a magician. You have been deceived.'

At this, the prince returned to the next land, and went to the same shore, where once again he came upon the man in full evening dress.

'My father, the king, has told me who you are,' said the young prince indignantly. 'You deceived me last time, but not again. Now I know that those are not real islands and real princesses, because you are a magician.'

The man on the shore smiled.

'It is you who are deceived, my boy. In your father's kingdom there are many islands and many princesses. But you are under your father's spell, so you cannot see them.'

The prince returned pensively home. When he saw his father, he looked him in the eyes.

'Father, is it true that you are not a real king, but only a magician?'

The king smiled and rolled back his sleeves.

'Yes my son, I am only a magician.'

'Then the man on the shore was God.'

'The man on the shore was another magician.'

'I must know the real truth, the truth beyond magic.'

'There is no truth beyond magic,' said the king.

The prince was full of sadness.

He said, 'I will kill myself.'

The king by magic caused death to appear. Death stood in the door and beckoned to the prince. The prince shuddered. He remembered the beautiful but unreal islands and the unreal but beautiful princesses.

'Very well,' he said. 'I can bear it.'

'You see, my son,' said the king, 'you too now begin to be a magician.'

From *The Magus* © John Fowles, published by Jonathan Cape, 1977.

REFRAMING AND THE TRANSFORMATION OF MEANING

There is nothing either good or bad, but thinking makes it so.

William Shakespeare

Mankind has always searched for meaning. Events happen, but until we give them meaning, relate them to the rest of our life, and evaluate the possible consequences, they are not important. We learn what things mean from our culture and individual upbringing. To ancient peoples, astronomical phenomena had great meaning: comets were portents of change, and the relationship of the stars and planets influenced individual destinies. Now scientists do not take eclipses and comets personally. They are beautiful to see and confirm the universe still obeys the laws we have made up for it.

What does a rainstorm mean? Bad news if you are out in the open without a raincoat. Good news if you are a farmer and there has been a drought. Bad news if you are the organizer of an open-air party. Good news if your cricket team is close to defeat and the match is called off. The meaning of any event depends on the frame you put it in. When you change the frame, you also change the meaning. When the meaning changes so do your responses and behaviour. The ability to reframe events gives greater freedom and choice.

One person we knew well fell and injured his knee quite badly. This was painful, and meant he could not play squash, a game he enjoyed very much. He framed the accident as an opportunity rather than a limitation, consulted a number of doctors and physiotherapists, and found out how the muscles and ligaments of the knee worked. Fortunately, he did not need surgery. He devised an exercise programme for himself and six months later his knee was stronger than it had been, and he was fitter and healthier too. He corrected the postural habits that had led to his knee becoming weak in the first place. Even his squash improved. Hurting his knee was very useful. Misfortune is a point of view.

Metaphors are reframing devices. They say in effect, 'This *could* mean that . . .' Fairy tales are beautiful examples of reframes. What seems to be unlucky turns out to be helpful. An ugly duckling is a young swan. A curse is really a blessing in disguise. A frog can be a prince. And if whatever you touch turns to gold, you are in big trouble.

Inventors make reframes. There is the well-known example of the man who woke one night with the sharp end of a rusty spring in his old mattress digging into him. What possible use could an old bedspring have? (Besides depriving him of sleep.) He reframed it as a stylish egg-cup and started a successful company on the strength of the idea.

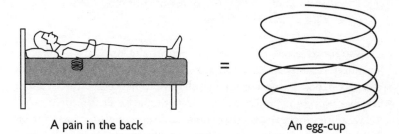

A pain in the back   An egg-cup

Jokes are reframes. Nearly all jokes start by setting events in a certain frame and then suddenly and drastically changing it. Jokes involve taking an object or situation and putting it suddenly in a different context, or suddenly giving it another meaning.

Why do anarchists drink herbal tea? (*Answer at end of chapter.*)

Sleight of Mouth Patterns

Here are some examples of different viewpoints on the same statement:

'My job is going badly and I feel depressed.'

Generalize: Perhaps you're just feeling down generally, but your job is OK.

Apply to self: Maybe you are making yourself depressed by thinking that.

Elicit values or criteria: What is important about your job that you think is going wrong?

Positive outcome: It could make you work harder to get over this particular problem.

Change outcome: Perhaps you need to change jobs.

Setting a further outcome: Can you learn something useful from the way your job is going at the moment?

Tell a metaphor: It's a bit like learning to walk . . .

Redefine: Your depression might mean you are feeling angry because your job is making unreasonable demands on you.

Step down: Which particular parts of your job are going badly?

Step up: How are things generally?

Counter examples: Has your work ever gone badly without you being depressed?

Positive intention: That shows you care about your job.

Time frame: It's a phase, it will pass.

Reframing is not a way of looking at the world through rose-coloured spectacles, so that everything is 'really' good. Problems will not vanish of their own accord, they still have to be worked through, but the more ways you have of looking at them, the easier they are to solve.

Reframe to see the possible gain, and represent an experience in ways that support your own outcomes and those you share with others. You are not free to choose when you see yourself pushed by forces beyond your control. Reframe so you have some room to manoeuvre.

There are two main types of reframe: *context* and *content*.

CONTEXT REFRAMING

Nearly all behaviours are useful *somewhere*. There are very few which do not have value and purpose in some context. Stripping off your clothes in a crowded high street will get you arrested, but in a nudist camp you might be arrested if you do not. Boring your audience in a seminar is not recommended, but the ability is useful for getting rid of unwelcome guests. You will not be popular if you tell bizarre lies to your friends and family, but you will be if you use your imagination to write a fictional bestseller. What about indecision? It might be useful if you could not make up your mind whether to lose your temper . . . or not . . . and then forget all about it.

Context reframing works best on statements like, 'I'm too . . .' Or, 'I wish I could stop doing . . .' Ask yourself:

'When would this behaviour be useful?'
'Where would this behaviour be a resource?'

When you find a context where the behaviour is appropriate, you could mentally rehearse it in just that context, and make up fitting behaviour in the original context. The New Behaviour Generator can be helpful here.

If a behaviour looks odd from the outside, it is usually because the person is in downtime and has set up an internal context which does not match the world outside. Transference in psychotherapy is an example. The patient responds to the therapist in the same way that he or she responded to parents many years ago. What was appropriate for a child is no longer useful to the adult. The therapist must reframe the behaviour, and help the patient develop other ways of acting.

CONTENT REFRAMING

The content of an experience is whatever you choose to focus on. The meaning can be whatever you like. When the two-year-old daughter of one of the authors asked him what it meant to tell a lie, he explained in grave, fatherly tones (taking due account of her age and understanding), it meant saying something that was not true on purpose, to make someone else think something was right when it wasn't. The little girl considered this for a moment and her face lit up.

'That's *fun!*' she said. 'Let's do it!'

The next few minutes were spent telling each other outrageous lies. Content reframing is useful for statements like, 'I get angry when people make demands on me.' Or, 'I panic when I have a deadline to meet.'

Notice that these types of statement use cause–effect Meta Model violations. Ask yourself:

'What else could this mean?'
'What is the positive value of this behaviour?'
'How else could I describe this behaviour?'

Politics is the art of content reframing par excellence. Good economic figures can be taken as an isolated example showing up an overall downward trend, or, as an indication of prosperity, depending on which side of the House of Commons you sit. High interest rates are bad for borrowers, but good for savers. Traffic jams are an awful nuisance if you are stuck in one, but they have been described by a government minister as a sign of prosperity. If traffic congestion were eliminated in London, he was reported as saying, this would mean the death of the capital as a job centre.

'We are not retreating,' said a general, 'We are advancing backwards.'

Advertising and selling are other areas where reframing is very important. Products are put in the best possible light. Advertisements are instant frames for a product. Drinking this coffee *means* that you are sexy, using this washing powder *means* that you care about your family, using this bread *means* that you are intelligent. Reframing is so pervasive you will see examples wherever you look.

Simple reframes are unlikely to make a drastic change, but if they are delivered congruently, perhaps with a metaphor, and bring in important issues to that person, they can be very effective.

INTENTION AND BEHAVIOUR

At the heart of reframing is the distinction between behaviour and intention: what you do, and what you are actually trying to achieve by doing it. This is a crucial distinction to make when dealing with any behaviour. Often what you do does not get you what you want. For example, a woman may constantly worry about her family. This is her way of showing she loves and cares for them. The family see it as nagging and resent it. A man may seek to demonstrate his love for his family by working very long hours. The family may wish he spent more time with them, even if it meant having less spending money.

Sometimes behaviour does get you what you want, but does not fit in well with the rest of your personality. For example an office worker may flatter and humour the boss to get a rise, but hate himself for doing it. Other times you actually may not know what a behaviour is trying to achieve, it just seems a nuisance. There is always a positive intention behind every behaviour – why else would you do it? Everything you do is fashioned towards some goal, only it may be out of date. And some behaviours (smoking is a good example) achieve many different outcomes.

The way to get rid of unwanted behaviours is not to try and stop them with will-power. This will guarantee they persist because you are giving them attention and energy. Find another, better way to satisfy the intention, one that is more attuned to the rest of your personality. You do not rip out the gas lights until you have installed electricity, unless you want to be left in the dark.

We contain multiple personalities living in uneasy alliance under the same skin. Each part is trying to fulfil its own outcome. The more these can be aligned and work together in harmony the happier a person will be. We are a mixture of many parts, and they often conflict. The balance shifts constantly; it makes life interesting. It is difficult to be totally congruent, totally committed to one course of action, and the more important the action, the more parts of our personality have to be involved.

Habits are difficult to give up. Smoking is bad for the body, but it does relax you, occupy your hands and sustain friendships with others. Giving up smoking without attending to these other needs leaves a vacuum. To quote Mark Twain, 'Giving up smoking is easy. I do it every day.'

SIX STEP REFRAMING

> We are as unlike ourselves as we are unlike others.
>
> Montaigne

NLP uses a more formal reframing process to stop unwanted behaviour by providing better alternatives. This way, you keep the benefits of the behaviour. It is a bit like going on a journey. Horse and cart seems to be the only way to get where you want to go, uncomfortable and slow as it is. Then, a friend tells you there is actually a train service and regular flights – different and better ways of reaching your destination.

Six step reframing works well when there is a part of you that is making you behave in a way you do not like. It can also be used on psychosomatic symptoms.

1. First identify the behaviour or response to be changed.
It is usually in the form: 'I want to . . . but something stops me.' Or, 'I don't want to do this, but I seem to end up doing it just the same.' If you are working with someone else, you do not need to know the actual problem behaviour. It makes no difference to the reframing process what the behaviour is. This can be secret therapy.

Take a moment to express appreciation for what this part has done for you and make it clear that you are not going to get rid of it. This may be difficult if the behaviour (let's call it X) is very unpalatable, but you can appreciate the intention, if not the way it was accomplished.

2. Establish communication with the part responsible for the behaviour.
Go inside and ask, 'Will the part responsible for X communicate with me in consciousness, now?' Notice what response you get. Keep all your senses open for internal sights, sounds, feelings. Do not guess. Have a definite signal, it is often a slight body feeling. Can you reproduce that exact signal consciously? If you can, ask the question again until you get a signal that you cannot control at will.

This sounds strange, but the part responsible is unconscious. If it were under conscious control, you would not be reframing it, you would just stop it. When parts are in conflict there is always some indication that will reach consciousness. Have you ever agreed with someone's plan while harbouring doubts? What does this do to your tone of voice? Can you control that sinking feeling in the pit of your stomach if you agree to work when you would rather be relaxing in the garden? Head shaking, grimacing and tonality changes are obvious examples of ways that conflicting parts express themselves. When there is a conflict of interest, there is always some involuntary signal and it is likely to be very slight. You have to be alert. The signal is the *but* in the 'Yes, *but* . . .'

Now you need to turn that response into a yes/no signal. Ask the part to increase the strength of the signal for 'yes' and decrease it for 'no'. Ask for both signals one after the other, so they are clear.

3. Separate the positive intention from the behaviour.

Thank the part for co-operating. Ask, 'Will the part that is responsible for this behaviour let me know what it is trying to do?' If the answer is the 'yes' signal, you will get the intention, and it may be a surprise to your conscious mind. Thank the part for the information, and for doing this for you. Think about whether you actually want a part to do this.

However, you do not need to know the intention. If the answer to your question is 'no', you could explore circumstances where the part would be willing to let you know what it is trying to achieve. Otherwise assume a good intention. This does not mean you like the behaviour, simply that you assume the part has a purpose, and that it benefits you in some way.

Go inside and ask the part, 'If you were given ways that enabled you to accomplish this intention, at least as well, if not better than what you are doing now, would you be willing to try them out?' A 'no' at this point will mean your signals are scrambled. No part in its right mind could turn down such an offer.

4. Ask your creative part to generate new ways that will accomplish the same purpose.

There will have been times in your life when you were creative and resourceful. Ask the part you are working with to communicate its positive intention to your creative, resourceful part. The creative part will then be able to make up other ways of accomplishing the same intention. Some will be good, some not so good. Some you may be aware of consciously, but it does not matter if you are not. Ask the part to choose only those it considers to be as good, or better than the original behaviour. They must be immediate and available. Ask it to give the 'yes' signal each time it has another choice. Continue until you get at least three 'yes' signals. You can take as long as you wish over this part of the process. Thank your creative part when you have finished.

5. Ask the X part if it will agree to use the new choices rather than the old behaviour over the next few weeks.

This is future pacing, mentally rehearsing a new behaviour in a future situation.

If all is well up to now, there is no reason why you will not get a 'yes' signal. If you get a 'no', assure the part it can still use the old behaviour, but you would like it to use the new choices first. If you still get a no, you can reframe the part that objects by taking it through the whole six step reframing process.

6. *Ecological check*

You need to know if there are any other parts that would object to your new choices. Ask, 'Does any other part of me object to any of my new choices?' Be sensitive to any signals. Be thorough here. If there is a signal, ask the part to intensify the signal if it really is an objection. Make sure the new choices meet with the approval of all interested parts, or one will sabotage your work.

If there is an objection you can do one of two things. Either go back to step 2 and reframe the part that objects, or ask the creative part, in consultation with the objecting part, to come up with more choices. Make sure these new choices are also checked for any new objections.

Six step reframing is a technique for therapy and personal development. It deals directly with several psychological issues.

One is *secondary gain:* the idea that however bizarre or destructive a behaviour appears, it always serves a useful purpose at some level, and this purpose is likely to be unconscious. It does not make sense to do something that is totally contrary to our interests. There is always some benefit, our mixture of motives and emotions is rarely a harmonious one.

Another is *trance.* Anyone doing six step reframing will be in a mild trance, with his focus of attention inwards.

Thirdly, six step reframing also uses negotiation skills between parts of one person. In the next chapter we will look at negotiation skills between people in a business context.

TIMELINES

We can never be anywhen else but 'now' and we have a time machine inside our skulls. When we sleep time stands still. And in our daydreams and night dreams we can jump between present, past and future without any difficulty. Time seems to fly, or drag its feet, depending on what we are doing. Whatever time really is, our subjective experience of it changes all the time.

We measure time for the outside world in terms of distance and motion – a moving pointer on a clock face – but how do our brains deal with time? There must be some way, or we would never know whether we had done something, or were going to do it; whether it belonged to our past or our future. A feeling of *déjà vu* about the future would be difficult to live with. What is the difference in the way we think of a past event and a future event?

Perhaps we can get some clues from the many sayings we have about time: 'I can't see any future,' 'He's stuck in the past,' 'Looking back on events,' 'Looking forward to seeing you.' Maybe vision and direction has something to do with it.

Now, select some simple repetitive behaviour that you do nearly every day, such as brushing your teeth, combing your hair, washing your hands, having breakfast or watching TV.

Think of a time about five years ago when you did this. It does not have to be a specific instance. You know that you did it five years ago, you can pretend to remember.

Now think of doing that same thing one week ago.

Now think what it would be like if you do it right this instant.

Now one week hence.

Now think about doing it in five years' time. It does not matter that you do not know where you may be, just think of doing that activity.

Now take those four examples. You probably have some sort of picture of each instance. It may be a movie or a snapshot. If a gremlin suddenly shuffled them all around when you were not looking, how could you tell which was which?

You may be interested to find out for yourself how you do it. Later, we will give you some generalizations.

Look at those pictures again. What are the *differences* between each of the pictures in terms of the following submodalities?

Where are they in space?

How large are they?

How bright?

How focused?

Are they all coloured equally?

Are they moving pictures or still?

How far away are they?

It is difficult to generalize about timelines, but a common way of organizing pictures of the past, present and future is by location. The past is likely to be on your left. The further into the past, the further away the pictures will be. The 'dim and distant' past will be furthest. The future will go off to your right, with the far future far away at the end of the line. The pictures on each side may be stacked or offset in some way so that they can be seen and sorted easily. Many people use the visual system for representing a sequence of memories over time,

but there may well be some submodality differences in the other
systems as well. Sounds may be louder when closer to the present,
feelings may be stronger.

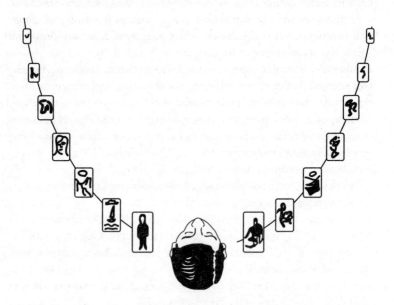

Happily, this way of organizing time allies itself with normal eye
accessing cues (and reading English), which may explain why it is a
common pattern. There are many ways to organize your time line.
While there are no 'wrong' time lines they all have consequences.
Where and how you store your timeline will affect how you think . . .

For example, suppose your past was straight out in front of you. It
would always be in view, and attracting your attention. Your past
would be an important and influential part of your experience.

Big, bright pictures in the far future would make it very attractive
and draw you towards it. You would be future-oriented. The
immediate future would be difficult to plan. If there were big, bright
pictures in the near future, long-range planning might be difficult. In
general, whatever is big, bright and colourful (if these are critical
submodalities for you) will be most attractive and you will pay most
attention to it. You can really tell if someone has a murky past or a
bright future.

The submodalities may change gradually. For example, the brighter
the picture, or the sharper the focus, the nearer to the present. These
two submodalities are good at representing gradual change.

Sometimes a person might sort their pictures in a more discrete way using definite locations, each memory detached from the last. Then the person will tend to use staccato gestures when talking about the memories, rather than using more fluent, sweeping gestures.

The future may be spaced out a long way in front of you, giving you trouble meeting deadlines, which will seem far away until they suddenly loom large. On the other hand if the future is too compressed with not enough space between future pictures, you may feel pressed for time, everything looks like it has to be done at once. Sometimes it is useful to compress the timeline, other times, to expand it. It depends what you want. It is common sense that people who are oriented towards the future generally recover from illness more quickly, and medical studies have confirmed this. Timeline therapy could aid recovery from serious illness.

Timelines are important to a person's sense of reality, and so they are difficult to change unless the change is ecological. The past is real in a way that the future is not. The future exists more as potential or possibilities. It is uncertain. Future submodalities will usually reflect this in some way. The timeline may split into different branches, or the pictures may be fuzzy.

Timelines are important in therapy. If a client cannot see a future for himself, a lot of techniques are not going to work. Many NLP therapy techniques presuppose an ability to move through time, accessing past resources or constructing compelling futures. Sometimes the timeline has to be sorted out before this can be done.

IN TIME AND THROUGH TIME

In his book *The Basis of Personality*, Tad James describes two main types of timelines. The first he calls 'through time', or the Anglo-European type of time where the timeline goes from side to side. The past is on one side, the future on another and both are visible in front of the person. The second type he calls 'in time', or Arabic time, where the timeline stretches from front to back so that one part (usually the past) is behind you, and invisible. You have to turn your head to see it.

Through time people will have a good sequential, linear idea of time. They will expect to make and keep appointments precisely. This is the timeline that is prevalent in the business world. 'Time is money.' A through time person is also more likely to store their past as dissociated pictures.

In time people do not have the advantage of the past and future spread out in front of them. They are always in the present moment, so deadlines, business appointments and time-keeping are less important than they are for a through time person. They are associated to their timeline, and their memories are more likely to be associated. This model of time-keeping is common in Eastern, especially Arabic, countries, where business deadlines are more flexible than in the Western world. This can be very exasperating for a Western businessman. The future is looked on much more like a series of 'nows' so the urgency goes out of acting this very minute. There are plenty more 'nows' where those come from.

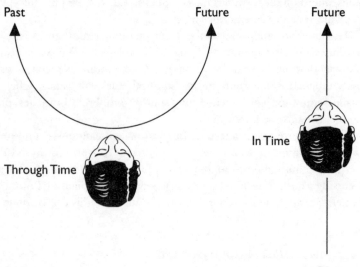

A summary of some generalizations about in time and through time differences:

Through Time	*In Time*
Western	Eastern
Left to right	Back to front
Past/present/future	Time happens now
In front	Not all in front
Orderly existence	Time is flexible
Memories usually dissociated	Usually associated memories

Time schedules important	Time schedules not so important
Harder to stay in the moment	Easy to focus on present

TALKING WITH TIME

Language affects brains. We respond to language at an unconscious level. Ways of talking about events will programme how we represent them in our minds, and therefore how we respond to them. We have already investigated some of the consequences of thinking with nominalizations, universal quantifiers, modal operators and other such patterns. Even verb tenses are not exempt, were they?

Now, think of a time when *you were walking.*

The form of that sentence is likely to make you think of an associated moving picture. If I say, think of the last time *you took* a walk, you are likely to make a dissociated, still picture. The form of words has taken the movement out of the picture. Yet both sentences mean the same thing, don't they?

Now, think of a time when you *will take* a walk. Still dissociated. Now a time when you *will be walking.* Now your idea is likely to be an associated movie.

Now I am going to invite you to be in the distant future, thinking about a past memory, which has actually not yet occurred. Tricky? Not at all; read the next sentence:

Think of a time when you *will have taken* a walk.

Now, remember when you are. You influence others and orient them in time with what you say. Knowing this, you have a choice about how you wish to influence them. You cannot stop yourself doing it. All communication does something. Does it do what you want it to do? Does it serve your outcome?

Imagine an anxious person visiting two different therapists. The first says, 'So you have felt anxious? Is that how you have been feeling?'

The second says, 'So you feel anxious? What things will make you feel anxious?'

The first dissociates her from the experience of feeling anxious and puts it the past. The second associates her into feeling anxious and programmes her to feel anxious in the future.

I know which therapist I would rather see.

This is just a small taste of how we influence each other with language in ways we are normally unaware of.

So now, as you think about how elegant and effective your communication can be . . . and you look back with these resources on what you used to do before you changed . . . what was it like to have been like that . . . and what steps did you take to change . . . as you sit here now . . . with this book in hand?

Why do anarchists drink herbal tea? *Answer:* Because property is theft.

7

CONFLICT AND CONGRUENCE

Everyone lives in the same world, and because we make different models of it, we come into conflict. Two people can look at the same event, hear the same words, and make completely different meanings. From these models and meanings we get the rich plurality of human values, politics, religions, interests and motives. This chapter explores negotiation and meetings to reconcile conflicting interests, and some of the ways these are being successfully used in the world of business.

Some of the most important parts of our map are the beliefs and values that shape our lives and give them purpose. They govern what we do and may bring us into conflict with others. Values define what is important to us; conflict starts if we insist that what is important to us should be important to others too. Sometimes our own values coexist uneasily, and we have to make difficult choices. Do I tell a lie for a friend? Should I take the boring job with more money, or the exciting work that is badly paid?

Different parts of us embody different values, follow different interests, have different intentions, and so come into conflict. Our ability to go for an outcome is radically affected by how we reconcile and creatively manage these different parts of ourselves. It is rare to be able to go wholeheartedly or completely congruently for an outcome, and the larger the outcome, the more parts of ourselves will be drawn in and the more possibility of conflicting interests. We have already dealt with the six step reframing technique, and in the next chapter we will further explore how to resolve some of these internal conflicts.

Internal congruence gives strength and personal power. We are congruent when all our verbal and non-verbal behaviour supports our outcome. All parts are in harmony and we have free access to our resources. Small children are nearly always congruent. When they want something they want it with their whole being. Being in harmony does not mean all the parts are playing the *same* tune. In an orchestra, the different instruments blend together, the total tune is more than any one instrument could produce on its own, and it is the difference between them which gives the music its colour, interest and harmony. So when we are congruent, our beliefs, values and interests act together to give us the energy to pursue our aims.

When you make a decision and you are congruent about it, then you know you can proceed with every chance of success. The question becomes, how do you know when you are congruent? Here is a simple exercise to identify your internal congruence signal:

IDENTIFYING YOUR CONGRUENCE SIGNAL

Remember a time when you really wanted something. That particular treat, present or experience you really looked forward to. As you think back and associate to that time and event, you can *begin to recognize what it feels like to be congruent.* Become familiar with this feeling so that you can use it in the future to know if you are fully congruent about an outcome. Notice how you feel, notice the submodalities of the experience as you think back to it. Can you find some internal feeling, sight or sound that will unmistakably define that you are congruent?

Incongruence is mixed messages – an instrument out of tune in an orchestra, a splash of colour that does not fit into the picture. Mixed internal messages will project an ambiguous message to the other person and result in muddled actions and self-sabotage. When you face a decision and are incongruent about it, this represents invaluable information from your unconscious mind. It is saying that it is not wise to proceed and that it is time to think, to gather more information, to create more choices, or explore other outcomes. The question here is, how do you know when you are incongruent? Do the following exercise to increase your awareness of your incongruence signal.

IDENTIFYING YOUR INCONGRUENCE SIGNAL

Think back to a time when you had reservations about some plan. You may have felt it was a good idea, but something told you it could lead to trouble. Or you could see yourself doing it, but still got that uncertain feeling. As you think about the reservations you had, there will be a certain feeling in part of your body, maybe some particular image or sound that lets you know that you are not fully committed. That is your incongruence signal. Make yourself familiar with it; it's a good friend, and could save you a lot of money. You may want to check it for several different experiences in which you know you had doubts or reservations. Being able to detect incongruence in yourself will save you from making many mistakes.

Used-car salesmen have a poor reputation for congruence. Incongruence also comes out in Freudian slips; someone who extols 'state of the *ark* technology' is clearly not really impressed with the software. Detecting incongruence in others is essential if you are to deal with them sensitively and effectively. For example, a teacher explaining an idea will ask if the student understands. The student may say 'Yes,' but her tone of voice or expression may contradict the words. In selling, a salesman who does not detect and deal with incongruence in the buyer is unlikely to make a sale, or if he does, he will generate buyer's remorse, and no further business.

VALUES AND CRITERIA

Our values powerfully affect whether we are congruent about an outcome. Values embody what is important to us and are supported by beliefs. We acquire them, like beliefs, from our experiences and from modelling family and friends. Values are related to our identity, we really care about them; they are the fundamental principles we live by. To act against our values will make us incongruent. Values give us motivation and direction, they are the important places, the capital cities, in our map of the world. The most lasting and influential values are freely chosen and not imposed. They are chosen with awareness of the consequences, and carry many positive feelings.

Yet values are usually unconscious and we seldom explore them in any clear way. To rise in a company you will need to adopt company values. If these are different to your own this could lead to incongruence. A company may only be employing half a person if a key worker has values that clash with his work.

NLP uses the word *criteria* to describe those values that are important in a particular context. Criteria are less general and wide-ranging than values. Criteria are the reasons you do something, and what you get out of it. They are usually nominalizations like wealth, success, fun, health, ecstasy, love, learning, etc. Our criteria govern why we work, whom we work for, whom we marry (if at all), how we make relationships and where we live. They determine the car we drive, the clothes we buy, or where we go for a meal out.

Pacing another person's values or criteria will build good rapport. If you pace his body but mismatch his values, you are unlikely to get rapport. Pacing other people's values does not mean you have to agree with them, but it shows you respect them.

Eliciting Criteria

Make a list of the 10 or so most important values in your life. You can do this alone, or with a friend to help you. Elicit your answers by asking such questions as:

What's important to me?
What truly motivates me?
What has to be true for me?

Criteria and values need to be expressed positively. Avoiding ill health might be a possible value, but it would be better to phrase it as good health. You may find it fairly easy to come up with the values that motivate you.

Criteria are likely to be nominalizations, and you need the Meta Model to untangle them. What do they mean in real, practical terms? The way to find this out is by asking for the evidence that lets you know the criterion has been met. It may not always be easy to find the answers, but the question to ask is:

How would you know if you got them?

If one of your criteria is learning, what are you going to learn about and how will you do it? What are the possibilities? And how will you know when you have learned something? A feeling? The ability to do something that you have not been able to do? These specific questions are very valuable. Criteria tend to disappear in a smoke screen when they come into contact with the real world.

When you have found out what these criteria really mean to you, you can ask whether they are realistic. If by success you mean a five-figure salary, a Ferrari, a town house, a country cottage and a high-powered job in the City all before your next birthday, you may well be disappointed. Disappointment, as Robert Dilts likes to say, requires adequate planning. To be really disappointed, you must have fantasized at great length about what you want to happen.

Criteria are vague and can be interpreted very differently by other people. I remember a good example from a couple I know well. For her, competence meant that she had actually done some task successfully. It was simply descriptive and not a highly valued criterion. For him, competence meant the feeling that he could do a task *if he put his mind to it*. Feeling competent in this way gave him self-esteem and it was highly valued. When she called him incompetent, he got very upset – until he understood what she actually meant. How different people see the criterion of male and female attractiveness is the force that makes the world go round.

HIERARCHY OF CRITERIA

Many things are important to us, and one useful step is to get a sense of the relative importance of your criteria. Since criteria are context-related, the ones you apply to your work will be different to the ones you apply to your personal relationships. We can use criteria to explore an issue like commitment to a job or a group of people. Here is an exercise to explore the criteria in this issue:

1. Suppose you had committed yourself to a group, what would have to be true for you to leave? Find the value or criterion that would motivate you to go. Do not jump to life or death issues at the start, think of something that would be just enough to tip the scales.
2. Next, ask what would have to be true to stay on even if (1) happened? Find the criterion that would override what you discovered at (1).
3. Then ask what would have to be true for you to leave given (1) and (2) have happened? Find a more important criterion.
4. Continue until you can go no further, so *nothing* would induce you to stay on if your last criterion (n) happened. You are sure to find some interesting ideas en route from (1) to (n).

You can use criteria in many ways. Firstly, we often do things for crummy reasons. Reasons that do not fully express our values. Equally we may want to do something in a vague sort of way, but it does not get done because other more important criteria stand in the way. This links back to outcomes in the first chapter. An outcome may need to be connected to a larger outcome that is sufficiently motivating because it is backed by important criteria. Criteria provide the energy for outcomes. If you can make something important to you by linking it to high criteria, obstacles will vanish.

Suppose you think it would be a good idea if you took regular exercise to get fit. Somehow, time goes on and you do not get round to it, because it is difficult to find the time in a busy week. Connecting regular exercise with looking attractive and having extra stamina for playing an enjoyable sport is likely to be far more motivating and can override the time factor, so that you create the time. There is usually time for what we really want to do. We do not have time for things that do not motivate us sufficiently.

The way you think about your criteria will have a submodality structure. The important ones may be represented by a bigger, closer or brighter picture, or a louder sound, or a stronger feeling, perhaps localized in a particular part of your body. What are the submodalities of your criteria, and how do you know which criteria are important to you? There are no rules that work in every case. It is worth exploring these ideas for yourself.

SNAKES AND LADDERS – STEPPING UP AND STEPPING DOWN

When you connect your actions to criteria, it is rather like playing a game of snakes and ladders. You can start with some small issue, but if you connect it to important criteria, you are taken very quickly to the top of the board. You will be motivated to do it, and you will think about it with submodalities that make it compelling.

How we connect events and ideas forms the substance of our maps, the roads between the cities. Understanding an issue means not only having the information, but also connecting it to other parts of our map. When we dealt with the size of our outcomes, we connected a smaller outcome to a larger one to give energy, and broke down a large outcome into a series of smaller ones to make it easier to handle. This was an example of a general idea which is known as *chunking* or *stepping* in NLP. Chunking is a term from the computer world, meaning to break things into bits. To chunk up or step up is to move from the specific to the general, or from a part to the whole. Chunking or stepping down moves from the general to the specific, or from the whole to a part.

The idea is simple. Take for example an everyday object such as a chair. To step up to the next level you would ask, 'What is this an example of?' One answer would be, 'An item of furniture.' You could also ask, 'What is this a part of?' One answer would be, 'A dining suite.' To step down, you ask the question in reverse, 'What is a specific example of the class of objects known as chairs?' One answer would be, 'An armchair.' The higher level always contains what is at the lower level.

You can also step sideways and ask, 'What is another example of this class of things?' To step sideways from a chair might come up with the answer, 'Table.' To step sideways from armchair might come to 'Deckchair.' The sideways example is always determined by what is at the next level up. You cannot ask for another example unless you know what it is another example of.

The Meta Model uses this idea; it explores the downward direction, making the idea more and more specific. The Milton Model goes up to the general level so as to take in all the specific examples below it.

If someone asks you for a drink and you give them a coffee, they may actually want a lemonade. Both coffee and lemonade are drinks. You need more specific information.

Stepping down goes to specifics, sensory-based, real-world events. (I want 25 fluid ounces of brand Fizzo lemonade in a tall glass at a temperature of 5° Centigrade, with three lumps of ice, shaken, not stirred.) Stepping up can eventually lead to outcomes and criteria (I want a drink because I am thirsty), if you start asking why at a high level.

Jokes, of course, make great use of stepping and then suddenly changing the rules on top. People connect things in weird and wonderful ways (according to our own map anyway). Do not assume they use the same rules as you do to connect ideas. Do not assume you know their rules at all. Like a game of Chinese whispers, the further you go with the rules slightly changing each time, the further away you will be from where you think you are.

Here is an exercise in stepping up in different ways. Coffee can be linked to each of the following in a different way. In the first example, tea and coffee are both members of a more general class called beverages. See if you can find a different step up for coffee and each of the others in turn:

1. Tea and coffee? Beverages.
2. Yams and coffee?

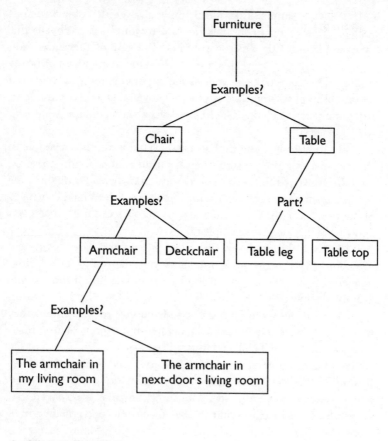

3. Clinic and coffee?
4. Amphetamines and coffee?
5. Ignatia and coffee?
(Answers at the end of the chapter.)

So it is possible to chunk sideways to some very different things and arrive in a very different place. It is like the oft-quoted idea that in this global village, six social relationships will bring you to anybody in the world. (I know Fred (1), who knows Joan (2), who knows Susy (3), who knows Jim (4), etc.)

So once again meaning depends on context. The links we make are important. Walls are held up not so much by the bricks as by the mortar that connects them. What is important to us, and how we connect ideas is important in meetings, negotiations and selling.

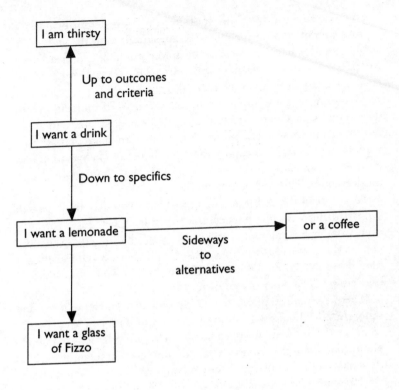

METAPROGRAMS

Metaprograms are perceptual filters that we habitually act on. There is so much information we could attend to, and most gets ignored as we have at most nine chunks of conscious attention available. Metaprograms are patterns we use to determine what information gets through. For example, think of a glass full of water. Now imagine drinking half of it. Is the glass half full or half empty? Both, of course, it's a matter of viewpoint. Some people notice what is positive about a situation, what is actually there, others notice what is missing. Both ways of looking are useful and each person will favour one view or the other.

Metaprograms are systematic and habitual, and we do not usually question them if they serve us reasonably well. The patterns may be the same across contexts, but few people are *consistently* habitual, so metaprograms are likely to change with a change of context. What holds our attention in a work environment may be different from what we pay attention to at home.

So metaprograms filter the world to help us create our own map.

You can notice other people's metaprograms both through their language and behaviour. Because metaprograms filter experience and we pass on our experience with language, certain patterns of language are typical of certain metaprograms.

Metaprograms are important in the key areas of motivation and decision-making. Good communicators shape their language to fit the other person's model of the world. So using language that accords with another person's metaprograms preshapes the information and ensures he can easily make sense of it. This leaves him more energy for decision-making and getting motivated.

As you read through these metaprograms you may find yourself sympathizing with one particular view in each category. You may even wonder how anyone could possibly think differently. This is a clue to the pattern you use yourself. Of the two extremes within a metaprogram pattern, there is likely to be one you can't stand or understand. The other is your own.

There are many patterns that might qualify as metaprograms, and different NLP books will emphasize different patterns. We will give some of the most useful ones here. No value judgment is implied about these patterns. None are 'better' or 'right' in themselves. It all depends on the context and the outcome you want. Some patterns work best given a particular type of task. The question is: can you act in the most useful way for the task you have to do?

Proactive–Reactive

This first metaprogram is about action. The *proactive* person initiates, he jumps in and gets on with it. He does not wait for others to initiate action.

The *reactive* person waits for others to initiate an action or bides her time before acting. She may take a long time to decide or never actually take any action.

A proactive person will tend to use complete sentences with a personal subject (noun or pronoun), an active verb and a tangible object, e.g. 'I am going to meet the managing director.'

A reactive person will tend to use passive verbs and incomplete sentences. He is also likely to use qualifying phrases and nominalizations, e.g. 'Is there any chance that it might be possible to arrange a meeting with the managing director?'

Even in such a short example there are many possibilities for making use of this pattern. A proactive person is motivated by phrases like 'Go to it', 'Do it' and 'Time to act.' In a sales situation, proactive people are more likely to go ahead and buy and make quick decisions. A reactive person would respond best to phrases like 'Wait', 'Let's analyse', 'Think about it' and 'See what the others think.'

Few people act out these patterns in such an extreme way. Most show a mixture of the two traits.

Towards–Away

The second pattern is about motivation and explains how people maintain their focus. People with a *towards* metaprogram stay focused on their goals. They go for what they want. *Away* people recognize problems easily and they know what to avoid, for they are clear about what they do not want. This can lead to problems for them in setting well-formed outcomes. Remember the old argument in business, education and parenting – whether to use the carrot or the stick approach? In other words, is it better to offer people incentives or threats? The answer of course is: it all depends whom you want to motivate. Towards people are energized by goals and rewards. Away people are motivated to avoid problems and punishment. Arguing which is best in general is futile.

It is easy to recognize this pattern from a person's language. Does she talk about what she wants, achieves or gains? Or does she tell you about the situations she wants to avoid and the problems to steer clear of? Towards people are best employed in goal-getting. Away from people are excellent at finding errors and work well in a job like quality control. Art critics usually have a strong away orientation as many a performing artist can testify!

Internal–External

This pattern is about where people find their standards. An *internal* person will have his standards internalized and use them to compare courses of action and decide what to do. He will use his own standards to make a comparison and a decision. In answer to the question, 'How do you know you have done a good piece of work?', he is likely to say something like, 'I just know.' Internal people take in information but will insist on deciding for themselves from their own standards. A strongly internal person will resist someone else's decision on their behalf, even if it is a good one.

External people need others to supply the standards and direction.

They know a job is well done when someone tells them so. Externals need to have an external standard. They will ask you about your standards. It looks as though they have difficulty deciding.

Internal people have difficulty accepting management. They are likely to make good entrepreneurs and are attracted to self-employment. They have little need of supervision.

External people need to be managed and supervised. They need the standard for success to come from the outside, otherwise they are unsure if they have done things correctly. One way you can identify this metaprogram is by asking: 'How do you know you have done a good job?' Internal people will tell you they decide. External people tell you they know because someone else has confirmed it.

Options–Procedures

This pattern is important in business. An *options* person wants to have choices and develop alternatives. He will hesitate to follow well-worn procedural paths, however good they are. The *procedures* person is good at following set, laid down courses of action, but not very good at developing them, being more concerned with how to do something than why she might want to do it. She is likely to believe there is a 'right' way to do things. It is obviously not a good idea to employ a procedures person to generate alternatives to the present system. Nor is it useful to employ an options person to follow a fixed procedure where success depends on following the procedure to the letter. They are not strong on following routines. They may feel compelled to be creative.

You can identify this metaprogram by asking: 'Why did you choose your current job?' Options people will give you reasons why they did what they did. Procedures people will tend to tell you how they came to do what they did or just give facts. They answer the question as if it were a 'how to' question.

Options people respond to promotional ideas that expand their choices. Procedures people respond to ideas that give them a clear-cut, proven path.

General–Specific

This pattern deals with chunking. General people like to see the big picture. They are most comfortable dealing with large chunks of information. They are the global thinkers. The specific person is most comfortable with small pieces of information, building from small to large, and so is comfortable with sequences, in extreme cases only being able to deal with the next step in the sequence he is following. Specifics people will talk about 'steps' and 'sequences' and give precise descriptions. They will tend to specify and use proper names.

The general person, as you might expect, generalizes. He may leave out steps in a sequence, making it hard to follow. He will see the whole sequence as one chunk rather than a series of graded steps. The general person deletes a lot of information. I bought some juggling balls some time ago and the instructions that came with them were clearly written by a very general person. They went as follows: 'Stand erect, balanced with your feet shoulder width apart. Breathe evenly. Start to juggle.'

General people are good at planning and developing strategies. Specific people are good at small step sequential tasks that involve attention to detail. You can tell from a person's language whether he is a general or a specific thinker. Does he give you details or the big picture?

Match–Mismatch

This pattern is about making comparisons. Some people notice what is the same about things. This is called *matching*. (It is not related to the rapport pattern.) *Mis*matchers notice what is different when making comparisons. They point out the differences and often get involved in arguments. A person that chunks down and mismatches will go over information with a fine toothcomb looking for discrepancies. If you match and think in big chunks, he will drive you crazy. Look at the three triangles below. Take a moment to answer this question silently to yourself: What is the relationship between them?

There is no right answer, of course, as their relationship involves points of similarity and difference.

The question highlights four possible patterns. There are people who *match*, who notice things that are the same. They might say that all three triangles are the same. (As indeed they are.) Such people will often be content in the same job or the same type of work for many years, and they are good at tasks that remain essentially the same.

There are people who notice *sameness with exception*. They notice similarities first, then differences. Looking at the diagram, they may answer that two triangles are the same and one is different, being upside down. (Quite right.) Such people usually like changes to occur gradually and slowly, and like their work situation to evolve over time. When they know how to do a job, they are ready to do it for a long time and are good at most tasks. They will use comparatives a lot, e.g. 'better', 'worse', 'more', 'less'. They respond to promotional material that uses words like 'better', 'improved' or 'advanced'.

Difference people are the *mismatchers*. They would say all three triangles are different. (Right again.) Such people seek out and enjoy change, often changing jobs rapidly. They will be attracted to innovative products, advertised as 'new' or 'different'.

Differences with exception people will notice differences first, then similarities. They might say the triangles are different and two of them are the same way up. They seek out change and variety, but not to the extent of the difference people. So to find out this metaprogram ask, 'What is the relationship between these two things?'

Convincer Patterns

There are two aspects to how a person becomes convinced of something. Firstly, what *channel* the information comes through, and secondly how the person manages the information once they have it (the *mode*).

First the channel. Think of a sales situation. What does a customer need to do to be convinced that the product is worthwhile? Or what evidence does a manager need to be convinced that someone is good at her job? The answer to this question is often related to a person's primary representational system. Some people need to *see* the evidence (visual). Others need to *hear* from others. Some people need to *read* a report; for example the Consumers' Association reports compare and give information about many products. Others have to *do* something. They may need to use the product to evaluate it or work alongside a new employee before deciding she is competent. The question to ask to determine this metaprogram is: 'How do you know someone is good at his job?'

A *visual* person needs to see examples. A *hear* person needs to talk to people and gather information. A *read* person needs to read reports or references about someone. A *do* person has to actually do the work with a person to be convinced she is good at her job.

The other side to this metaprogram is how people learn new tasks most easily. A visual person learns a new task most easily if he is shown how to do it. A hear person will learn best if she is told what to do. A read person learns best by reading instructions. A do person learns best by going and doing it for him or herself, getting 'hands-on experience'.

The second part of this metaprogram is about how the person manages the information and how it needs to be presented. Some people need to be presented with the evidence a particular number of times – perhaps two, three or more – before they are convinced. These are people who are convinced by a *number of examples*. Other people do not need much information. They get a few facts, imagine the rest and decide quickly. They often jump to conclusions on very little data. This is called the *automatic pattern*. On the other hand, some people are never really convinced. They will only be convinced for a particular example or a particular context. This is known as the *consistent pattern*. Tomorrow you may have to prove it to them all over again, because tomorrow is another day. They need convincing all the time. Lastly some people need to have their evidence presented over a *period of time* – a day, a week – before becoming convinced.

This is a very brief survey of some of the main metaprograms. They were originally developed by Richard Bandler and Leslie Cameron Bandler, and were further developed for use in business by Rodger Bailey as the 'Language and Behaviour Profile'. Criteria are often referred to as metaprograms, but they are not patterns, they are the values and things that really matter to you, so we have treated them separately.

Orientation in time is often referred to as a metaprogram. Some people will be *in* time, that is, associated with their timeline. Some people are *through* time, that is, primarily dissociated from their timeline. Another pattern that is often referred to as a metaprogram is preferred perceptual position. Some people spend most of their time in first position, in their own reality. Others empathize more and will spend a lot of time in second position. Others prefer third position.

Different books will have varying lists of metaprogram patterns, and there is no right answer, except to use those patterns that are useful to you and ignore the rest. Remember everything is likely to change with context. A man who weighs 90 kilograms will be heavy in the context of an aerobics class. He will be at the extreme end of scale there. Put him in a gymnasium full of Sumo wrestlers and he will be at the light end of the scale. A person who appears very proactive in one context may seem reactive in another. Similarly, a person may be very specific in a work context, yet very general in his leisure pursuits.

Metaprograms may also change with emotional state. A person may become more proactive under stress and more reactive when comfortable. As with all the patterns presented in this book, the answer is always the person in front of you. The pattern is only the map. Metaprograms are not another way of pigeonholing people. The important questions are: Can you be aware of your own patterns? What choices can you give others? They are useful guiding patterns. Learn to identify only one pattern at a time. Learn to use the skills one at a time. Use them if they are useful.

Metaprogram Summary

1. Proactive–Reactive
   The proactive person initiates action. The reactive person waits for others to initiate action and for things to happen. He will take time to analyse and understand first.
2. Towards–Away
   The towards person stays focused on his or her own goals and is motivated by achievement. The away person focuses on problems to be avoided rather than goals to be achieved.
3. Internal–External
   The internal person has internal standards and decides for him or herself. The external person takes standards from outside and needs direction and instruction to come from others.
4. Options–Procedures
   Options people want choices and are good at developing alternatives. Procedures people are good at following set courses of procedures. They are not action-motivated and are good at following a fixed series of steps.
5. General–Specific
   General people are most comfortable dealing with large chunks of information. They do not pay attention to details. Specific people pay attention to details and need small chunks to make sense of a larger picture.

6. Match–Mismatch

People who match will mostly notice points of similarity in a comparison. People who mismatch will notice differences when making a comparison.

7. Convincer patterns

Channel:

Visual: Need to see the evidence.

Hear: Need to be told.

Read: Need to read.

Do: Need to act.

Mode:

Number of Examples: Need to have the information some number of times before becoming convinced.

Automatic: Need only partial information.

Consistent: Need to have the information every time to be convinced, and then only for that example.

Period of time: Need to have the information remain consistent for some period of time.

SELLING

Sales psychology already has given rise to whole libraries of books, and we will only touch on it lightly here, to show some of the possibilities using NLP ideas.

Selling is often misunderstood, like advertising. A popular definition describes advertising as the art of arresting human intelligence long enough to get money from it. In fact, the whole purpose of sales, as the book *The One Minute Sales Person* by Spencer Johnson and Larry Wilson puts very eloquently, is to help people to get what they want. The more you help people to get what they want, the more successful a salesperson you will be.

Many NLP ideas will work towards this purpose. Initial rapport is important. Anchoring resources will enable you to meet challenges in a resourceful state. Feeling good about your work lets you do good work.

Future pacing can help to create the situations and feelings that you want, by mentally rehearsing them first. Setting well-formed outcomes is an invaluable skill in selling. In Chapter 1 you applied the well-formedness criteria to your own outcomes. The same questions that you used there can be used to help others become clear about what they want. This skill is crucial in selling because you can only satisfy the buyer if you know exactly what they want.

The idea of stepping up and down can help you find out what people need. What are their criteria? What is important to them about a product?

Do they have an outcome in mind about what they are buying, and can you help them to realize it?

I remember a personal example. There is a high street near where I live which has many more than its fair share of hardware shops. The one that does the best business is a small, rather out of the way shop. The owner always makes a genuine attempt to find out what you are doing and what you want the tool or equipment for. Although he does not always get good rapport, for sometimes his interrogation verges on the third degree, he makes sure that he does not sell you anything that does not specifically help you achieve what you want to do. If he does not have the right tool, he will direct you to a shop that does. He survives very well in the face of strong competition from big chain stores with substantially lower prices.

In our model he steps up to find out the criteria and outcome of his customers, and then steps down to exactly the specific tool they need. This may involve a step sideways from what the customer actually asked for in the first place. (It always does when I go there.)

Stepping sideways is very useful to find out what a person likes about a product. What are the good points? Where are the points of difference that means a person chooses one product rather than another? Exploring what a person wants in these three directions is a consistent pattern of top salespeople. Congruence is essential. Would a salesperson use the product he is selling? Does he really believe in the advantages he recites? Incongruence can leak out in tonality and posture, and make the buyer uneasy.

FRAMES

Framing in NLP refers to the way we put things into different contexts to give them different meanings; what we make important at that moment. Here are five useful ways of framing events. Some have been implicit in other aspects of NLP, and it is worth making them explicit here.

Outcome Frame

This is evaluating in terms of outcomes. Firstly know your own outcome, and make sure it is well-formed. Is it positive? Is it under your control? Is it specific enough and the right size? What is the evidence? Do you have the resources to carry it out? How does it fit with your other outcomes?

Secondly, you may need to elicit outcomes from any other people involved, to help them get clear what they want, so you can all move forward. Thirdly, there is dovetailing outcomes. Once you have your outcome and the other person's outcome, you can see how they fit together. You may need to negotiate over any differences between them.

Lastly, by keeping outcomes in mind you can notice if you are moving towards them. If you are not, you need to do something different.

The outcome frame is an extremely useful pair of spectacles with which to view your actions. In business, if executives do not have a clear view of their outcome, they have no firm basis for decisions and no way of judging if an action is useful or not.

Ecology Frame

Again this has been dealt with explicitly with outcomes and implicitly throughout the book. How do my actions fit into the wider systems of family, friends, professional interests? Is it expressive of my overall integrity as a human being? And does it respect the integrity of the other people involved? Congruence is the way our unconscious mind lets us know about ecology, and is a prerequisite of acting with wisdom.

Evidence Frame

This concentrates on clear and specific details. In particular, how will you know when you have attained your outcome? What will you see, hear and feel? This forms part of the outcome frame, and is sometimes useful to apply on its own, especially to criteria.

As If Frame

This frame is a way of creative problem-solving by pretending that something has happened in order to explore possibilities. Start with the words, 'If this happened . . .' or, 'Let's suppose that . . .' There are many ways this can be useful. For example, if a key person is missing from a meeting, you can ask, 'If X *were* here, what would she do?' If someone knows X well the answers they come up with can be very helpful. (Always check back with X later if important decisions are to be made.)

Another way of using the idea is to project yourself six months or a year into a successful future, and looking back, ask, 'What were the steps that we took then, that led us to this state now?' From this perspective you can often discover important information that you cannot see easily in the present because you are too close to it.

Another way is to take the worst case that could happen. What would you do if the worst happened? What options and plans do you have? 'As if' can be used to explore the worst case as a specific example of a more general and very useful process known as downside planning. (A process insurance companies make a great deal of money from.)

Backtrack Frame

This frame is simple. You recapitulate the information you have up to that point using the other person's key words and tonalities in the backtrack. This is what makes it different to a summary, which often systematically distorts the other person's words. Backtrack is useful to open a discussion, to update new people in a group, and to check agreement and understanding of the participants in a meeting. It helps build rapport and is invaluable any time you get lost; it clarifies the way forward.

Many messages seem to come to agreement, but the participants go away with totally different ideas about what was agreed. Backtrack can keep you on course towards the desired outcome.

MEETINGS

Although we will describe meetings in a business context, the patterns apply equally to any context where two or more people meet for a common purpose. As you read through the rest of this chapter, think of each pattern in whatever context is appropriate to you.

NLP has a lot to offer in a business context. The greatest resource of any business is the people in it. The more effective the people become, the more effective the business will be. A business is a team of people working towards a common goal. Their success will depend mainly on how well they deal with these key points:

a) Goal Setting.
b) Communicating effectively within the group and to the outside world.
c) Reading their environment accurately. Keeping customer needs and responses in mind.
d) Commitment to success: congruence.

The resourcefulness, flexibility, perceptual filters, presentation and communication skills of the individuals in the business determine how successful it is. NLP addresses the precise skills that create success in the business world.

NLP goes to the heart of a business organization by refining and developing the effectiveness of each individual member carrying out these tasks. Business meetings are one place many of these skills will come together. We will start by dealing with co-operative meetings where most people will broadly agree about the outcome. Meetings where there are apparently conflicting outcomes will be dealt with under negotiation.

Meetings are purposeful and the purpose of co-operative meetings is likely to be explicit, for example to meet with colleagues once a week to exchange information, make decisions and allocate responsibility. Other examples would be planning next year's budget, a performance appraisal, or a project review.

As a participant in an important meeting you need to be in a strong, resourceful state, and congruent about the part you have to play. Anchors can help, both before a meeting to get you in a good state, and during a meeting if things start to go awry. Remember other people will be anchors for you, and you are an anchor to others. The room itself may be an anchor. An office is often a place full of the trappings of personal power and success of the person behind the desk. You may need all the resources you can get.

The membership and agenda of the meeting need to be settled in advance. You must be clear about your outcome. You also need an evidence procedure: how you will know if you achieve it. You need to be very clear about what you would want to see, hear and feel. If you have no outcome for the meeting, you are probably wasting your time.

The basic format for successful meetings resembles the three minute NLP seminar in Chapter 1:

1. Know what you want.
2. Know what others want.
3. Find ways in which you can all get it.

This seems simple and obvious, but it is often lost in the rough and tumble, and step 3 may be difficult if there are widely conflicting interests.

When the meeting starts, get consensus on a shared outcome. It is important that all agree on an outcome for the meeting, some common issue to be dealt with. When you have the outcome, anchor it. The easiest way to do this is to use a key phrase, and write it up on a board or flip chart. You will also need to agree on the evidence that will show that the outcome has been achieved. How will everyone know when they have it? Use the evidence frame.

Once again, rapport is an essential step. You will need to establish rapport with the other participants, if you do not have it already, by using non-verbal skills and matching language. Be sensitive to any incongruence in any of the participants about the shared outcome. There may be hidden agendas, and it is better to know about these at the outset, rather than later.

During the discussion, the evidence, ecology, backtrack, and As If frames may be useful. One problem that besets meetings is that they go off track. Before you know it, the time is up and the decision or outcome has not been achieved. Many a meeting has gone off at a tempting tangent and ended up in a cul-de-sac.

The outcome frame can be used to challenge the relevance of any contribution and so keep the meeting on track. Suppose a colleague makes a contribution to the discussion that does not seem to relate to the mutually-agreed outcome. It may be interesting, informative and true, but not relevant. You could say something like, 'I have trouble seeing how that could bring us nearer to our outcome; can you tell us how it fits into this meeting?' You can anchor this relevancy challenge visually with a hand or head movement. The speaker must show how his contribution is relevant. If it is not, then valuable time is saved. The contribution may be important in another context, in which case recognize it as such, and agree that it be dealt with at another time. Close and summarize each issue as it arises, fitting it into the agreed outcome, or agree to defer it to another meeting.

If someone is disrupting a meeting or leading it seriously off track, you might say something like, 'I appreciate that you feel strongly about this issue and it is clearly important to you. However, we agreed that this is not the place to discuss it. Can we meet later to settle this?' Calibrate for congruence when you make these sorts of proposals. Calibration may tell you that X lights a cigarette when she is happy with the outcome. Y always looks down when he objects (so you ask what he would need to feel OK about the issue). Z bites his nails when unhappy. There are so many ways that you can be aware on a deeper level how the meeting is progressing and sidestep trouble before it arises.

At the close of the meeting, use the backtrack frame and get agreement on progress and the outcome. Clearly define and get agreement on what actions are to be taken and by whom. Sometimes there is not a full agreement, so the close is dependent on certain actions. So you say something like, 'If this happened and if X did this and if we persuade Y that this is alright, then we proceed?' This is known as a conditional close.

Anchor the agreement with key words and future pace. What will remind the participants to do what they have agreed? Project the agreement out of the room and make sure it is connected to other independent events that can act as signals to remind the people to take the agreed action.

Research has shown that we remember things best when they occur in the first or last few minutes of a meeting. Take advantage of this and place the important points at the beginning and the end of the meeting.

Meeting Format Summary

A) Before the meeting:
1. Set your outcome(s) and the evidence that will let you know that you have reached it (them).
2. Determine the membership and agenda for the meeting.

B) During the meeting:
1. Be in a resourceful state. Use resource anchors if necessary.
2. Establish rapport.
3. Get consensus on a shared outcome and the evidence for it.
4. Use the relevancy challenge to keep the meeting on track.
5. If information is not available, use the As If frame.
6. Use the backtrack frame to summarize key agreements.

7. Keep moving towards your outcome, by using the Meta Model or any other tools needed.

C) Closing the meeting:
1. Check for congruence and agreement of the other participants.
2. Summarize the actions to be taken. Use the backtrack frame to take advantage of the fact that we remember endings more easily.
3. Test agreement if necessary.
4. Use a conditional close if necessary.
5. Future pace the decisions.

NEGOTIATION

Negotiation is communicating for the purpose of getting a joint decision, one that can be congruently agreed on both sides. It is the process of getting what you want from others by giving others what they want, and takes place in any meeting where interests conflict.

Would that it were as easy to do as it is to describe. There is a balance and a dance between your integrity, values and outcomes, and those of the other participants. The dance of communication goes back and forth, some interests and values will be shared, some opposed. In this sense, negotiation permeates everything we do. We are dealing here with the process of negotiation, rather than what you are actually negotiating over.

Negotiation often takes place about scarce resources. The key skill in negotiation is to dovetail outcomes: to fit them together so that everyone involved gets what they want (although that may not be the same as their demand at the beginning of the negotiation). The presupposition is that the best way to achieve your outcome is to make sure that everyone involved achieves theirs too.

The opposite of dovetailing outcomes is manipulation, where other people's wants are disregarded. There are four dragons that lie in wait for those that practise manipulation: remorse, resentment, recrimination and revenge. When you negotiate by seeking to dovetail outcomes the other people involved become your allies, not your opponents. If a negotiation can be framed as allies solving a common problem, the problem is already partially solved. Dovetailing is finding that area of overlap.

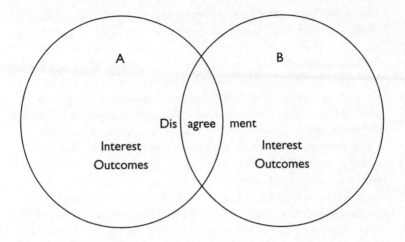

Separate the people from the problem. It is worth remembering that most negotiations involve people with whom you have, or want, an ongoing relationship. Whether you are negotiating over a sale, a salary or a holiday, if you get what you want at the other person's expense, or they think you have pulled a fast one, you will lose goodwill that may be worth much more in the long run than success in that one meeting.

You will be negotiating because you have different outcomes. You need to explore these differences, because they will point to areas where you can make trade-offs to mutual advantage. Interests that conflict at one level may be resolved if you can find ways of each party getting their outcome on a higher level. This is where stepping up enables you to find and make use of alternative higher level outcomes. The initial outcome is only one way of achieving a higher level outcome.

For example, in a negotiation over salary (initial outcome), more money is only one way of obtaining a better quality of life (higher level outcome). There may be other ways of achieving a better quality of life if money is not available – longer holidays, or more flexible working hours, for example. Stepping up finds bridges across points of difference.

People may want the same thing for different reasons. For example, imagine two people quarrelling over a pumpkin. They both want it. However, when they explain exactly why they want it, you find that one wants the fruit to make a pie, and the other wants the rind to make a Halloween mask. Really they are not fighting over the same thing at all. Many conflicts disappear when analysed this way. This is a small example, but imagine all the different possibilities there are in any apparent disagreement.

If there is a stalemate, and a person refuses to consider a particular step, you can ask the question, 'What would have to happen for this not to be a problem?' or, 'Under what circumstances would you be prepared to give way on this?' This is a creative application of the As If frame and the answer can often break through the impasse. You are asking the person who made the block to think of a way round it.

Set your limits before you start. It is confusing and self-defeating to negotiate with yourself when you need to be negotiating with someone else. You need what Roger Fisher and William Ury in their marvellous book on negotiation, *Getting to Yes,* call a BATNA, or Best Alternative To Negotiated Agreement. What will you do if despite all the efforts of both parties you cannot agree? Having a reasonable BATNA gives you more leverage in the negotiation, and a greater sense of security.

Focus on interests and intentions rather than behaviour. It is easy to get drawn into winning points and condemning behaviour, but really nobody wins in these sorts of situations.

A wise and durable agreement will take in community and ecological interests. A mutually satisfying solution will be based on a dovetailing of interests, a win/win, not a win/lose model. So what is important is the problem and not the people, the intentions not the behaviour, the interests of the parties not their positions.

It is also essential to have an evidence procedure that is independent of the parties involved. If the negotiation is framed as a joint search for a solution, it will be governed by principles and not pressure. Yield only to principle, not pressure.

There are some specific ideas to keep in mind while negotiating. Do not make an immediate counter-proposal immediately after the other side has made a proposal. This is precisely the time when they are least interested in your offering. Discuss their proposal first. If you disagree, give the reasons first. Saying you disagree immediately is a good way to make the other person deaf to your next few sentences.

All good negotiators use a lot of questions. In fact two good negotiators will often start negotiating over the number of questions. 'I've answered three of your questions, now you answer some of mine . . .' Questions give you time to think, and they are an alternative to disagreement. It is far better to get the other person to see the weakness in his position by asking him questions about it, rather than by telling him the weaknesses you perceive.

Good negotiators also explicitly signal their questions. They will say something like, 'May I ask you a question about that?' By doing so they focus the attention of the meeting on the answer and make it difficult for the person questioned to evade the point if he has agreed to answer the question.

It would seem that the more reasons you give for your point of view the better. Phrases like 'the weight of the argument' seem to suggest it is good to pile arguments on the scales until it comes down on your side. In fact the opposite is true. The fewer reasons you give, the better, because a chain is only as strong as its weakest link. A weak argument dilutes a strong one, and if you are drawn into defending it, you are on poor ground. Beware of a person who says, 'Is that your *only* argument?' If you have a good one, say, 'Yes'. Do not get drawn into giving another, necessarily weaker one. The follow-up may be, 'Is that *all?*' If you take this bait you will just give him ammunition. Hopefully, if the negotiation is framed as a joint search for a solution, this sort of trick will not occur.

Finally, you could use the as if frame and play the devil's advocate to test the agreement ('No, I don't really think this is going to work, it all seems too flimsy to me . . .'). If other people agree with you, you know that there is still work to be done. If they argue, all is well.

Negotiation Checklist

A) *Before the negotiation:*
Establish your BATNA and your limits in the negotiation.

B) *During the negotiation:*
1. Establish rapport.
2. Be clear about your own outcome and the evidence for it. Elicit outcomes of the other participants together with their evidence.
3. Frame the negotiation as a joint search for a solution.
4. Clarify major issues and obtain agreement on a large frame. Dovetail outcomes, step up if necessary to find a common outcome. Check that you have the congruent agreement of all parties to this common outcome.
5. Break the outcome down to identify areas of most and least agreement.
6. Starting with the easiest areas, move to agreement using these trouble-shooting techniques:

Negotiation going off course ...	Relevancy challenge.
Conflicting outcomes ...	Stepping up and down to common outcome.
Uncertainty ...	Backtrack.
Lack of information ...	As If and the Meta Model.
Stalemate ...	What would have to happen?

Backtrack as agreement is reached in each area, and finish with the most difficult area.

C) *Closing the negotiation:*
1. Backtrack frame.
2. Test agreement and test congruence.
3. Future pace.
4. Write agreement down. All participants have a signed copy.

Answers: 1. Tea and coffee – Beverages. 2. Yams and coffee – Cash crops. 3. Clinic and coffee – Six-letter words beginning with 'c'. 4. Amphetamines and coffee – Stimulants. 5. Ignatia and coffee – Diuretics.

8

PSYCHOTHERAPY

The first NLP models came from psychotherapy. However NLP is not restricted to psychotherapy, it was simply by historical accident that John and Richard had access to exceptional performers in the domain of psychotherapy when they began modelling. *Structure of Magic 1* explored how we can limit our world by the way we use language, and how to use the Meta Model to break free of these limitations. *The Structure of Magic 2* developed the theme of representational systems and family therapy. From this basis, NLP has created many powerful psychotherapy techniques, and this chapter will deal with three of the main ones: the phobia cure, the swish pattern and internal negotiation. It will also give some guide as to where they are best used.

The overall frame around all such techniques is to use them with wisdom, appreciating the person's external relationships and internal balance. The intention of NLP is always to give more choices, never to take them away.

There are two essential aspects for any therapist, or anyone who is helping another person make changes in their life. The first is relationship. Build and maintain rapport to establish an atmosphere of trust. The second is congruence. You need to be completely congruent about what you do to help the other person; incongruence on your part will give mixed messages, and reduce the effectiveness of the change process. This means that you need to act congruently as if you believe the techniques will work. Relationship and congruence are at a higher logical level than any technique that you can apply within them. Use the outcome frame to gather information about the present state, the desired state, and the resources needed to move from one to the other. Within this outcome frame, be sensitive to what you are seeing, hearing and feeling, and willing to respond to the person's changing concerns. Only inside all these frames do you apply a technique. The techniques are fixed means. Be prepared to vary them or abandon them and use others to achieve the outcome.

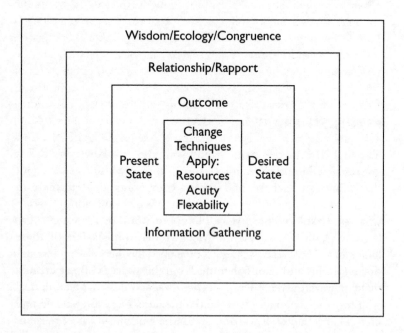

FIRST ORDER CHANGE

Here is one way to think about where to apply these techniques. The simplest case would be where you want a single outcome: a different state or response in a given situation. This is called a *first order change*. For example, you may find yourself always getting angry with a particular person, or always feeling uncomfortable dealing with someone at work. Stage fright would be another example where public speaking or performing 'makes' you feel nervous and inadequate.

Simple reframes are a good way to start to change this sort of situation, discovering when this response would be useful, and what else it could mean. Anchoring techniques are also suitable here. Collapsing, stacking or chaining anchors will bring over resources from other contexts. The original behaviour or state was anchored, so you are using the same process to change the stuck state as was used to create it. The New Behaviour Generator and mental rehearsal also work well if you need a new skill or behaviour.

Sometimes these anchoring techniques will not work because a person has an overwhelming response to an object or situation. Past events can make it difficult to change direction in the present. Change Personal History may not work because there are traumatic past experiences that are difficult even to think about without feeling bad. These may have created a phobia, where an object or situation generates instant panic because they are associated with the past trauma. Phobias can vary enormously: fear of spiders, fear of flying, fear of open spaces. Whatever the cause, the response is overwhelming anxiety. Phobias can take years to cure by conventional methods; NLP has a technique that can cure phobias in one session. It is sometimes known as Visual/Kinesthetic (or V/K) dissociation. Remember to reread the cautionary note on page 55 before practising these techniques.

THE PHOBIA CURE

You can only feel in the present moment. Any bad feeling from an unpleasant memory must come from the *way* you are remembering it. You felt bad back then. Once is enough.

The easiest way to re-experience the bad feelings of a past event is to remember it as an associated picture. You must be there, seeing what there was to see through your own eyes and feeling it again. Thinking back on a memory in a dissociated way by looking at yourself in the situation reduces the feeling in the present.

This is the crucial fact that allows you to erase the bad feelings associated with past events (what an apt phrase that is), so you can simply look back at them in perspective. If you want to work with a phobia or a very unpleasant memory of your own, it is best to have a friend or colleague guide you through these steps. Another person will give you invaluable support when you are dealing with difficult personal issues. The technique is described from the point of view of the guide or therapist.

1. The client is going on a difficult journey into the past, so set up a powerful safety anchor. You can either establish a here-and-now anchor, or you can ask the client to think, associated, to a past experience where they felt very safe. Have them see the scene, hear the sounds, feel the secure feelings. Anchor this security kinesthetically, by touch. Make sure your touch brings a feeling of

security. Holding hands works well; you will literally be in touch with what the person is feeling. You can hold the anchor throughout, or use it when required.

2. Ask the client to imagine himself in a cinema or watching television, with a still, frozen image on the screen. When that is established, ask the client to imagine floating out to watch himself or herself watching the screen.

3. Have the client float back along their timeline to the unpleasant event, or to the very first incident that set up the phobia. It may not always be possible to get the first, but get the earliest possible. Have the client run a film of this incident from just before the start, when he was safe, through to a point when the immediate danger was past, and he was safe again. That has taken one sentence to describe, but will take some time in reality. The client will be seeing this in a double dissociated state, watching himself watching a younger self go through the experience on screen. This maintains the necessary emotional distance. From this position A in the diagram, the client watches his own physiology in position B as he watches the screen. If his physiology starts to collapse into the phobic state, have him blank the screen immediately. Ask him to start the movie again, and ask him to change the submodalities of the picture on the screen, for example making it darker, smaller, or further away, in order to reduce the intensity of the negative feelings. This is all part of coming to terms with the experience.

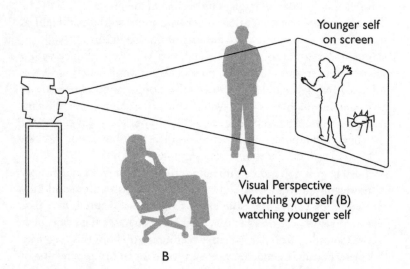

Younger self on screen

A
Visual Perspective
Watching yourself (B)
watching younger self

B

This takes time and your exquisite attention. Be creative and flexible to help the client within the basic process. You need to be precise with your language as you guide the client through the experience, speaking to him, here, now, watching himself, there, watching his younger self in the picture, back then. If at any time the client falls back into the feeling, come back to the here and now, reestablish the comfort anchor and start again. (Only if the client wishes, of course.) Yo may need to reassure the client by saying something like, 'You are safe, here, pretending to watch a movie.' This stage is complete when the client has watched it all the way through in comfort.

4. When the film is over, congratulate the client for having re-experienced this for the first time without collapsing into those old negative feelings and have the client float back into his body. In the diagram, A joins back to B. This will integrate the visual perspective with the actual body position.

5. Now the client imagines stepping into the screen to give his younger self much needed support and encouragement. He can reassure his younger self, 'I am from the future, you survived, it's OK. You never have to go through it again.' The present-day person with strength and resources, knowing what he knows, can cope with the incident. If the original incident involved genuine danger, it is still alright to have some anxiety about it. For example, if the phobia was of snakes, it is still useful to have a healthy respect for snakes and the danger they may pose, but the disabling fear is useless, and will have vanished.

6. When the younger person understands, ask the client to bring the younger self back from the screen into his own body, and allow some quiet time to recover and integrate the profound changes that will have taken place.

7. Future pace. Ask the client to imagine (associated) the next time that he would have expected to feel the fear. This may bring a slight anxiety, but not the previous full-blown fear. We all carry some burden on our shoulders of past fear and limitation. Easing this load is a fine gift to give yourself and others.

In a way phobias are quite an achievement; a strong, dependable response based on just one experience. People never forget to have the phobic response. The closest to having a 'good phobia' seems to be 'love at first sight'. It would be nice to give ourselves and others good phobias. How is it that someone can learn to be consistently and dependably frightened of spiders and yet not learn in the same dependable consistent way to feel good at the sight of a loved person's face?

Marriages can and do break up because one or both of the partners does an unconscious 'phobia cure' on their good feelings, dissociating from the good times, and associating with the bad.

The *swish pattern* is a powerful technique that uses critical submodality changes. It works on a specific behaviour you would rather be without, or responses you would rather not make. It is a good technique to use on unwanted habits. The swish pattern changes a problem state or behaviour by going in a new direction. It does not simply replace the behaviour, but produces a generative change.

THE SWISH PATTERN

1. First identify a specific behaviour that you wish to change. Nail biting, overeating, or smoking would be examples. You could also take a situation where you would like to respond more resourcefully, perhaps in dealing with a particular person.
2. Treat this limitation as an achievement. How do you know when to have the problem or behaviour? What are the specific cues that generate it? Imagine you have to teach someone this limitation, what would they have to do?

    There must always be a definite and specific cue that triggers the response. If the cue is internal, generated from your thoughts, make it an image exactly as you experience it. If it is an external cue, picture it exactly as it happens: as an associated picture. For example, the cue for nail biting might be a picture of your hand approaching your mouth. (The swish is easiest with visual images, although it is possible to do it with auditory or kinesthetic cues by working with auditory or kinesthetic submodalities.)
3. Identify at least two visual submodalities of the cue picture that change your reaction to it. Size and brightness usually work well. For a majority of people increasing the size and the brightness of an image will give it greater impact. However, there may be others that are equally effective. Test these two submodalities on another image to check they have the desired effect. They must be submodalities that you can vary continuously over a range.

    Break state by thinking of something different for a moment before continuing.

4. Next, think how you would really like to be, the sort of person who would respond differently, who would not have this limitation. How would you see yourself if you had made the desired change? You would have more choices, be more capable, you could come closer to the person you really want to be. The image should be of yourself with desired qualities, not behaving in a specific way. The picture must be dissociated to be motivating and attractive. An associated picture will give you the feeling that you have the change already, and therefore it will not motivate you.

Check that the new self-image is ecological, and fits into your personality, environment and relationships. You may need to make some adjustments as you try it on.

Think about the resources this self-image would have. It will need resources to deal with the intention of the old behaviour. Make sure the image is balanced, believable and not closely tied to any particular situation. Also be sure that the image is compelling enough that it produces a marked shift to a more positive state.

Now break state and think of something different.

5. Take the cue picture and make it bright and large if those are the identified critical submodalities. In the corner of this picture put a small, dark picture of the new self-image. Now, take the large bright image of the limitation and very quickly make it small and dark, while at the same time making the new self-image picture large and bright. Speed is of the essence. Make sure the old image fades as the new one grows simultaneously. It can help if you imagine, or actually say a sound that represents this, 'Whoosh!' or 'Swish!' Let the sound represent the excitement you feel about becoming the new self-image. Clear the screen. Repeat this five times fast.

Brains work fast. Have you ever had the experience of describing a process to someone, and feeling that she was doing it as you described it? You are right. She was. (Think of your front door . . . but not just yet!)

Clear the screen briefly after each swish by seeing something different. A 'reverse swish' will just cancel the positive swish. Make sure it is a one-way ticket. If it does not work after five repeats, do not keep doing something that does not work. Be creative. The critical submodalities may need to be adjusted, or perhaps the desired self-image is not compelling enough. The process works. Who in their right mind would keep a problem behaviour in the face of a set of such alluring, new capabilities?

6. When you are satisfied, test the result by future pacing. Think of the cue. Does it produce the same response? Next time you are in the situation look for the new response. NLP techniques, like brains, work fast and efficiently. We effectively swish ourselves into all kinds of trouble without ever realizing it. Now we can consciously use the same process to go somewhere more appealing. These techniques show you can quickly change your direction without strain or pain.

SECOND ORDER CHANGE

Second order change is when there are multiple outcomes and secondary considerations involved. All therapy probably involves second order change, as the new resource or response will need to be supported by some growth and rebalancing in the rest of the personality. First order change is where this takes care of itself, or is slight enough to be ignored.

Second order change is best used to describe what is needed where the secondary outcomes are strong enough to block the main desired outcome. Six step reframing is a good technique for dealing with secondary outcomes.

INTERNAL CONFLICT

If there are different ideas in conflict, negotiation skills can be used between the different parts of our personality. Resolving a problem involves achieving a balance in the present that is at least as powerful as the old one.

Because balance is dynamic and not static, conflicts are bound to develop between different parts of our personality that embody different values, beliefs and capabilities. You may want incompatible experiences. There may be familiar situations when you are interrupted by another part with conflicting demands. Yet if you yield to that, the first part makes you feel bad. The upshot is often that you enjoy neither activity. When you are relaxing, another part will conjure up vivid visions of all the work you should be doing. If you work, all you want to do is relax. If this sort of conflict is familiar and spoiling both activities, it is time for a truce.

Internal Conflict Resolution

1. Clearly identify and separate the parts. They will seem to be making conflicting demands. For example, one part may want freedom and leisure, another the security of a steady income. Or one may be very careful with money, the other very extravagant. One part may be overly concerned with pleasing people, while the other resents the demands they make. Each part will make negative value judgements about the other. Some parts are built on parental values, and these may coexist uneasily with parts you have built from your own life experience. All parts have something valuable to offer.

2. Get a clear representation of each part. If there are two parts, one could go on each hand, or you could seat them beside you on chairs. Get a full visual, kinesthetic and auditory representation of each part. What do they look like? How do they feel? What do they sound like? Are there any words or phrases that could characterize them? Have both parts survey your timeline, present and future, to define themselves, their personal history and direction.

3. Find out the intention of each part. Appreciate they each have a positive intention. Step up to as high a level as you need to for the parts to agree on a shared outcome. Both will probably agree on your continued well-being, and both must agree to reach an agreement. Start to negotiate, just as if you were dealing with real people. If the parts are seriously at odds, the only shared agreement might be the continued survival of the person.

4. Negotiate. What resources does each part have that would help the other part to realize its concerns? What trade-offs can be made? How might they co-operate? What does each part want from the other for each to be satisfied? It will become clear that their conflict is actually preventing them from realizing their intentions. Get each part to agree to give a signal when something is needed, like more time, permission, attention or appreciation.

5. Ask each part if it is willing to integrate with the other to solve their shared problems. It is not crucial that they do come together. It may be better for the parts to stay apart (in a manner of speaking). But if they are willing to integrate, bring them both into your body physically in a way that feels right for you. If the parts have been in your hands, visually squash them, by clasping your hands together. Then create a picture, sound and feeling of the new, integrated part and take it into yourself only as fast

as feels right. Allow some quiet time to appreciate the change. This new part may like to review your timeline, reframing past events and experiences in the light of your new knowledge and understanding.

During this negotiation other parts may surface. The deeper the conflict, the more likely that this will happen. All may need to join the negotiation. Virginia Satir used to arrange 'Parts Parties' where different people would enact the different parts of the client, who would direct the unfolding drama.

Parts negotiation is a powerful means of resolving conflicts on a deep level. You can never banish conflict. Within limits, it is a healthy and necessary preliminary to rebalancing. The richness and wonder of being human comes from diversity, and maturity and happiness from balance and co-operation between the different aspects of yourself.

9

LEARNING AS MODELLING

As human beings, we are all naturally gifted learners. For many of us, this process slows down as we grow older. For some, learning continues unabated for a lifetime. When we are growing up, we teach ourselves to walk and talk by being with people who do these things. On a daily basis, we take actions (our first tentative steps), notice our results (falling over repeatedly), and change our actions accordingly (leaning on chairs and people). In essence, this is learning by modelling. As we grow older, we tend to reinterpret this natural learning process as a series of tiny 'successes' and 'failures'. With reinforcement from parents and peers, we begin to long for the 'successes' and fear the 'failures'. It seems that this fear of 'doing it wrong', more than anything else, is how we learn to inhibit our natural learning processes. Mark Twain once said that if people learned to walk and talk the way they were taught to read and write, everyone would limp and stutter.

So what are some of the differences between the way we learn naturally and the ways that do not work so well? It may be useful at this point to compare this natural learning process with John and Richard's first exploration of modelling.

HOW NLP MODELLING BEGAN

When John and Richard met and became friends at the University of California, Santa Cruz, in 1972, John was an Assistant Professor of Linguistics and Richard was in his final year at the college. Richard had a strong interest in Gestalt therapy. He had done a study and made some video tapes of Fritz Perls at work for his friend Bob Spitzer, who owned the publishers Science and Behaviour

Books. These tapes later went to make up a book called *Eyewitness To Therapy.*

Bob Spitzer owned property near Santa Cruz, and used to let it out to his friends. Gregory Bateson was living there at the time, and Richard moved into a house on the same property, a stone's throw from Bateson. Richard started leading weekly Gestalt encounter groups, charging participants $5.00 a night. He re-established contact with John Grinder and got him interested enough in Gestalt to come to these groups.

When John came, he was intrigued. Richard knew he could successfully run Gestalt groups, but he wanted to know exactly how he did it, and which patterns were effective. There is a big difference between having a skill and knowing explicitly how you succeed with it. John and Richard made a deal. Richard would show John how he did Gestalt therapy, and John would teach Richard what it was that he was doing. So John would go to the Monday night group and model Richard, Richard would indicate what he believed were the important patterns by pointing with his eyes and using different voice intonations.

John learnt very quickly. It took him two months to unpack the patterns and be able to perform like Richard. He used to do what they called a 'repeat miracle' group on Thursday night. People got the same miracles in their lives on Thursday night from John that others had already had on Monday night from Richard.

Richard then got a job observing and videotaping a month-long training programme that Virginia Satir was holding in Canada for family therapists. Richard had met Virginia before and they were already on friendly terms. Throughout the programme, he was isolated in his own little recording room except for the microphones to the seminar room. He had a split earphone and would monitor recording levels through one ear and play tapes of Pink Floyd through the other. In the last week Virginia had set up a counselling situation and asked how the participants would deal with it, using the material that she had been teaching them. The participants seemed stuck. Richard came storming down from his room and successfully dealt with the problem. And Virginia said, 'That's exactly right.' Richard found himself in the strange situation of knowing more about Virginia's therapeutic patterns than anyone else, without consciously trying to learn them at all. John modelled some of Virginia Satir's patterns from Richard and made them explicit. Their efficiency was improving. This time they did it in three weeks, instead of two months.

Now they had a double description of effective therapy, two complementary and contrasting models: Virginia Satir and Fritz Perls. The fact that they were totally different characters and would not have been able to coexist amicably in the same room made them especially valuable examples. The therapeutic patterns they had in common were much clearer because their personal styles were so different.

They continued and modelled Milton Erickson next, adding a rich collection of hypnotic patterns. The process of modelling out the skills of outstanding performers in business, education, health care, etc., is unusually productive and has grown rapidly in range and sophistication since the early days.

MODELLING

So modelling is at the heart of NLP. NLP is the study of excellence, and modelling is the process that makes explicit the behavioural patterns of excellence. What are the behavioural patterns of successful people? How do they achieve their results? What do they do that is different from people who are not successful? What is the difference that makes the difference? The answers to these questions have generated all the skills, techniques and presuppositions associated with NLP.

Modelling can be simply defined as the process of replicating human excellence. Explanations of *why* some people excel more than others usually cite inborn talent. NLP by-passes this explanation by exploring *how* we can excel as quickly as possible. By using our mind and body in the same way as a peak performer, we can immediately increase the quality of our actions and our results. NLP models what is possible, because real human beings have actually done it.

There are three phases in the full modelling process. The first phase involves being with your model while he is doing the behaviour that you are interested in. During this first phase, you imagine yourself in his reality, using second position skills, and do what he does until you can create roughly the same results. You focus on *what* he does (behaviour and physiology), *how* he does it (internal thinking strategies) and *why* he does it (the supporting beliefs and assumptions). The *what* you can get from direct observation. The *how* and *why* you explore by asking questions.

In the second phase you systematically *take out* elements of the model's behaviour to see what makes a difference. If you leave something out, and it makes little difference, then it is not necessary.

If you leave something out and it does make a difference to the results you get, then it is an essential part of the model. You refine the model and begin to understand it consciously during this phase. This is the exact opposite of traditional learning patterns. Traditional learning says add pieces a bit at a time, until you have them all. However, this way you cannot easily know what is essential. Modelling, which is the basis of accelerated learning, gets all the elements, and then subtracts to find what is needed.

The third and final phase is designing a way to teach the skill to others. A good teacher will be able to create an environment, so her students learn for themselves how to get the results.

Models are designed to be simple and testable. You do not need to know why they work, just as you do not need to understand why or how cars work to drive one. If you are lost in the maze of human behaviour, you need a map to find your way around, not a psychological analysis of why you want to find your way out of the labyrinth in the first place.

Modelling in any field gives results and techniques, and also further tools for modelling. NLP is generative because its results can be applied to make it even more effective. NLP is a 'bootstrap programme' for personal development. You can model your own creative and resourceful states and so be able to enter them at will. And with more resources and creativity at your disposal you can become yet more resourceful and creative . . .

If you model successfully, you will get the same results as your model, and you do not *have* to model excellence. To find out how a person is creative, or how he manages to become depressed, you ask the same key questions. 'If I had to stand in for you for a day, what would I have to do to think and behave like you?'

Each person brings his own unique resources and personality to what he does. You cannot become another Einstein, Beethoven, or Edison. To achieve and think exactly like them you would need their unique physiology and personal history. NLP does not claim anyone can be an Einstein, however it does say that anyone can think like an Einstein, and apply those ways of thinking, should he choose, in his life; in doing this, he will come closer to the full flower of his own personal genius, and his own unique expression of excellence.

In summary, you can model any human behaviour if you can master the beliefs, the physiology and the specific thought processes, that is, the strategies, that lie behind it. Before going on to explore these in more detail, it is worth remembering that we are only touching the surface of a domain as vast as our own future potential.

BELIEFS

The beliefs that we each have about ourselves, others and the way the world is have a major impact on the quality of our experience. Because of the 'self-fulfilling prophecy effect', beliefs influence behaviour. They can support particular behaviour or inhibit it. This is why modelling beliefs is so important.

One of the simplest ways to model the beliefs of people with outstanding abilities is to ask them questions about *why* they do what they do. The answers they give you will be rich with insights into their beliefs and values. There is a story of a child in Rome who spent hours watching a strange young man working intently. Finally, the boy spoke. 'Signore, why are you hitting that rock?' Michelangelo looked up from his work and answered, 'Because there's an angel inside and it wants to come out.'

Beliefs will generally take one of three main forms. They can be beliefs about what things mean. For example, if you believe that life is basically a competitive struggle and then you die, you are likely to have a very different experience of life than if you believe that it is a kind of spiritual school with many rich and fulfilling lessons on offer.

Beliefs can also be about what causes what (cause and effect) and so give rise to the rules we choose to live by. Or again they can be beliefs about what is important and what matters most, so giving rise to our values and criteria.

In modelling out beliefs, you want to focus on those that are most relevant to and supportive of the particular skills and competencies that you are interested in. Some good questions to elicit beliefs and metaphors are:

1. Why do you do what you do?
2. What does that mean to you?
3. What would happen if you didn't do that?
4. What is that like? What do you compare it to?
5. What is empowering to you about this?

Once you have elicited the beliefs of your model, you can begin to experiment with them for yourself. When you go beyond simple understanding and actually 'try on a belief' to 'see how it fits', the difference can be profound. You do this by simply acting for a time as if the belief were true and noticing what changes when you do. One of Einstein's core beliefs was that the universe is a friendly place.

Imagine how different the world might seem if you were to act as if that were true.

What new actions would you take if you believed that?
What would you do differently?
What else would you be capable of?

If you realize that the only thing between you and what you want is a belief, you can begin to adopt a new one by simply acting as if it were true.

PHYSIOLOGY

Imagine for a moment that you are looking at a very small baby. As the baby looks up at you, eyes open wide, you flash it an enormous smile. The baby coos in delight and smiles right back at you. By matching your physiology, in this instance your smile, the baby experiences a bit of your delight in watching it. This is a phenomenon known as *entrainment* – where babies unconsciously begin to mimic exactly the expressions, patterns and movements of the people around them. As adults, taking on the expressions, tonalities and movements of the people around us can enable us to replicate their inner state, which will allow us access to previously untapped emotional resources. Take a moment now to think of someone you admire or respect. Imagine how he would be sitting if he were reading this book. How would he be breathing? What kind of expression would he have on his face? Now actually shift your body until you are sitting and breathing in the same way with the same expression. Notice the new thoughts and feelings that arise as you do this.

With some skills, replicating physiology may be the most important part. To model an excellent skier, for example, you would watch him ski until you begin to move your body in the same way. This will give you an experience of what it is like to do what he does, and you may even have some intuitions about what it is like to be that person, or at least to be inside that body. By precisely mirroring the patterns of movement, posture and even breathing, you will begin to feel the same way as him on the *inside*. You will have gained access to resources that may have taken him years to discover.

STRATEGIES

Thinking strategies are perhaps the least obvious component of modelling. For that we reason, we will look at strategies in depth before moving on to look at other aspects of modelling.

Strategies are how you organize your thoughts and behaviour to accomplish a task. Strategies always aim for a positive goal. They can be switched on or off by beliefs; to succeed in a task, you need to believe you can do it, otherwise you will not commit yourself fully.

You must also believe you deserve to do it, and be prepared to put in the necessary practice or preparation. Also, you must believe it is worth doing. The task must engage your interest or curiosity.

The strategies we use are part of our perceptual filters; they determine how we perceive the world. There is a little game that eloquently makes this point. Read the following sentence and count how many times you see the letter 'F'.

> FINISHED FILES ARE THE RE-
> SULT OF YEARS OF SCIENTIF-
> IC STUDY COMBINED WITH THE
> EXPERIENCE OF MANY YEARS.

Easy? The interesting thing is that different people see different numbers of 'F's and they are all sure they are right. And so they are, each in their own reality. Most people get three 'F's on their first pass, but a few see more. Remember, if what you are doing is not working, do something different. In fact do something very different. Go through the sentence backwards letter by letter. How many 'F's were you conscious of at first and how many were you unconscious of?

The reason you missed some of them was probably because you said the words to yourself and were relying on the sound of the 'F's to alert you to their presence. 'F' sounds like 'V' in the word 'of'. As soon as you *look* at every word *backwards* so that the letters do not link together to make a familiar word, the 'F's are easily seen. We asked how many times you see the letter 'F', not how many times you hear it. The world seems different when you change strategies.

A RECIPE FOR SUCCESS

To understand strategies think of a master chef. If you use his recipe, you will probably be able to cook as well as he does, or very close.

A strategy is a successful recipe. To make a wonderfully tasty dish, you need to know three basic things. You need to know what the ingredients are. You need to know how much of each ingredient to use, and the quality of each ingredient. And you need to know the correct order of steps. It makes a big difference to the cake whether you add the eggs before, during, or after you put it in the oven to bake. The order in which you do things in a strategy is just as crucial, even if it all happens in a couple of seconds. The ingredients of a strategy are the representational systems, and the amounts and quality are the submodalities.

To model a strategy you need:
1. The ingredients (representational systems).
2. The amounts and quality of each (submodalities).
3. The sequence of the steps.

Suppose you have a friend who is very skilled in some field. It could be interior design, buying clothes, teaching maths, getting up in the morning, or being the life and soul of the party. Have your friend either do that behaviour, or think back to a specific time when he was doing it. Make sure you have rapport and he is in an associated congruent state.

Ask, 'What was the very first thing you did, or thought, in this situation?' It will be something they saw (V), heard (A) or felt (K).

When you have this, ask, 'What was the very next thing that happened?' Continue until you have gone all the way through the experience.

Your questions and observations, perhaps using the Meta Model, will find out what representation systems the person is using and in what order. Then ask about the submodalities of all the VAK representations you discovered. You will find accessing cues and predicates very helpful in directing your questions. For example, if you ask, 'What comes next?' and the person says, 'I don't know,' and looks up, you might ask if they are seeing any mental picture as the next step for them could be visual internal. If you ask and the person replies, 'I don't know, it just *seems clear* to me,' you again would ask about internal pictures.

In the strategy the senses may be turned towards the outside world, or be used internally. If they are being used internally, you will be able to discover if they are being used to remember or construct by watching the eye accessing cues.

For example, someone may have a motivation strategy that starts by looking at the work he has to do (visual external) (V^e). He then constructs an internal picture of the work finished (visual internal constructed) (V^i_c), gets a good feeling (kinesthetic internal) (K^i) and tells himself he had better get started (auditory dialogue) (A^{id}). If you wanted to motivate this person you would say something like, 'Look at this work, think how good you'll feel when it's finished, here, (hear, phonological ambiguity), you'd better get started.'

Total strategy $V^e > V^i_c > K^i > A^{id}$

You would need a quite different approach for someone who looks at the work (V^e), and asks himself (A^{id}), 'What would happen if I did not complete this?' He constructs possible consequences (V^i_c), and feels bad (K^i). He does not want this feeling and those consequences, so he starts. The first person is going for the good feeling. The second person is avoiding the bad feeling. You could motivate the first person by giving him tempting futures and the second by threatening reprisals.

Teachers, managers, trainers all need to motivate people, so knowing these strategies is very useful. Everyone has a buying strategy, and good salespeople will not give everybody the same set talk. Some people need to see a product, talk it over with themselves until they get the feeling they want it. Others may need to hear about it, feel it is a good idea and see themselves using it before buying. Good salesmen change their approach accordingly if they really want to satisfy their customers.

It is essential for teachers to understand and respond to different children's learning strategies. Some children may need to listen to the teacher and then make internal pictures to understand a idea. Others may need some visual representation first. A picture may be worth a thousand words, but a lot depends on who is looking at it. Some students would rather have a thousand words any day. A teacher who insists that there is only one right way of learning is liable to be insisting that everyone ought to use his strategy. This makes it hard for many of his students who do not share it.

Insomniacs could learn a strategy for going to sleep. They could start by attending to the relaxed bodily sensations (K^l) while telling themselves in a slow, drowsy voice (A^{ld}) how comfortable they are. Their existing strategy may involve paying attention to all the uncomfortable sensations in their body, while listening to a loud, anxious internal voice telling them how difficult it is to go to sleep.

Add some fast moving, bright and colourful pictures and they have an excellent strategy for staying awake, quite the opposite of what they want.

Strategies create results. Are they the results you want? Do you arrive where you want to go? Any strategy, like a train, works perfectly well, but if you get on the wrong one . . . you will go somewhere you do not want to go. Don't blame the train.

MUSIC STRATEGY

A good example of some of these ideas comes from a study carried out by one of the authors on the way talented musicians memorize music; how they are able to retain sequences of music after only one or two hearings. The students were asked to clap or sing back short pieces of music, and their strategy was elicited by asking questions, watching accessing cues and noticing predicates.

The most successful students shared several patterns. They consistently adopted a particular posture, eye position and breathing pattern, usually with the head tilted to one side and the eyes looking downwards while listening. They tuned their bodies to the music.

As they listened, (A^e), they got an overall feeling for the music (K^i). This was often described as the 'mood' or 'imprint' of the piece. This feeling represented the piece as a whole, and their relationship to it.

The next step was to form some visual representation of the music. Most students visualized some sort of graph with the vertical axis representing the rise and fall of pitch, and the horizontal axis used to represent duration in time (V^i_c).

The longer or more difficult the piece, the more the students relied on this image to guide them through. The image was always bright, clear, focused, and at a comfortable distance to read. Some students visualized a stave with the exact note values just like a score, but this was not essential.

The feeling, sound and picture were built up together on the first listening. The feeling gave an overall context for the detailed image. Subsequent hearings were used to fix parts of the tune that were still uncertain. The harder the tune, the more important these feeling and visual memories were. The students reheard the tune mentally immediately after it had finished, in its original tonality, and usually at a much faster speed, rather like the fast forward mode on a video recorder (A^i_c).

All students reheard the tune, usually in its original tonality (A^i_r), while singing or clapping it back. They also reviewed the picture, and kept the overall feeling in mind. This gave them three ways of storing and retrieving the piece. They broke the music down into smaller sections, and noticed repetitive patterns in both pitch and rhythm. These were remembered visually, even after one hearing.

Remembering music seems to involve a strong auditory memory, but this study showed it is a synesthesia. It is hearing the picture of the feeling of the tune. They heard the tune, created a feeling to represent the piece as a whole, and used what they heard and felt to form a picture of the music.

The basic strategy is $A^e > K^i > V^i_c > A^i$. This strategy illustrates some general points about effective memorization and learning. The more representations you have of the material the more you are likely to remember it. The more of your neurology you commit, the stronger the memory. The best students also had the ability to move between representational systems, sometimes concentrating on the feeling, sometimes on the picture, depending on the sort of music they heard. All the students believed in their ability. Success could be summed up as commitment, belief and flexibility.

Before leaving music strategies, here is a fascinating extract from a letter by Wolfgang Amadeus Mozart about how he composed:

> All this fires my soul, and provided I am not disturbed, my subject enlarges itself, becomes methodised and defined, and the whole, though it be long, stands almost complete and finished in my mind, so that I can survey it like a fine picture or a beautiful statue at a glance. Nor do I hear in my imagination the parts successively, but I hear them as it were, all at once. What a delight this is I cannot tell!

> From a letter Mozart wrote in 1789, quoted in E. Holmes,
> *The Life of Mozart, Including his Correspondence*,
> Chapman and Hall, 1878

MEMORY STRATEGY

Do you have a good memory? This is a trick question because memory is a nominalization, you cannot see, hear or touch it. The process of remembering is the important thing. Nominalizations are actions that are frozen in time. Memory is static, you cannot influence it. Better to look at how you memorize, and how you can improve.

What is your memory strategy? How would you memorize the following sequence? (And pretend for a moment it is very important to retain it.)

DJWI8EDL42IS

You have THIRTY SECONDS STARTING NOW . . .

Time's up.

Cover the page, take a deep breath and write down the sequence.

How did you do? And more importantly, whatever your success, what did you do?

Twelve digits is beyond the capacity of the conscious mind to retain as separate units. You need a strategy to chunk them together in a smaller number of blocks to remember them all.

You may have repeated the sequence over and over again to form a tape loop (A^i). Tape loops last only a very short time. You may have recited it rhythmically. You may have written it out (K^e). You may have looked at it carefully and seen it again internally (V^i_c), as you looked up to your left. Perhaps you used colour or another submodality to help you remember your internal picture.

Pictures are retained in long-term memory, tape loops in short-term memory. If you use this little test on someone you know, you will probably be able to tell what strategy they are using without asking. You might see their lips move soundlessly, or see their eyes scanning it over and over. Perhaps they smile as they make some amusing connection.

One thing that is very helpful, is to give this random sequence some meaning. For example it might translate into Don Juan (living in W1) 8ed (hated) L (hell) for (4) 21 Seconds. Spending your half minute giving it some meaning is a good way of memorizing. Good because it accords with how the brain works naturally. If you made a mental picture of Don Juan in Hell etc. you will probably be unable to forget the sequence until the end of this chapter, however much you try in vain.

Robert Dilts tells a story about a woman describing her strategy in a demonstration workshop. The sequence was: A2470558SB. She was a Cordon Bleu cook. First, she said, it started with the first letter of the alphabet. Next came 24: the age she qualified as a chef. Next was 705. That meant that she was five minutes late for breakfast. The 58 was difficult to remember so she saw it in a different colour in her mind. S was on its own so she made it big: S. And the last letter was B the second of the alphabet, linking with A at the beginning.

Now . . . cover the book and write out that sequence of letters and numbers. Don't forget the one that was bigger than the others . . .

You probably did well. And you did not even try. If you can remember that without trying what could you do if you tried?

A lot worse. Trying uses mental energy and the word itself presupposes a difficult task and probable failure. The harder you try, the more difficult it becomes. The very effort you use becomes a barrier. A good efficient strategy will make learning easy and effortless. An inefficient strategy makes it hard.

Learning to learn is the most important skill in education, and needs to be taught from reception class onwards. The educational system concentrates mostly on what is taught, the curriculum, and omits the learning process. This has two consequences. First, many students have difficulty picking up the information. Secondly, even if they do learn it, it has little meaning for them, because it has been taken out of context.

Without a learning strategy, students may become information parrots, forever dependent on others for information. They are information enabled, but learning disabled. Learning involves memory and understanding: fitting information into context to give it meaning. Focus on failure and its consequences further distract students. Everyone needs permission to fail. Good learners do make mistakes, and use these as feedback to change what they are doing. They keep their goal in mind and stay resourceful.

Marks and grades have no effect on the strategy a student uses. They are merely a judgement on the performance, and serve only to separate students out into a hierarchy of merit. Students may try harder with the same ineffective strategy. If learners were all taught a range of good strategies, then large differences between them in performance would disappear. Teaching efficient strategies would improve the results of all the students. Without this, education functions as a way of ordering people into hierarchies. It keeps the status quo, labels the sheep and the goats, and sorts one from the other. Inequality is reinforced.

Teaching involves gaining rapport, and pacing and leading the student into the best strategies or ways of using the body and mind to make sense of the information. If students fail and continue to fail, they are likely to generalize from performance, to capability, to belief and think that they cannot do the task. This then becomes a self-fulfilling prophecy.

Many school subjects are anchored to boredom and unhappiness, and so learning becomes difficult. Why is education often so painful and time-consuming? Most of the content of a child's full-time education could be learned in less than half their time at school if the children were motivated and given good learning strategies.

All our thinking processes involve strategies, and we are usually unconscious of the strategies we use. Many people use only a handful of strategies for all their thinking.

SPELLING STRATEGY

Spelling is an important skill, and one many people find difficult. You get credit for creative writing, but not for creative spelling. Robert Dilts teaches the process that good spellers use and has organized it into a simple, effective strategy.

Good spellers nearly always go through the same strategy, and you may like to check this if you do spell well or you know someone who does. Good spellers look up or straight ahead as they spell; they visualize the word as they spell it, and then look down to check with their feeling that they are correct.

People who spell poorly usually try to do it from the sound. This is not so effective. Spelling involves writing down the word, representing it visually on paper. The obvious step is first to represent it visually internally. English words do not follow simple rules where the sound corresponds to the spelling. In the extreme case 'Ghoti' could be a phonetic spelling of 'fish' – 'gh' as in cough; 'o' as in women and 'ti' as in condition. A phonetic spelling system cannot even spell its own title correctly.

Good spellers will report seeing a mental image of the word with a feeling of familiarity. They just feel that it looks right. Copy editors who have to be expert spellers just have to look down a page and they report that wrong spellings seem to jump out at them.

If you want to be an expert speller, or if you are already, and are interested in checking what you do, here are the steps of the strategy:

1. Think of something that feels familiar and pleasant. When you have that feeling, look at the word you want to spell for a few

seconds. It may help to actually place the word up and to your left in the visual accessing area.

2. Next, look away and move your eyes up and to your left and remember what you can of the correct spelling. Notice the gaps (if any) and look back at the word, review the letters which fit in the gaps and repeat the process until you can picture the word in its entirety.

3. Look up at your mental image and then write down what you see. Check that it is correct, if not, go back to Step 1, take another look and get the image clear in your mind.

4. Look up at your mental image and spell the word backwards. This will really make sure the image is clear. No phonetic speller can possibly spell a word backwards.

There are some helpful ideas you can use with this basic strategy:

a) Use the submodalities that make your images the clearest and most memorable. Think of some scene that is really memorable. Where in your mind do you see it? What are the submodalities? Put the word you want to spell in the same place and give it the same submodalities.

b) It may help to picture the word in your favourite colour.

c) It may also help to put it on a familiar background.

d) Make parts that you find difficult stand out by submodality changes. Make them bigger, closer, or vary the colour.

e) If the word is a long one, break it down into chunks of three or four letters. Make the letters small enough so that you can see the whole word easily, and big enough to read without strain. Do not run out of mental space. You may like to trace the letters in the air as you see them, or if you are strong kinesthetically, trace them on your arm to build your picture with added feeling.

This strategy was tested at the University of Moncton, New Brunswick in Canada. A number of average spellers were split into four groups. A spelling test was set up using nonsense words the students had never seen before. The first group (A) was shown the words and told to visualize them while looking up and to the left. The second group (B) were told to visualize the words, but not told any eye position. The third group (C) were simply told to study the words in any way they wished. The fourth (D) were told to visualize the words looking down and to the right.

The test results were interesting. Group A showed a 20 per cent increase in correct spellings on previous test results. Group B showed a 10 per cent increase. Group C stayed roughly the same as you would expect, they had not changed their strategy. The scores of group D had actually worsened by 15 per cent, because they were trying to visualize, using an eye accessing position that made it extremely difficult to do so.

Good spelling is a capability. If you follow this strategy you will be able to spell *any* word correctly. Learning lists of words by rote may help you to spell those words but it does not make you a good speller. Learning by rote does not build capability.

This spelling strategy has been used with success on children that have been labelled as dyslexic. Often these children simply are more auditory or kinesthetic than other children. Wun wunders why foenick spelling methuds arr stil tort in skools.

STRATEGY FOR CREATIVITY

> I prefer to entertain people in the hope that they learn, rather than teach people in the hope that they are entertained.
>
> Walt Disney

Robert Dilts has created a model of the strategy used by Walt Disney, a remarkably creative and successful man, whose work continues to give pleasure to countless people all over the world. He would have made a fine business consultant, because he used a general creative strategy which can be used for any type of problem.

Walt Disney had a wonderful imagination; he was a very creative dreamer. Dreaming is the first step towards creating any outcome in the world. We all dream of what we want, what we might do, how things could be different, but how can we manifest those dreams in the real world? How to avoid the pie in the sky from turning to egg on the face? And how do you make sure the dreams are well received by the critics?

He first created a dream or vision of the whole film. He got the feelings of every character in the film by imagining how the story appeared through their eyes. If the film was a cartoon, he told the animators to draw the characters from the standpoint of those feelings.

He then looked at his plan realistically. He balanced money, time, resources, and gathered all the necessary information to make sure that the film could be successfully made: that the dream could become reality.

When he had created the dream of the film, he took another look at it from the point of view of a critical member of the audience. He asked himself, 'Was it interesting? Was it entertaining? Was there any dead wood, regardless of his attachment to it?'

Disney used three different processes: the Dreamer, the Realist and the Critic. Those who worked with him recognized these three positions, but never knew which one Disney would take at a meeting. He probably balanced the meeting, supplying the one that was not well-represented.

Here is the strategy you can use formally:

1. Select the problem you are going to deal with, it can be as difficult as you like. Do not think about it yet. Choose three places in front of you that you can step into. One for your Dreamer, one for your Critic and one for your Realist.
2. Think of a time when you were really creative, when your Dreamer really generated some creative choices. Step into the Dreamer position in front of you and relive that time. You are anchoring your resources and strategy as a Dreamer to that actual place.

   If you find difficulty accessing a creative reference experience, find a metaphor for the problem that could help you think creatively. Or you could model someone you know who is a good creative dreamer. Go and ask them how they get themselves into that state before you come back to this process. You may need to break the problem up into more manageable chunks. Do not think realistically, that comes later. Do not edit or evaluate. You could even distract the conscious mind by listening to a tune, or by doing some physical activity. When you have dreamed as much as you like, step out again to the uninvolved position.
3. Think back to a time when you were careful and realistic about some plan, either your own or someone else's. Some time when you put a plan into action in an elegant and effective way. If you have difficulty, think of a person you can model. Either ask how they think about putting plans into action, or pretend to be them. 'If I were X, how would I put these plans into action?' Act as if you were X.

   When you are ready, step into the Realist position. You are anchoring your realist state and resources to that spot. When you have relived your experience, step back to the uninvolved position.

4. Finally the evaluation. The Critic. Remember a time when you criticized a plan in a constructive way, saw the weaknesses as well as the strengths, and identified the problems. It may have been one of your own projects, or a project of a colleague. Again, if this is difficult, model a good critic you know. When you have a reference experience, step into the third place you have identified and relive the experience. When you have finished step out.

What you have done is to anchor the Dreamer, the Critic and the Realist into three different places. You can use three places in your workroom, or even three separate rooms. You will probably find one position is much easier for you to access than the others. You might like to draw some conclusions from this about the plans you make. Each of these positions in fact is a strategy in itself. This creative strategy is a super-strategy, three separate strategies rolled into one.

5. Take the problem or outcome you want to work with. Step into the Dreamer location and let your mind be free. The Dreamer does not have to be realistic. Dreams are usually visual and your Dreamer is likely to use visual constructed thoughts. The sky is the limit. Do not let reality damp your thoughts. Brainstorm. What would you do if you could not fail? The Dreamer could be summed up in the phrase, 'I wonder if . . .' When you have finished, step back to the uninvolved position. Despite what you were told at school, daydreaming can be a useful, creative and enjoyable way to pass the time.

6. Step into the Realist position and think about the plan you have dreamed about. Organize your ideas. How could it be put into practice? What would have to change to make it realistic? When you are satisfied step into the outside position again. The phrase for the realist is, 'How can I do this . . .' The Realist in you is liable to be predominantly kinesthetic, the 'man or woman of action'.

7. Next, step into the Critic position and check and evaluate the plan. Is there anything missing? If the plan needs other people's co-operation, what is in it for them? What do you get out of it? Is it interesting? Where is the payoff? The Critic asks, 'What's missing? . . . What's in it for me?' The Critic seems to operate mostly by internal dialogue.

8. Step back into the Dreamer and change the plan creatively to take in what you have learnt from the realist and the critic. Continue to go through the three positions until the plan congruently fits

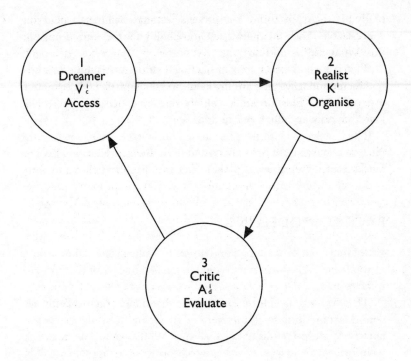

Disney Creative Strategy

each one. You will have a different physiology and neurology in each of the positions, make sure that there is a continuity of outcome from one to the other.

To make sure the criticism is constructive rather than destructive, remember that the Critic is no more realistic than the Dreamer. It is just another way of thinking about the possibilities. The Critic must not criticize the Dreamer or the Realist. The Critic must criticize the plan. Some people criticize themselves and feel bad, instead of using criticism as useful feedback about their *plans*. Sometimes the Critic comes in too soon and picks the dream or the Dreamer apart.

Some people use this strategy naturally. They have a special place or room where they think creatively, an anchor for their Dreamer. There is another place for the practical planning, and another for the evaluation and criticism. When these three ways of thinking are cleanly sorted spatially, each can do what they do best without interference. Only if the finished idea works in each place are they ready to act. At the end of this process you may well have a plan that is irresistible. Then the question is not 'Shall I do this?' but, 'I must do this. What else would I do?'

This is a good example of a balanced strategy. All three primary representational systems are involved, so all channels of information are available. The Dreamer usually operates visually, the Realist kinesthetically and the Critic auditorily.

There needs to be some external step outside the strategy in case the internal processing gets into a loop and goes nowhere. Here you have an outside position to review the whole process and call a halt in real time.

BACK TO MODELLING

As we move out of strategies and go on to look at some other aspects of modelling, it is worth mentioning in passing one point that troubles some people.

There is a strange idea in our culture that finding out explicitly *how* you do something will interfere with doing it well, as though ignorance is a prerequisite to excellence. While you are doing a task, your focus of conscious attention is, of course, on doing the task. The car driver does not consciously think about everything she does as she is doing it, and the musician does not consciously keep track of every note she plays. However, both could explain to you afterwards what it is that they have just done.

One difference between a competent performer and a master in any field is that the master can go back and tell you exactly what it is that he has just done, and how he did it. Masters have unconscious competence and the ability to make that competence explicit. This last skill is referred to as *metacognition*.

With metacognition, you have the possibility of becoming aware of how you perform a task. Knowing how you do something gives you the ability to pass it on to others. Also, by identifying the difference between what you are doing when things are going well and what you are doing when they are not, you can increase the likelihood of peak performance on an ongoing basis.

Exploring the process of modelling also raises questions of whom you model. This depends on the outcomes you are going for. You need to first identify the skills, competencies or qualities that you are most interested in acquiring. Then you consider who would serve as your best role-model.

The next question is how you go about modelling. There is a whole spectrum of possibilities, which range from the unconscious and informal modelling that we all do to the very sophisticated research and modelling strategies used by people like Robert Dilts in his recent modelling project for Fiat on leadership skills for the future. An informal and simple way to incorporate modelling skills in your development is to choose role-models from people you admire and respect. Alexander the Great modelled himself on an image he had of the legendary warrior Achilles, Thomas à Kempis had perhaps loftier ambitions when he wrote *The Imitation of Christ*. In more recent times, Stravinsky borrowed heavily from Mozart, claiming that he had the right because he so loved Mozart's music. Ray Charles modelled Nat King Cole, saying that he 'breathed Cole, ate him, drank him and tasted him, day and night' until he developed his own special brand of musicianship.

By 'breathing, eating, drinking and tasting' your model, whether in books, television or film, you will gain access to the kinds of states and mental resources that your model uses. If you are sitting down, try a little experiment. Most people sub-vocalize when they read, that is, they say the words aloud in their head as they read them. Notice what happens if you go back to the beginning of this paragraph right now and allow the voice in your head to transform into the voice of someone you really admire. For many people, just changing the voice inside their head to that of a role-model gives them access to new and different resources.

Often people get caught up in the mystique of modelling and think that it is something they cannot do until they have learned how to do it 'properly'. But anyone who is curious about people cannot *not* do it! You do it already.

When I look back over the ten years since I first encountered NLP, I realize that most of my useful learning has come from informal modelling.

For example, I was visiting some friends recently and discovered for the first time that the lady of the house writes romantic fiction. She had been a little discreet about it, but in a half-hour social conversation I discovered some writing strategies that provided me with just what I was looking for. In brief, she used daydream time creatively to generate her material and jotted down keyword notes in a notebook she always carries. This reminds her of the content when she next sits down to write. She loves her creative daydreaming time, so it has a motivation strategy built in. Elegant.

You can be more sophisticated about modelling if you have identified a specific skill that you want to learn. Remember those three basic elements of any behaviour: belief, physiology and strategy. For example, to write this book, I need to believe that I can, and that it is worth doing. I need a set of strategies (sequences of images, sounds and feelings) with which to generate the content, and I need to feel comfortably relaxed as I sit and let my fingers dance on the keyboard.

If you wanted to enrich this minimal model, you would probably want to see me in action, or perhaps I should say 'see me in *in*action', since much of the process takes place unconsciously in the background as I do other things. You would probably want to ask me a lot of questions, some key ones being:

'In what context do you commonly use this skill?'
'What outcomes guide your actions in applying this skill?'
'What do you use as evidence to let you know you are achieving these outcomes?'
'What exactly do you do to achieve these outcomes?'
'What are some specific steps and actions?'
'When you get stuck, what do you do to get yourself unstuck?'

These questions are TOTE elicitation questions based on the TOTE model (Text–Operate–Text–Exit) in Chapter 4. The kind of model you are building is a system of recursively nested TOTEs or, to put it more simply, skills within skills, rather like a set of Chinese boxes, each contained within another.

With the answers to these kinds of questions you can start building a model of what I am doing with my nervous system. To know what questions to ask next, you run this model in your nervous system to find out what works and what is missing. This is rather like when someone gives you a set of directions to follow and you try them out in your imagination to see if they make sense.

There are many more skills to modelling than can be covered here or learned from a book. For example, you need good second position skills to penetrate the 'wall of consciousness'. What is this wall of consciousness? At its simplest, when talented people try to explain or teach what they do, they discover that many of their skills are completely unconscious. It is as if the conscious scaffolding of the learning process has been taken away from the finished house, leaving no trace of how it was constructed.

At the other end of the spectrum from informal modelling is the full-blown high-quality modelling project usually done in the world of business. This involves having a full set of modelling skills at your fingertips. A typical sequence of events might be as follows:

1. Preliminary interviews with the organization to identify which set of competencies is most worth modelling, who the top performers are and how many people to model. Typically there may be three top performers who are contrasted with three average performers (controls) to highlight the critical differences. Finally an action plan is agreed.
2. Spend at least a couple of days with each role-model watching them in action in different contexts. Record their actions and interview each model to unpack beliefs, strategies, states, metaprograms, etc. Interview their colleagues to get their descriptions. Repeat all of the above with the 'control' role-models. Often, the controls are not told that they are controls, to save embarrassment.
3. Take time to map out explicitly what you think you have got and what is still missing. This stage is often done with a co-modeller. Contrastive analysis clarifies the differences that make the difference between the top performers and the controls.
4. At this stage you will need to go back to confirm the patterns that you think you have found and to explore the gaps with more observation and questions. You may need to do this several times.
5. Write up the full report to include the original brief, the methodology and the explicit model. This model covers the levels from identity, beliefs, capabilities through to specific external and internal behaviours.
6. Design a training programme with their trainers to enable others to reproduce these skills. Run the training programme and use the feedback that you get to refine it. Train their trainers to run it. Exit.

Steps 1 to 5 are likely to take somewhere in the order of 20 days' work, with step 6 taking perhaps half as long again. This kind of back-to-back modelling-training package is very effective in organizations where the same work role is replicated many times over, for example team supervisors or shop managers. Modelling without the training input is also beginning to be used in this country to fine tune the process of effective recruitment for specific work roles. Large organizations are beginning to appreciate the value of applied modelling.

NLP, MODELLING AND ACCELERATED LEARNING

This has been a brief introduction to modelling, ranging from the informal through to formal business projects. So here we are in the nineties with sophisticated modelling skills that all came from modelling language in the early days.

When Richard asked John to help him become aware of his Gestalt patterns, John approached it as he would approach learning a new language. To do a study of a language you did not speak was absurd. John had to be able to do the patterns before he could study them. This is the direct opposite of traditional learning, which analyses the pieces first before putting it all together. Accelerated learning is learning to do something and only later learning how you are doing it. You do not examine the learning until it is stable and consistent and voluntarily available to you. Only then will it be stable enough to stand the scrutiny of the conscious mind.

This is a profoundly different way to learn than the four stages outlined in Chapter One, which began with unconscious incompetence, and ended in unconscious competence. To start from intuition and then analyse is the basis of modelling and accelerated learning. You can go straight to unconscious competence in one stage. We have come a full circle from Chapter 1.

NLP began from a basis of intuition, rather like the way we learn our native language. Taking the whole study of excellence as the starting point, you can analyse all the way down to submodalities, the smallest building blocks of our thoughts.

What goes down must come up again. The analysis you have done ensures that you do not simply step up back to the place you were before. You emerge at a point of greater understanding. This stepping back up in a sense is coming back to the roots and knowing that place for the first time. This new point gives the basis for a whole new set of intuitions which can be stepped down again, and so the process continues.

You learn on each of these steps by testing each discovery to its limits. By using each idea or technique on every possible problem, you soon find out its true value, and where its limits are. Only by acting as if it works, do you find out if it does or not, and what its limits are.

First the Meta Model went through this process. Then representational systems, then eye accessing cues, then submodalities and so on. Each piece is pushed to its limit and the next piece takes its place. A constant loss of balance, followed by a constant rebalancing.

The value of NLP lies in the learnings you make in exploring these processes. The roots of NLP lie in the systematic patterns that underlie behaviour. You do whatever it takes to create results, within ethical constraints, and then refine it to make it as simple as possible, so discovering the difference that makes the difference. The purpose of NLP is to increase human choice and freedom.

USER'S GUIDE

So as you are coming to the end of the last chapter of this book, you may already have started to wonder how to get the most from it. Each of us finds our own way of doing this and sometimes we don't even know we are doing it. One thing you may want to decide on a conscious level is whether you find this material interesting and useful enough to want to pursue it further, by buying books or attending training courses.

You may find yourself talking over the ideas with like-minded friends as you make sense of your new learnings and understandings. You may find yourself unexpectedly becoming more aware of some of the different patterns you have begun exploring, of rapport and subtle shifts in body language, of the dance of eyes as people think, of the delicate and profound shifts in your own emotional states and others. You may find yourself becoming increasingly aware of your own thoughts and thinking processes, noticing which ones serve you and which are mere ghosts of the past. You play with changing the content of your thoughts and you play with changing the form of your thoughts and you wonder at the impact as you discover how to create more emotional choice for yourself and others.

Perhaps you have already discovered the extraordinary effectiveness of developing the habit of setting outcomes, of thinking of problems as opportunities to explore, to do something different, and to learn something new and exciting.

You might have found yourself having more insights and intuitions into other people's realities, or being more grounded in your own. It is as though your unconscious mind is integrating your new learnings in its own time and way; a new relationship is evolving between your conscious mind and your unconscious wisdom. As though by rediscovering yourself, you are more aware of what matters to you and to the people that you are close to.

In listening to your own internal dialogue you discover yourself applying the Meta Model questions, you become increasingly curious as you discover more about your own own beliefs, and you continue changing the limiting ones to empowering ones that enable you to be more of who you always wanted to be.

In becoming increasingly aware of your own identity it seems as though you have far more choice than to be the slave of your past history. You think differently about your future and this influences who you are becoming in the present.

You may find a growing richness and intimacy in your relationships with your close friends and you may want to spend more time with other explorers of the rich world of human experience.

And as more of us become aware of how we make up our reality, we can begin to enjoy making it up more the way we would like it to be, so creating a better world for all.

EPILOGUE

This book so far has described the main ideas of NLP in a practical way. NLP did not develop by logical steps, and it is not easy to describe. Trying to describe NLP in a logical sequence is like trying to describe a hologram by pulling it apart bit by bit, but each part of a hologram contains all of it. Here are some final and more speculative thoughts on NLP and its place in our culture.

We believe that NLP is the next generation of psychology. It has been called the New Learning Paradigm and the New Language of Psychology. As a model of the structure of human experience, it may be as profound a step forward as the invention of language. At the very least it is a powerful process that will continue to generate ways of achieving excellent results in a wide range of different fields. Because it is about subjective experience and communication, it is in a sense about everything and nothing. Gregory Bateson described NLP as the first systematic approach to learning to learn; it is the first applied epistemology.

Learning is no longer enough; learning to learn is essential. There is so much to learn and so little time to learn it. Not only are we gaining knowledge and technology more quickly, but the rate at which we gain it is accelerating. We are on an evolutionary journey that is like a roller-coaster ride – it starts slowly, but the further we go, the faster it gets. And we have not yet found any brake. Unfortunately, mere accumulation of knowledge and technical know-how is not bringing with it the wisdom we need to use it well for the good of the planet, and everyone on it. We are clever, but not yet wise.

Huge changes are taking place. Ninety per cent of all scientific knowledge has been accumulated over the lifetime of the generation born at the beginning of this century. They have seen the science fiction of their childhood become science fact. Paradoxically the increase in knowledge makes us feel more ignorant and impotent. The more knowledge there is, the more ignorant we become, for the more we do not know, and the more we have to rely on experts to do the simplest things.

The science and technology that has led to this vast expansion of knowledge and power has had some unfortunate consequences that we are only just becoming aware of, they are what makes the roller-coaster ride so potentially dangerous. Events are moving so fast we can actually see our direction for the first time. We can actually watch the destruction of the Brazilian rain forests on television, and we can read of global warming in the newspapers. Scientists can monitor the holes in the ozone layer. Now it is not a question of whether the future will be different, nor even by how much. It is a question of whether we have one.

The world is now too dangerous for anything less than Utopia.

Buckminster Fuller

As we look around, how many of us are satisfied with what we see? Each one of us experiences the increasing pressure for change. And we each have a part to play if this roller-coaster of untrammelled technology and power is not to go out of control with disastrous planetary consequences. We have to control it, we cannot jump off. The question is how?

It is the individual that is the source of creativity that enables social evolution to happen; and it is the level of consciousness of the individuals in a society that makes up the level of consciousness of that society.

Social change begins with individual change. We face many social and ecological problems. If we are to develop a society that can deal effectively with them, we have to act now. As time passes and knowledge grows, two questions become more and more urgent: What is worth knowing? What is worth doing?

We have devastated the outer world with the products of science and technology. The attitude and world view that has given us this science and technology is deeply entrenched in our culture, and has had profound effects on our inner world.

Science has grown up through a series of controlled and repeatable experiments on nature in order to try to formulate mathematical laws and theories. Man no longer considers himself part of nature in any practical way. Man, the experimenter, must stand apart from nature, his experiment. And he does not admit that his very experiment changes nature or influences the result, for that would mean he forgoes his claim to objectivity. To try to get an objective result would mean another experimenter would have to monitor the first experimenter. This creates an impossible and infinite regress like a painter attempting to paint the whole landscape including himself. He can never paint the painter that is painting the picture.

We have come to treat nature as a machine, with laws imposed upon it from without, instead of as an organism.

A machine should be inherently predictable. In theory all you have to do is to find all the rules and discover all the bits. So the hunt was on to paint a more and more complete picture of nature, and the painter was forgotten.

Knowledge was divorced from experience. It became something you learned at second hand, an abstract body of theory existing independently of the knower and growing all the time. All that mattered was the final product, the theory, not the experience of learning it.

This way of objectifying knowledge severely limits the kind of knowledge you can deal with. At the extreme, emotions, art and relationships are devalued, because they rely on subjective experience. Scientific laws no longer seem to relate to the real world of human experience.

Scientific theories are metaphors about the world, they are not true, they are a way of thinking about the world, in the same way that a painting is one way of representing the landscape. We are rapidly finding that our way of thinking about the world up to now has been useful in some directions and catastrophic in others.

The metaphor of a predictable, objective world has been shaken by the quantum theories of physics. The more deeply we investigate, the more it becomes clear both that the observer has an effect on what he observes, and that the observer is an integral part of any scientific experiment. Light will act as particles or waves, depending on what sort of experiment you set up. You can never exactly pinpoint both where a particle is, and when it is there. The world is fundamentally indeterminate. Quantum physics is displacing the clockwork universe as the prevailing scientific metaphor.

The new explorations and ideas of systems theory, and the study of chaos and order, are showing us that even in simple systems you cannot keep track of all the variables, and slight variations can change the whole system. It is the beginning of a revolution; it is changing the whole way we see nature.

Chaos is predictable randomness, which is epitomized by the so-called Butterfly Effect. This is named after a talk by the American meteorologist Edward Lorenz, entitled 'Does the Flap of a Butterfly's Wings in Brazil Set Off a Tornado in Texas?' Lorenz had been using a computer model for tracking weather. He tired of typing in long numbers and thought it would make no difference if he rounded them off to a few decimal places. He was surprised to find that this threw the world's weather predictions completely out. A tiny change in the right place can have huge consequences. This underlines how the whole of nature is a system and not something apart from us that we can experiment on with impunity. As Gregory Bateson says in *Steps to an Ecology of Mind,* 'Lack of systemic wisdom is always punished.'

These new scientific metaphors allow us to be part of nature again. In the same way NLP as a metaphor connects us back to our subjective experience, and expresses the systemic nature of our inner experience.

We now know about the complexity of the external world and we know something of the impact that we, the invisible observers, are having on the external world. The consequences of how we think are faithfully mirrored back by the outside world. The universe is a perfect feedback device. What we think is what we get. If we want to change the world, we must first change ourselves. We must explore and change our internal experience if we are to influence and shape the external world with wisdom.

NLP, as the study of the structure of subjective experience, enables us to explore ourselves. For it is a study of how we make models. It does not take the models we have made and confuse them with reality.

As a way of creating excellence it is infiltrating and influencing many fields. In a way, when this process is complete, NLP could cease to exist as a separate discipline. It would be assimilated into everyday life like the teacher who succeeds by making herself redundant, because her students can now learn for themselves.

NLP is part of a movement that is growing steadily stronger. A movement towards acting in the world more effectively, using the skills and knowledge that we have, with grace, wisdom and balance. We can learn much from the Balinese maxim, 'We have no art, we just do things as well as possible.'

We are discovering ourselves and our capacity for awakening in a beautiful and alluring world of endless surprises.

> People travel to wonder
> at the height of the mountains,
> at the huge waves of the sea,
> at the long courses of rivers, at the vast compass of the ocean,
> at the circular motion of the stars,
> and they pass themselves by without wondering.
>
> St Augustine

INVESTING IN YOURSELF

Increasingly more of us are looking to find satisfaction on an inner level. Different people will call it by different names: personal development, personal evolution, self-development, self-actualization, spiritual development, or realizing more of our potential.

According to Peter Russell in his excellent book *The Awakening Earth*, the personal development field is a growing area and is roughly doubling every four years. Personal development in its widest sense covers a range of different activities including meditation, yoga and tai chi, counselling, Gestalt, psychotherapy, groupwork, transactional analysis, rebirthing, assertiveness training, stress management, prosperity consciousness, relationship training, and many more including, of course, NLP.

Each of us becomes drawn to one or another personal development path in different ways and at different times. The fact that you are reading this book indicates that you are at the moment drawn to explore NLP.

You are the best judge of which path is most appropriate for you at the moment. Whichever pathways you pursue, they will involve some investment in terms of time and money. They will involve organizing and travelling, buying books or tapes, and doing courses. You, in effect, invest some proportion of the money that flows through you in your own personal development. Each of us spends a different proportion at different times.

It is well worth taking a few minutes to work out roughly what percentage of your income you have invested in yourself over the last few years. First make a list of what you consider to be the personal development activities in your life. As a guideline here, these will have a lasting effect that is in some way generative. They go on producing benefits. Meditation has this quality, ice-cream does not.

Now make a rough estimate of the financial cost of each of these activities. Notice, too, the benefits you have got from each. Now total the cost. What percentage is this of your total income over the period?

It is worth comparing this to the proportion of income that companies spend on training and developing their people. For most companies in this country it is around one or two per cent. For the most successful companies it is nearer ten per cent.

The percentage of your income that you invest in yourself is a reflection of how much you value yourself. You are your own most valuable resource and investing in yourself may be the best investment you can make.

Do you invest as much in yourself as you want to? Quite apart from the inner benefits, there can be financial benefits too.

I have a friend who became dissatisfied with her life. She worked as a cook earning about £7,000 a year. Over three or four years, she invested about ten per cent of her income in her own development and training, including NLP training. She has transformed herself and her lifestyle. She now finds life much more satisfying and also earns £20,000 a year.

The flow of money in our lives accurately reflects the flow of thoughts in our minds. So, if you want to change your bank balance, change your thinking. This is a central notion of prosperity consciousness.

On a more general level, if you want to change your external reality, change your inner reality first.

NLP is about changing our inner reality. Unless the benefits are sufficiently clear, there is no motivation to commit time and money. What are the benefits of investing in NLP training?

Everyone brings their own unique personality and potential to an NLP training course, and the benefits will vary from person to person. What you will get depends mainly on what you want to get, so it is well worth being clear about your personal outcomes.

Many people come primarily for personal development. They may be going through a period of change in their life, and want skills and tools for making changes. Others may simply be aware that there could be more to their life.

Some come mainly for professional reasons, although personal and professional development go hand in hand. NLP skills are invaluable as interpersonal skills. Many professionals use NLP in their work: teachers, trainers, counsellors, therapists, psychiatrists, nurses, social workers, probation officers, management consultants and salespeople. NLP improves effectiveness at work and gives an enhanced sense of well-being. Many professionals use NLP to become more successful financially, so getting a tangible return in kind on their investment.

Participants often report a new dimension to experience, a new perspective on life, more choices, creative ideas and new skills to apply. Enhanced awareness and flexibility revitalize both personal and professional life.

Last, but not least, NLP is fun. A course is something to look forward to, an occasion to enjoy and meet interesting people.

You can learn NLP from books, but NLP is experiential. It involves having the perceptual filters, the patterns and the skills in your behaviour, rather than just as ideas in your head. Personal experience with others has so much more meaning and impact than the written word. NLP is to be used at the level of experience if it is to be of any value.

An NLP training seminar gives a safe environment in which to learn the patterns experientially with sympathetic people, under skilled supervision.

There is an old Chinese saying:

I hear and I forget.
I see and I remember.
I do and I understand.

Your investment in training is considerably more than your investment in books and warrants careful consideration. There are considerably more benefits too.

The only way you will find out if NLP training is for you is to do it. In the next section we offer our thoughts on how you go about choosing the course that is best for you.

CHOOSING NLP TRAINING

This section gives some guidelines to help you choose which NLP training to do.

NLP courses are being offered in greater numbers and varieties all the time. At the moment you can choose from two-day introduction courses, more advanced courses, including specialized courses for particular applications, and longer NLP trainings. Many organizations offer free introductory evenings so you can find out more about them and the courses they offer.

There is a range of courses specifically aimed at applying NLP in particular areas such as education, business, selling, presentations, meetings, negotiations, music, acupuncture, counselling, psychotherapy and hypnotherapy. There are also update courses offering new and recent NLP patterns and developments.

Practitioner or diploma level training is a substantial step. This normally involves around 150 hours training spread over some 20 or more days. Increasingly, more training organizations are offering a short training first with a variety of different names, and an optional longer part to bring this up to the diploma or practitioner level.

Following on from this, is master practitioner or advanced diploma level training, involving a similar time commitment. There are also courses in new developments, and trainings for trainers.

In practical terms, the first question to ask yourself is what sort of training do you want? You may be clear from the start, or you may need to formulate your ideas by gathering information. Do you simply want NLP training or do you want it specialized in an area of application? If so, which one? Do you want a certificate or qualification from the training?

The cost of the course is an obvious consideration, and where the course takes place is an important factor, both in terms of convenience and time. Remember to add travel and accommodation costs to the course fees.

How long does the course last? How does it fit in with your other commitments?

How flexible are the arrangements? Do you buy a whole course that you are then locked into whether you like it or not, or is it organized in units that you can take or leave at your convenience? What are the deposit and cancellation terms? How is the course spread over time? Is it on weekends or weekdays? In practitioner trainings there will often be some practice evenings that you will need to attend.

The trainers will have a big influence on the course. Some organizations use internationally known trainers. This will add to the cost, but it is worth bearing in mind that these trainers will usually have had a long involvement with NLP and be more experienced.

Perhaps most important are your own personal feelings and assessment of the training and the trainers. NLP is about subjective experience. Be aware of your personal evaluations of quality and what is important to you.

Do you like and respect the trainer/s? Do you have rapport and do they have a personal integrity you can trust? Trainers have very different personal styles. Does their style suit you? Can you learn well from them?

Find out as much as you can first. Telephone the organizations and ask about their courses. Tell them your requirements. Beware of training organizations that belittle others. This is unprofessional conduct and may be used to cover their own weaknesses. A good organization will not find it necessary to put down others. Many organizations have open evenings when you can go and speak to the trainers. For many people word of mouth recommendation is a key criterion. You may know of friends or acquaintances who have done training and they can give you invaluable feedback. Many people will prefer to take the recommendation of one particular friend that they trust and respect, whereas others will make up their own mind.

The Association for Neuro-Linguistic Programming, here in Britain, runs annual conferences where you can speak to many of the organizations and trainers. National conferences are excellent places to learn about NLP and find out more.

If you have enjoyed this book, you may like to know that the authors are also the longest established providers of NLP training courses in the UK. You can contact them directly for further information. See the section at the end of this book called 'About the Authors'.

NLP ORGANIZATIONS WORLDWIDE

In the first editions of this book we provided a comprehensive list of NLP organizations worldwide. However, this has grown to such an extent that it is no longer feasible. We have decided now to limit this section to national NLP organizations.

Our intention is to include as complete a list as possible at the present time, and we regret if there are any errors or omissions. Please send any corrections, updates and inclusions to the authors (see 'About the Authors' section for addresses).

NATIONAL NLP ORGANIZATIONS

FINLAND

Finnish Association of NLP
Vehkatie 25 as. 23
04400 Jarvenpaa

Tel: 0291 9834

or:

Stephen Molnar
Tschaikowsky Strasse 6
8000 Munich 60

Tel: 49 89 864 4379

GERMANY

See the book *Wer Trainert NLP?* by Inke Jochims (Junfermann, 1992) for a complete listing of German training organizations and trainers.

ITALY

IIPNL
Via Bandello 18
20123 Milano

Tel: 2 481 6500

HUNGARY

Hungarian Association for NLP
Budapest XIV
Thokoly O. 162

Tel: 0036 1 1832 835

SWITZERLAND

NLP World
International English language magazine.

NLP World
Les 3 Chasseurs
1413 Orzens
Vaud
Fax: 21 887 7976

UNITED KINGDOM

ANLP
28 Corser Street
Stourbridge
2013
DY8 2DQ

Tel: 01384 44 3935

NLP Publications in the UK:

Rapport
Published by ANLP (see above).

USA

NAANLP
7126 E. Shea Blvd., Suite B 184
Scottsdale, AZ 85254

Tel: 602 596 5893

NLP Publications in the USA:

Anchor Point Magazine
PO Box 286
Franktown, CO 80116
Tel: 303-841 8701

800-544 6480
Fax: 303-841 8705

Rapporter Newsletter
740 East Mingus Avenue No
Cottonwood, AZ 86326

Tel: 602-634 7646

The Vak Newsletter
240A Twin Dolphin Dr.
Redwood City, CA 94065

Tel: 415-595 7795
800-228 4069

NLP Book Publishers:

Metamorphous Press, Inc.
PO Box 10616
Portland, OR 97210-0616

Tel: 503-228 4972

Meta Publications
PO Box 565
Cupertino, CA 95015

A GUIDE TO NLP BOOKS

This is a list of books dealing with NLP and applications of NLP to particular fields. It is not an exhaustive list, and some books could be placed in more than one category. The general comments provide a guide to further reading.

The list is divided into four categories: *General, Business and Sales, Education* and *Health and Therapy*. Books are arranged by alphabetical order of author's name within each category.

Many NLP books are published in the USA and are not yet widely available. Contact the nearest NLP training organizations for details of NLP bookshops or see the NLP Resources Guide at the end of this section.

Our thanks to Michael Breen and Michael Neill for helping us compile this section.

GENERAL

Books are listed alphabetically by author.

Change Your Mind and Keep the Change
Steve and Connirae Andreas, Real People Press, 1987.
Edited transcript of seminars given by the authors. It gives many of Richard Bandler's submodality change techniques, swish, changing criteria, and the compulsion blowout. Also there is a chapter on timelines.

Heart of the Mind
Steve and Connirae Andreas, Real People Press, 1990.
NLP strategies applied to a wide range of ideas, including using timelines for personal change. One of the best collections of NLP in action.

An Insider's Guide To Submodalities
Richard Bandler and Will MacDonald, Meta Publications, 1988.
A book that gives a wide range of work with submodalities, including changing beliefs and variations on the swish. The most comprehensive guide to submodalities available at the moment.

Frogs into Princes
Richard Bandler and John Grinder, Real People Press, 1979.
An edited seminar transcript covering many of the main NLP patterns: anchoring, reframing, representational systems, rapport and eye accessing cues. There are many anecdotes and fascinating asides in the course of the book.

Magic in Action
Richard Bandler, Meta Publications, 1985.
This book is made up of edited transcripts of video tapes of Richard Bandler working with clients on problems such as agoraphobia, fear of authority figures and anticipatory loss. An appendix covers treating symptoms of post-traumatic stress disorders using NLP techniques.

Neuro-Linguistic Programming: Volume 1, The Study of the Structure of Subjective Experience
Richard Bandler, John Grinder, Robert Dilts, Judith DeLozier, Meta Publications, 1980.
A comprehensive guide to modelling, covering eliciting, designing, utilizing and installing strategies.

Reframing: Neuro-Linguistic Programming and the Transformation of Meaning
Richard Bandler and John Grinder, Real People Press, 1982.
A book of edited seminar transcripts dealing with reframing in detail. There are sections on negotiation between parts, creating new parts, six step reframing and reframing in systems such as families and organizations.

The Structure of Magic 1
Richard Bandler and John Grinder, Science and Behaviour Books, 1975.
The first NLP book to be published and the definitive one on the Meta Model, very detailed and with material on transformational grammar. The Meta Model is presented in an overall context of psychotherapy.

The Structure of Magic 2
Richard Bandler and John Grinder, Science and Behaviour Books, 1976.
Companion volume to *Magic 1*. Detailed account of synesthesias, incongruity and representational systems in a context of family therapy.

Using Your Brain For a Change
Richard Bandler, Real People Press, 1985.
Edited transcript of Richard Bandler's seminars about submodality patterns including the swish pattern. Some very entertaining asides occur in the development of the main ideas.

An NLP Workbook: Advanced Techniques Book 1
Phil Boas with Jane Brooks, Metamorphous Press, 1985.
A list of NLP exercises from a trainer's point of view. Not an introductory
text.

A Framework for Excellence
Charlotte Bretto, Grinder DeLozier Associates, 1989.
An excellent and detailed resource manual giving material and exercises
at practitioner level.

Emotional Hostage
Leslie Cameron-Bandler and Michael Lebeau, Future Pace Inc., 1985.
A practical book for dealing with emotional and relationship problems.

The Emprint Method
Leslie Cameron-Bandler, David Gordon and Michael Lebeau, Future
Pace Inc, 1985.
Detailed methods of modelling excellence in any field. A step-by-step
technical manual of the method.

Know How, Guided Programs to Inventing Your Own Best Future
Leslie Cameron-Bandler, Michael Lebeau and David Gordon, FuturePace,
1985.
Practical applications of the Emprint method to diet and health, children
and relationships.

Feeling Good about Feeling Bad
Pat Christopherson, Golden Egg Publishing, 1987.
On integrating pain and painful emotions as a part of your day-to-day life.

Results on Target
Bruce Dilman, Outcome Publications, 1989.
An excellent in-depth exploration of outcomes at work and at home.

Applications of Neuro-Linguistic Programming
Robert Dilts, Meta Publications, 1983.
A series of papers covering the Meta Model, and applications of NLP to
business communication, sales, education, creative writing and health.

Changing Belief Systems with NLP
Robert Dilts, Meta Publications, 1990.
A workshop-style book on changing beliefs. Very thorough and includes
the Meta-Mirror and the Failure into Feedback pattern.

Roots of Neuro-Linguistic Programming
Robert Dilts, Meta Publications, 1983.
A complex book which contains three early papers. The first integrates NLP material with theories of brain function, the second describes research into EEG readings and representational systems. The third contains material on the Meta Model, altered states and metaphor in a therapeutic context.

Tools for Dreamers
Robert Dilts and Todd Epstein, Meta Publications, 1991.
A treasure trove of strategies and techniques for creativity. Some of the most up-to-date writing on modelling available.

Various NLP Monographs
Robert Dilts, Dynamic Learning Center.
Spiral-bound monographs including 'Albert Einstein, Neuro-Linguistic Analysis of a Genius'; 'The Cognitive Patterns of Jesus of Nazareth'; 'Moshe Feldenkrais, NLP of the Body'; 'NLP and Life Extension' (with Jaap Hollander); 'NLP in Training Groups'; 'Overcoming Resistance to Persuasion with NLP' (with Joseph Yeager); 'The Parable of the Porpoise'; 'Spelling Strategy'; 'Walt Disney, the Dreamer, The Realist and the Critic'; 'Wolfgang Amadeus Mozart'. These are available directly from the Dynamic Learning Center (see addresses section).

Developing Co-operative Relationships
Gene Early, published by Gene Early, 1988.
A booklet that uses NLP for developing and maintaining co-operative relationships, where sharing and agreement are important. Useful for both personal and professional relationships.

The Happy Neurotic
Geoff Graham, Real Options Press, 1988.
English book containing aspects of NLP. Much of the material is available in *Using Your Brain for a Change*.

Trance-Formations: Neuro-Linguistic Programming and the Structure of Hypnosis
John Grinder and Richard Bandler, Real People Press, 1981.
Edited seminar transcript of hypnosis seminars. There are clear and detailed explanations of trance induction with exercises broken into small steps, also many interesting stories and examples of hypnotic patterns. Utilization techniques include reframing, New Behaviour Generator, pain control and amnesia.

Turtles All the Way Down
John Grinder and Judith DeLozier, Grinder DeLozier Associates, 1987.
Edited seminar transcript of John Grinder and Judith DeLozier's new
work on the prerequisites of genius and the necessary wisdom, style and
grace which must go with applications of NLP technology. A fascinating
and essential book for anyone with knowledge of and interest in NLP.

Leaves Before the Wind
John Grinder, Judith DeLozier and Charlotte Bretto, Grinder DeLozier
Associates, 1990.
A series of articles dealing with NLP and hypnosis, healing and artistry.

Challenge of Excellence
S. L. Gunn, Metamorphous Press, 1986.
Achieving excellence through physical competence, balanced physiology,
and appropriate patterns of thought. Useful for any teacher who wants to
develop NLP skills in conjunction with cooperative games or outdoor
pursuits.

The Excellence Principle
S. L. Gunn, Excellence Unlimited, 1981.
An introductory level NLP workbook based on the presupposition that
'fun is a prerequisite to excellence'.

Monsters and Magical Sticks
Steven Heller and Terry Steele, Falcon Press, 1987.
A clear and entertaining book on hypnosis and trance states.

The Secret of Creating your Future
Tad James, Advanced Neuro-Dynamics, 1989.
Learn about timelines through the metaphorical adventures of Milon
and the Wizard.

Timeline Therapy and the Basis of Personality
Tad James, Meta Publications, 1988.
A detailed and clear account of timelines, metaprograms and values.
Not an introductory book.

Fine Tune your Brain
Genie Laborde, Syntony Publishing, 1988.
Following on from *Influencing with Integrity*, this deals with communication
patterns, dovetailing outcomes, congruence and metaphors.

Magic Demystified
Byron Lewis and Frank Pucelik, Metamorphous Press, 1982.
An introduction to parts of NLP. It deals at length with the Meta Model, communication, how we make maps of the world, representation systems and accessing cues.

NLP: The Wild Days 1972–1981
Terry McClendon, Meta Publications, 1989.
A short, anecdotal account of John and Richard's early partnership.

Golf: The Mind Game
Tennis: The Mind Game
Marlin M. Mackenzie with Ken Denlinger, Dell, 1990.
Applying NLP to sport. Understandable to those without NLP training.

The Art of the Possible
Dawna Markova, Conari Press, 1991.
This is the most in-depth study of communication patterns based on representational systems, including identifying your own patterns.

Basic Techniques: An NLP Workbook
Linnaea Marvell-Mell, Metamorphous Press, 1982.
A workbook and cassette tape designed to teach basic patterns of reframing, anchoring, accessing cues and the Meta Model.

Introducing Neuro-Linguistic Programming
Joseph O'Connor and John Seymour, Mandala, 1990.
An excellent introduction to NLP, this book is designed for beginners. Comprehensive, clear and detailed, it contains an overview and all the main patterns. Good as a reference, it has an invaluable section on all the NLP books, a guide to choosing courses and an extensive glossary of NLP terms. Also available direct from John Seymour Associates.

Practitioner Manual for Introductory Patterns in NLP
Maryann Reese and Carol Yancar, Southern Press, 1986.
A manual taken from a practitioner training, an *aide memoire* to the training.

Programmer's Pocket Summary
Maryann Reese and Alan Densky, Reese and Densky, 1986.
Small, loose leaf binder which contains basic NLP patterns in a sort of recipe format. Not a book for beginners.

Awaken the Giant Within
Anthony Robbins, Simon and Schuster, 1992.
A book about the structure of destiny and the science of Neuro-Associative Conditioning (NAC!) Exciting and motivating, though not strictly NLP.

Unlimited Power
Anthony Robbins, Simon and Schuster, 1986.
A very good exposition of the basic principles of NLP and many personal applications. Written in a very personal and immediate style, very anecdotal.

Cognitive Harmony
Jerry Stocking, Moose Ear Press, 1991.
Subtitled 'An Adventure in Mental Fitness', this book introduces NLP concepts in the context of personal evolution.

Various NLP Monographs
Wyatt Woodsmall, Self published.
Spiral-bound monographs including 'Business Applications of NLP'; 'The Science of Advanced Behavioural Modelling'; 'Metaprograms'; 'Language Patterns and Timeline Therapy'; 'Strategies'; 'Lifeline Therapy'; 'Beyond Self Awareness'. Available from Advanced Behaviour Modelling, see training organizations addresses.
Basic Techniques, Book II
Clifford Wright, Metamorphous Press, 1989.
A collection of exercises from NLP practitioner training. Best done in groups of two or more.

Thinking About Thinking with NLP
Joseph Yeager, Meta Publications, 1985.
A book which deals more with the principles of NLP, an 'NLP state of mind', particularly applied to the business world, rather than with particular techniques. An interesting overview if you are already acquainted with the basic ideas of NLP.

BUSINESS AND SALES

Green Light Selling
Don Aspromonte and Diane Austin, Cahill Mountain Press, 1990. Aa NLP sales process that will be particularly useful for those salespeople who know their product, know their markets and know that they can do better.

Beyond Selling
Dan Bagley and Edward Reese, Meta Publications, 1987.
A well-written book covering an NLP approach to gaining and keeping
customers.

Instant Rapport
Michael Brooks, Warner Books, 1989.
A broad overview of rapport and anchoring skills.

What They Don't Teach You in Sales 101
Steven Drozdek, Joseph Yeager and Linda Sommer, McGraw Hill, 1991.
One of the best and most comprehensive applications of NLP to sales.
Includes an excellent section on 'keeping yourself going'.

Making the Message Clear
James Eicher, Grinder DeLozier Associates, 1987.
NLP applied to business, mainly to do with verbal communication.

Precision: A New Approach to Communication
John Grinder and Michael McMaster, Precision Models, 1980. A
systematic format for gathering information. The book is designed to
improve business planning, management and meetings.

Influencing With Integrity
Genie Laborde, Syntony Publishing Co., 1984.
Subtitled 'Management skills for communication and negotiation', it is a
fine introduction to NLP in a business context. Clearly written, it covers
such matters as outcomes, rapport, acuity and flexibility and their
applications in meetings and negotiation.

90 Days to Communications Excellence
Genie Laborde, Syntony Publishing Co., 1985.
A companion workbook to go with *Influencing with Integrity*, it breaks down
sensory acuity and pattern recognition into small learnable chunks.

Rapport on the Telephone
Genie Laborde, Syntony Publishing Co., 1991.
Designed as a notepad, each page contains a separate skill, from setting
outcomes to pacing and leading, and gathering referrals. Simple use of
NLP on the telephone.

Performance Management
Michael McMaster, Metamorphous Press, 1986.
Communication and training in management using NLP together with
other approaches.

Unlimited Selling Power
D. Moine and K. Lloyd, Prentice-Hall, 1990.
Subtitled 'How to Master Hypnotic Selling Strategies', this is basically the
Milton Model for salespeople.

Modern Persuasion Strategies
J. Moine and J. Herd, Prentice-Hall, 1985.
One of the best books on personal influence in the sales context. A clear
introduction to the theme of hypnotic language patterns in everyday life.

No Experience Necessary
Scott Nelson, Meta Publications, 1990.
Techniques for succeeding in telemarketing.

The Magic of Rapport
J. Richardson and J. Margoulis, Meta Publications, 1988. Deals with
rapport building and hypnotic persuasion techniques.

Sales: The Mind's Side
James E. Robertson, Metamorphous Press, 1989.
Sports psychology and mental training as it applies to sales. Focuses more
on the salesperson than selling strategies.

Successful Selling With NLP
Joseph O'Connor and Robin Prior, Thorsons, 1995.
Using NLP to increase congruence and satisfaction in the selling
profession. As well as being a practical workbook, it deals at length with
the sales process, why people buy, goals and values, and there is a section
on leadership in sales management.

Training with NLP
Joseph O'Connor and John Seymour, Thorsons, 1994.
A comprehensive organization of the fundamentals of training into a
practical primer and reference. Includes sections on presentation skills,
planning and evaluating the results of training.

EDUCATION

Master Teaching Techniques
B. Cleveland, Connecting Link Press, 1984.
Workbook format for teachers to apply the basic techniques of NLP in
the classroom. The exercises in the book are best practised with small
groups.

Righting the Educational Conveyor Belt
Michael Grinder, Metamorphous Press, 1989.
A good, detailed application of parts of NLP to classroom teaching.
A very useful, interesting and practical book.

Meta-Cation: Prescriptions for Some Ailing Educational Processes
Sid Jacobsen, Meta Publications, 1983.
NLP ideas such as metaphor, anchors, representational systems and
guided fantasy applied to individual educational counselling.

Meta-Cation 2
Sid Jacobsen, Meta Publications, 1987.
Companion book giving further applications and developments of
Volume 1.

Meta-Cation 3
Sid Jacobsen, Meta Publications, 1988.
Companion book giving further applications and developments of
Volumes 1 and 2.

Super-Teaching
Eric P. Jensen, Turning Point for Teachers, 1988.
A workbook of NLP, accelerated learning and other techniques for use in
the classroom, with many practical tips.

Classroom Magic
Linda Lloyd, Metamorphous Press, 1989.
Applies NLP skills to primary school classroom teaching in a series of daily
lesson plans. Presents many ideas to develop children's learning skills.

Listening Skills in Music
Joseph O'Connor, Lambent Books, 1989.
The results of modelling talented musicians, full account of the strategy
for musical memory and how to teach it. Includes a video of the
modelling process.

Not Pulling Strings
Joseph O'Connor, Lambent Books, 1987.
A book about learning and teaching music. Explains and uses basic NLP
ideas of rapport, representational systems and sub-modalities.

The Carnival
D. Spence, Southern Institute Press, 1987.
A story incorporating NLP techniques, designed to introduce NLP ideas
to children.

HEALTH AND THERAPY

Virginia Satir: The Patterns of her Magic
Steve Andreas, Science and Behaviour, 1992.
A full transcript of Virginia Satir working with 'forgiving parents'.
Includes detailed commentary and highlights many patterns.

Metamedicine
Vida Baron, Barez Publishing Company, 1990.
Simple and basic NLP frames applied to medicine.

Solutions
L. Cameron-Bandler, FuturePace Inc., 1985.
This is a revised and expanded edition of *They Lived Happily Ever After.*
Clear and detailed application of NLP to sexual and relationship
problems.

Beliefs: Pathways to Health and Wellbeing
Robert Dilts, Real People Press, 1990.
A book aptly described by the title, about how your beliefs affect your
health.

Therapeutic Metaphors
David Gordon, Meta Publications, 1978.
Presents a model for generating powerful metaphors to help people get in
touch with their resources. Ways of utilizing synesthesia, representational
systems and submodalities are included.

Patterns of Hypnotic Techniques of Milton H. Erickson M.D., Volume 1
John Grinder and Richard Bandler, Meta Publications, 1975. Clear
exposition of the artfully vague language patterns used by Milton Erickson.
Basic trance induction of pacing and leading, distracting the dominant
hemisphere and accessing the non-dominant hemisphere is explained.
Includes a session of Erickson working with Aldous Huxley. The second
NLP book to be published.

Patterns of Hypnotic Techniques of Milton H. Erickson M.D., Volume 2
John Grinder, Richard Bandler, Judith DeLozier, Meta Publications,
1977.
Companion to *Volume 1*, more technical and detailed, with transcripts of
Erickson working with clients.

Irresistible Communication: Creative Skills for the Health Professional
Mark King, Larry Novick and Charles Citrenbaum, W. B. Saunders &
Co., 1983.
Clear and practical introduction to NLP and communication for doctors,
nurses and social workers.

Get the Results You Want: A Systemic Approach to NLP
K. Kostere and L. Malatests, Metamorphous Press, 1985.
A clear introduction to NLP for therapists with transcripts of client
sessions.

Maps, Models and the Structure of Reality
K. Kostere and L. Malatesta, Metamorphous Press, 1992.
A fairly straightforward exploration of the philosophical underpinnings
of NLP and how they relate to the use of the techniques.

Practical Magic
Steven Lankton, Meta Publications, 1980.
Subtitled 'A translation of basic NLP into clinical psychotherapy'. Deals
with rapport, representational systems, anchors, the Meta Model,
strategies, trance and metaphors applied to psychotherapy.

Facticity: A Door to Mental Health and Beyond
Ragini Elizabeth Michaels, Facticity Trainings, 1991.
A book on recognizing and integrating the light and dark aspects of our
personality.

Changing With Families
Virginia Satir, John Grinder and Richard Bandler, Science and Behaviour
Books, 1976.
Excellent descriptions of Virginia Satir's work. Sorting representational
systems in families and non-verbal behaviour are extensively dealt with.

Your Balancing Act: Discovering New Life through Five Dimensions of Wellness
Carolyn Taylor, Metamorphous Press, 1988.
Presents a model of health through belief systems. The five areas are
physical, mental, emotional, social and spiritual. Makes great use of the
Disney character, Jiminy Cricket.

NLP RESOURCES GUIDE

Computer networking

There is an NLP section in the AIExpert forum on Compuserve Information Service (CIS), the international bulletin board.

For details of CIS in the UK, telephone 0800 289458 or write to:

15-16 Lower Park Row
PO Box 676
Bristol BS99 1YN

NLP Computer software

NLP Computer software is now available. See the *Business Consultancy* – 'About the Authors' section

Networking

There are lists of local NLP groups in *Rapport*, published by NLP (see above).

For general information on NLP training, books, audio and video tapes in the UK, contact

ANLP
PO Box 5
Haverfordwest
Wales
SA63 4YA
Tel: +44 (0) 870 870 4970
Website: www.anlp.org

Outside the UK, contact local NLP training centres or national associations.

NLP GLOSSARY

Accessing Cues	The ways we tune our bodies by breathing, posture, gesture and eye movements to think in certain ways.
'As-If' Frame	Pretending that some event has happened, so thinking 'as if' it had occurred, encourages creative problem-solving by mentally going beyond apparent obstacles to desired solutions.
Analogue	Continuously variable between limits, like a dimmer switch for a light.
Anchoring	The process by which any stimulus or representation (external or internal) gets connected to and triggers a response. Anchors can occur naturally or be set up intentionally.
Associated	Inside an experience, seeing through your own eyes, fully in your senses.
Auditory	To do with the sense of hearing.
Backtrack	To review or summarize, using another's key words and tonalities.
Behaviour	Any activity that we engage in, including thought processes.
Beliefs	The generalizations we make about the world and our operating principles in it.
Calibration	Accurately recognizing another person's state by reading non-verbal signals.
Capability	A successful strategy for carrying out a task.
Chunking or Stepping	Changing your perception by going up or down a *or* logical level. Stepping up is going up to a level that includes what you are studying. Stepping down is going to a level below for a more specific example

of what you are studying. This can be done on the basis of member and class, or part and whole.

Complex Equivalence	Two statements that are considered to mean the same thing, e.g. 'He is not looking at me, so he is not listening to what I say.'
Congruence	State of being unified, and completely sincere, with all aspects of a person working together toward an outcome.
Conscious	Anything in present moment awareness.
Content Reframing	Taking a statement and giving it another meaning, by focusing on another part of the content, asking, 'What else could this mean?'
Context Reframing	Changing the context of a statement to give it another meaning, by asking, 'Where would this be an appropriate response?'
Conversational Postulate	Hypnotic form of language, a question that is interpreted as a command.
Criterion	What is important to you in a particular context.
Cross over Mirroring	Matching a person's body language with a different type of movement, e.g. tapping your foot in time to their speech rhythm.
Deep Structure	The complete linguistic form of a statement from which the surface structure is derived.
Deletion	In speech or thought, missing out a portion of an experience.
Digital	Varying between two different states like a light switch that must be on or off.
Dissociated	Not in an experience, seeing or hearing it from the outside.
Distortion	The process by which something is inaccurately represented in internal experience in a limiting way.
Dovetailing Outcomes	The process of fitting together different outcomes, optimizing solutions. The basis of win-win negotiations.
Downtime	In a light trance state with your attention inwards to your own thoughts and feelings.

Ecology	A concern for the overall relationship between a being and its environment. Also used in reference to internal ecology; the overall relationship between a person and their thoughts, strategies, behaviours, capabilities, values and beliefs. The dynamic balance of elements in any system.
Elicitation	Evoking a state by your behaviour. Also gathering information either by direct observation of non-verbal signals or by asking Meta Model questions.
Eye Accessing Cues	Movements of the eyes in certain directions which indicate visual, auditory or kinesthetic thinking.
Epistemology	The study of how we know what we know.
First Position	Perceiving the world from your own point of view only. Being in touch with your own inner reality. One of three different Perceptual Positions, the others being Second and Third Position.
Frame	Set a context or way of perceiving something as in Outcome Frame, Rapport Frame, Backtrack Frame, etc.
Future Pace	Mentally rehearsing an outcome to ensure that the desired behaviour will occur.
Generalization	The process by which one specific experience comes to represent a whole class of experiences.
Gustatory	To do with the sense of taste.
Identity	Your self-image or self-concept. Who you take yourself to be. The totality of your being.
Incongruence	State of having reservations, not totally committed to an outcome, the internal conflict will be expressed in the person's behaviour.
Intention	The purpose, the desired outcome of an action.
Internal Representations	Patterns of information we create and store in our minds in combinations of images, sounds, feelings, smells and tastes.
Kinesthetic	The feeling sense, tactile sensations and internal feelings such as remembered sensations, emotions, and the sense of balance.

Leading Changing your own behaviours with enough rapport for the other person to follow.

Lead System The representational system that finds information to input into consciousness.

Logical Level Something will be on a higher logical level if it includes something on a lower level.

Map of Reality (Model of the World) Each person's unique representation of the world built from his or her individual perceptions and experiences.

Matching Adopting parts of another person's behaviour for the purpose of enhancing rapport.

Meta Existing at a different logical level to something else. Derived from Greek, meaning over and beyond.

Metacognition Knowing about knowing: having a skill, and the knowledge about it to explain how you do it.

Meta Model A model that identifies language patterns that obscure meaning in a communication through the processes of distortion, deletion and generalization, and specific questions to clarify and challenge imprecise language to connect it back to sensory experience and the deep structure.

Metaphor Indirect communication by a story or figure of speech implying a comparison. In NLP metaphor covers similes, parables and allegories.

Metaprograms Habitual and systematic filters we put on our experience.

Milton Model The inverse of the Meta Model, using artfully vague language patterns to pace another person's experience and access unconscious resources.

Mirroring Precisely matching portions of another person's behaviour.

Mismatching Adopting different patterns of behaviour to another person, breaking rapport for the purpose of redirecting, interrupting or terminating a meeting or conversation.

Modal Operator of A linguistic term for rules (should, ought, etc.)
Necessity

Modal Operator of Possibility	A linguistic term for words that denote what is considered possible (can, cannot, etc.).
Model	A practical description of how something works, whose purpose is to be useful. A generalized, deleted or distorted copy.
Modelling	The process of discerning the sequence of ideas and behaviour that enable someone to accomplish a task. The basis of accelerated learning.
Model of the World	Each person's unique representation of the world (Map built from his or her individual perceptions and experiences. The sum total of an of Reality) individual's personal operating principles.
Multiple Description	The process of describing the same thing from different viewpoints.
Neuro-Linguistic Programming	The study of excellence and a model of how individuals structure their experience.
Neurological Levels	Also known as the different logical levels of experience: environment, behaviour, capability, belief, identity and spiritual.
New Code	A description of NLP that comes from the work of John Grinder and Judith DeLozier in their book *Turtles All the Why Down*.
Nommalization	Linguistic term for the process of turning a verb into an abstract noun, and the word for the noun so formed.
Olfactory	To do with the sense of smell.
Outcome	A specific, sensory-based, desired result that meets the well-formedness criteria.
Overlap	Using one representational system to gain access to another, for example, picturing a scene and then hearing the sounds in it.
Pacing	Gaining and maintaining rapport with another person over a period of time by joining them in their model of the world. You can pace beliefs and ideas as well as behaviour.
Parts	Sub-personalities with intentions, sometimes conflicting.

Perceptual Filters	The unique ideas, experiences, beliefs and language that shape our model of the world.
Perceptual Position	The viewpoint we are aware of at any moment can be our own (First Position), someone else's (Second Position), or an objective and benevolent observer's (Third Position).
Phonological Ambiguity	Two words that sound the same, but there/their difference is plain/plane to see/sea.
Physiological	To do with the physical part of a person.
Predicates	Sensory-based words that indicate the use of one representational system.
Preferred System	The representational system that an individual typically uses most to think consciously and organize his or her experience.
Presuppositions	Ideas or statements that have to be taken for granted for a communication to make sense.
Punctuation Ambiguity	Ambiguity created by merging two separate sentences into one can always try to make sense of them.
Quotes	We read a definition of this once that said, 'Linguistic pattern in which your message is expressed as if by someone else.'
Rapport	The process of establishing and maintaining a relationship of mutual trust and understanding between two or more people, the ability to generate responses from another person.
Reframing	Changing the frame of reference round a statement to give it another meaning.
Representation	An idea: a coding or storage of sensory-based information in the mind.
Representation System	How we code information in our minds in one or more of the five sensory systems: Visual, Auditory, Kinesthetic, Olfactory (smell) and Gustatory (taste).
Requisite Variety	Flexibility of thought and behaviour.
Resources	Any means that can be brought to bear to achieve an outcome: physiology, states, thoughts, strategies, experiences, people, events or possessions.

Resourceful State	The total neurological and physical experience when a person feels resourceful.
Second Position	Perceiving the world from another person's point of view. Being in tune and in touch with their reality. One of three different Perceptual Positions, the others being First and Third Position.
Sensory Acuity	The process of learning to make finer and more useful distinctions about the sense information we get from the world.
Sensory-Based Description	Information that is directly observable and verifiable by the senses. It is the difference between 'The lips are pulled taut, some parts of her teeth are showing and the edges of her mouth are higher than the main line of her mouth' and 'She's happy' - which is an interpretation.
State	How you feel, your mood. The sum total of all neurological and physical processes within an individual at any moment in time. The state we are in affects our capabilities and interpretation of experience.
Stepping	See *Chunking*.
Strategy	A sequence of thought and behaviour to obtain a particular outcome.
Submodality	Distinctions within each representational system, qualities of our internal representations, the smallest building blocks of our thoughts.
Surface Structure	Linguistic term for the spoken or written communication that has been derived from the deep struture by deletion, distortion and generalization.
Synesthesia	Automatic link from one sense to another.
Syntactic Ambiguity	Ambiguous sentence where a verb plus 'ing' can serve either as an adjective or a verb, e.g. Influencing people can make a difference.
Third Position	Perceiving the world from the viewpoint of a detached and benevolent observer. One of three different Perceptual Positions, the others being First and Second Position.

Timeline	The way we store pictures, sounds and feelings of our past, present and future.
Trance	An altered state with an inward focus of attention on a few stimuli.
Triple Description	The process of perceiving experience through First, Second and Third Positions.
Unconscious	Everything that is not in your present moment awareness.
Unified Field	The unifying framework for NLP. A three-dimensional matrix of Neurological Levels, Perceptual Positions and Time.
Universal Quantifiers	Linguistic term for words such as 'every', and 'all' that admit no exceptions; one of the Meta Model categories.
Unspecified Nouns	Nouns that do not specify to whom or to what they refer.
Unspecified Verbs	Verbs that have the adverb deleted, they do not say how the action was carried out. The process is not specified.
Uptime	State where the attention and senses are committed outwards.
Values	What is important to you.
Vestibular System	Representational system that deals with the sense of balance.
Visual	To do with the sense of sight.
Visualization	The process of seeing images in your mind.
Well-Formedness Criteria	A way of thinking about and expressing an outcome which makes it both achievable and verifiable. They are the basis of dovetailing outcomes and win/win solutions.

INDEX

ABOUT THE AUTHORS AND BUSINESS CONSULTANCY SERVICES

Joseph O'Connor is one of the best-known and respected trainers of NLP and coaching in the world. He has taught in North and South America, Hong Kong and Singapore (where he was awarded the medal of the National community Leadership Institute), New Zealand and many European countries. Joseph has been a visiting member of the faculty for NLP University in Santa Cruz, California, and a visiting trainer with NLP Comprehensive.

Joseph has worked with many companies as a trainer and consultant, including BA, HP Invent, Interbrew and the United Nations Industrial Development Organization (UNIDO) in Vienna, consulting on industrial co-operation projects in developing countries.

He is the author of seventeen books, translated into twenty-one languages, including many bestselling and highly respected books. He was the first author outside the United States to write an NLP book. *Introducing NLP* has been used for over ten years as the basic reference book for NLP study and has sold over 100,000 copies.

Joseph lived in the UK for many years and now lives in Brazil. He is co-founder of Lambent do Brasil, a company based in Sao Paulo that works internationally with training, coaching and consultancy.

The company runs the following trainings:

- International Coaching Community Certification programmes
- NLP Practitioner
- NLP Master Practitioner
- NLP Trainer
- Systemic Thinking

For a full list, please visit our website at www.lambentdobrasil.com

Contact Joseph at joseph@lambentdobrasil.com

International Community of NLP (ICNLP)

ICNLP is an association for all who are interested in building an international community of NLP based on shared standards and ethics. It is open to all who are interested in NLP and offers practitioner, master practitioner and trainer training in NLP.

For details, see www.ICNLP.org

The International Coaching Community (ICC)

Through our training programmes, we are creating an international community of certified coaches who work to the highest standards of skill and ethics. The International Coaching Community is a group of highly qualified coaches who have successfully completed the International Coaching Certification Training.

Members of the ICC have:

- A listing in the ICC database so they are part of the referral network of the ICC
- A monthly electronic magazine
- An Internet chatroom for networking
- Peer networking
- Established standards and a common language for coaching

See www.internationalcoachingcommunity.com

John Seymour is one of the best-known names in professional NLP training in the UK. He is a Master Trainer of NLP; business consultant; speaker; author and founder of John Seymour Associates Ltd, Britain's longest established NLP training organization. John has been providing professional NLP skills training since 1985. Drawing on his wide experience of business and education, he has run thousands of training days and introduced tens of thousands to the field. He also works hand in hand with blue chip companies and consulting organizations. John was chosen to introduce NLP at national level to the health and education services.

His NLP background includes training with both the main co-developers of NLP. He is a certified NLP Trainer (twice); a certified NLP Master; a fellow of the North American Association for NLP; and he sits on the advisory board of the international NLP journal, *NLP World*.

With postgraduate degrees in Education and Psychology, John has a gift for skills training–he makes the complex profoundly simple and inspiring. His passions include the rapid evolution of personal and organizational development, and he integrates a wide range of skills and knowledge into his work. This leads to a style of NLP that has a unique quality of width, depth and integrity.

John Seymour Associates Ltd

As the longest established NLP training organization in the UK, our aim is to provide the highest quality NLP training for professional communicators. The JSA Practitioner course is fully recognized by the British Association for NLP (ANLP). Unique to JSA is the Accelerated Personal Development' course. Investing in these generative learning skills may be the best investment you can make. All public courses are covered by a full money-back guarantee.

Please phone for further information on any of the following:

NLP Seminars for the Public

- Free brochure on professional NLP training courses in London and Bristol
- Dates for intensive two-day NLP Introduction courses

Three six-day NLP Diplomas which make up the:

- Trainer Training courses
- Twenty-day Master Practitioner courses
- Assistants' programme (for NLP Practitioners and above)
- Apprentice NLP Trainer programme (for Master Practitioners and above)

Consultancy, In-House and Bespoke Training

- Available both nationally and internationally:
- Free advice on how to use NLP for effective results
- Keynote speaking functions
- Change management and culture change
- Trainer training
- NLP introductions
- Diagnosis of, and practical solutions to, a wide range of common business problems
- 1:1 sessions with CEOs and MDs

Products

Books : Introducing NLP and Training with NLP
Video: NLP in Education

John Seymour Associates Ltd
Park House
10 Park Street
Bristol BS1 5HX
Tel: +44 (0) 845 6580654
Fax: +44 (0) 117 9154547
e-mail: enquiries@johnseymour-nlp.co.uk
website: www.johnseymour-nlp.co.uk

TRAINING WITH NLP

Skills for managers, trainers and communicators

Joseph O'Connor and John Seymour

Training is already a ?3 billion per year business in the UK. Changes in technology and organization development make it likely that 75 per cent of people working today are likely to need training within the next 10 years. Training can be one of the most effective ways to learn the new skills and knowledge needed for the future. The opportunities for outstanding trainers are immense.

What are the differences between outstanding trainers and the rest? There is now a practical answer to this question, provided by NLP modelling skills:

- Discover how the skills of top trainers can work for you
- Communicate at different psychological levels simultaneously
- Learn to improve your presentation skills
- Enhance your self-confidence
- Turn difficult questions to your advantage
- Design and evaluate more effective training
- Increase your influence on training strategy

'A monumental feat...the organisation of the fundamentals of training into a practical primer and valuable reference for anyone who wants to know more about designing effective ways to train.'
– Christina Hall, MA, The NLP Connection

SUCCESSFUL SELLING WITH NLP

The way forward in the New Bazaar

Joseph O'Connor and Robin Prior

Sales is changing to a culture dominated by relationship, integrity and influence for a win–win result: the New Bazaar. NLP, the study of how we communicate with each other, offers powerful ways for salespeople and customers to get what they want in the New Bazaar. This book will help you:

- Create and maintain excellent relationships with customers both on the telephone and face to face
- Learn questions to discover what your customers really want and what they value
- Speak the customers' language, using words that are important to them
- Know how customers decide to buy
- Take care of your own well-being
- Be a leader as well as a manager
- Learn skills for powerful presentations

'A well written book which not only translates the theory of Neuro-Linguistic Programming into effective selling practice but goes beyond this to teach many of the techniques which distinguish successful sales professionals.'

– David Mercer, Head of the Centre for
Strategy and Policy, The Open University

NLP & SPORTS

How to achieve your own peak performance

Joseph O' Connor

Winning matters!

But before you can be your best on court, track, field – or life – you have to win at the mind game because you have two opponents – your limitations and your competitors.

You play the mind game to beat your limitations so you can succeed against your competitors. The goal of the game is to play at your best – and enter 'the zone' – that state of flow where everything you do turns out right.

This practical book will give you the winning ways of thinking that apply to every competitive endeavor so that you can:

- enter the zone more often
- maintain your concentration and focus
- play to the top range of your skill regardless of circumstances
- learn from your mistakes and your successes
- take care of yourself and deal effectively with sports injuries
- make your self-talk work for you and not against you.

This book will help you not only to win but also to enjoy competition.

NLP & RELATIONSHIPS

Simple strategies to make your relationships work

Joseph O'Connor & Robin Prior

Do you make relationships or do they seem to happen to you? Do you have the relationships you deserve? Have you ever wondered why men read so few books on relationships? Never before have we known so much about why people find each other attractive, yet relationships break up more quickly now than ever before. Does nature play a trick by making us want close, satisfying relationships, yet giving us qualities that make this impossible.

Your relationships can work if you want them to.

This book will show you how to:

- choose a partner who will really suit you
- release your passion
- be yourself in a relationship and not what someone else wants you to be
- enjoy – not struggle! – with the differences between men and women.

LEADING WITH NLP

Essential leadership skills for influencing and managing people

Joseph O'Connor

Why be a leader? To be involved in what really matters to you. To be able to do what is important to you with others who share your passion.

Leadership is a natural part of life, a skill that can be learned, not a magical quality you are born with. It does not depend on high profile and glamour. It is an essential skill in modern business.

Leading with NLP tells you how to:

- develop and learn your own natural leadership style
- create shared vision
- use strategic thinking
- create trust
- overcome resistance and reluctance to move forward.

You cannot be a leader on your own. Others make you a leader. *Leading with NLP* is about the beliefs and actions that will make you a leader for yourself and others, and gives practical ways to develop the skills you need.

PRINCIPLES OF NLP

Joseph O'Connor & Ian McDermott

Neuro-Linguistic Programming (NLP) is the psychology of excellence. It is based on the practical skills that are used by all good communicators to obtain excellent results. These skills are invaluable for personal and professional development. This introductory guide explains:

- what NLP is
- how to use it in your life personally, spiritually and professionally
- how to understand body language
- how to achieve excellence in everything you do.

MINDSTORE

The ultimate mental fitness programme

Jack Black

Have you ever looked at people who are successful, either socially or professionally, and thought to yourself, 'How gifted', 'How lucky'? Yet the truth is, 'How unlikely'. Either intentionally or subconsciously, successful people have developed a programme of mind management which has enabled them to be different. This power is present in everyone, not just a 'gifted' few.

Jack Black, a leading motivational speaker and the founder of MindStore, has dedicated his life to discovering the techniques, beliefs, strategies and visions of success. For the first time in book from, his message is now available to all. Entertaining, dynamic and above all easy to learn, discover for yourself how to:

- Master emotions, finances and relationships
- Let go of your 'I can't' philosophy
- Gain renewed energy for life
- Manage stress
- Achieve your dreams

MindStore has worked for thousands of people, including leading sports personalities and company directors. Now let it work for you.

TAKE CHARGE OF YOUR LIFE

How not to be a victim

Louis Proto

It's not life that makes us victims, but how we perceive it. In *Take Charge of your Life* Louis Proto shows us that more often than not we can choose our reaction to what happens to us. Handing us the tools of analysis and support – including visualization, relaxation and meditation – he explains how we can use our experiences to grow and become more whole.

Taking time and space for ourselves, creating more harmonious relationships, and emerging from financial and emotional pressures can all be achieved by learning how to become aware of our own needs and get back the power we have given away. Once we take responsibility for our own experiences, we can use our energy to create the quality of life we want for ourselves.